Teacher Induction Policy in Global Contexts

A volume in
Teacher Induction Research, Policy, and Practice: A Global Perspective
Jian Wang, *Series Editor*

Teacher Induction Policy in Global Contexts

Intentions, Implementations, and Influences

edited by

Jian Wang
Texas Tech University

INFORMATION AGE PUBLISHING, INC.
Charlotte, NC • www.infoagepub.com

Library of Congress Cataloging-in-Publication Data

A CIP record for this book is available from the Library of Congress
http://www.loc.gov

ISBN: 979-8-88730-738-1 (Paperback)
      979-8-88730-739-8 (Hardcover)
      979-8-88730-740-4 (E-Book)

Copyright © 2024 Information Age Publishing Inc.

All rights reserved. No part of this publication may be reproduced, stored in a retrieval system, or transmitted, in any form or by any means, electronic, mechanical, photocopying, microfilming, recording or otherwise, without written permission from the publisher.

Printed in the United States of America

CONTENTS

Introduction—Teacher Induction Policy in Global Contexts:
An Introduction vii
Jian Wang

PART I

NATIONAL INDUCTION POLICY DEVELOPMENT IN CENTRALIZED SYSTEM

1. The Evolution of Teacher Induction Policy in Brunei Darussalam 3
   *Masitah Shahrill, Rosmawijah Jawawi,
   and Shamsiah Zuraini Kanchanawati Tajuddin*

2. Teacher Induction and Professional Development Policy:
   The Case of Israel 23
   Noy Dali and Dorit Tubin

3. Economic, Social, and Educational Contexts and Development
   of Teacher Induction Policy in Malaysia: Enhancing Novice
   Teachers' Intellectual Capitals 43
   Nor Asniza Ishak and Hazri Jamil

4. Teacher Induction Policies and Practices in Singapore 61
   Yanping Fang, Rachel Goh, and Kenneth Kang Neng Loon

PART II

NATIONAL INDUCTION POLICY DEVELOPMENT IN DECENTRALIZED SYSTEM

5 Beginning Teacher Induction in Australia: Current Policy Trends and Future Challenges 83
Sean Kearney

6 Teacher Induction Policy in Chile 101
Beatrice Ávalos and Erika Castillo

7 Quality Teacher Induction Policy in Germany: Development, Implementation, and Impact of the "Quality Initiative of Teacher Education" 121
Hans-Georg Kotthoff and Katharina Hellmann

PART III

PROVINCIAL AND STATE INDUCTION POLICY DEVELOPMENT IN DECENTRALIZED SYSTEM

8 Teacher Induction Policy in Canada: Development and Implementation of Ontario's New Teacher Induction Program ... 145
Benjamin Kutsyuruba, Lorraine Godden, and Keith Walker

9 Policy Related to Teacher Induction and Instructional Coaching in the United States 167
Peter Youngs, Jacob Elmore, and Rachel van Aswegen

PART IV

LOCAL INDUCTION POLICY DEVELOPMENT IN DECENTRALIZED SYSTEM

10 Teacher Induction Policies and Programs in Brazil 189
Aline Maria de Medeiros Rodrigues Reali, Ana Paula Gestoso de Souza, and Rosa Maria Moraes Anunciato

11 Newly Qualified Teachers and Their Support in Finland 213
Vilhelmiina Harju and Hannele Niemi

About the Editor 229

INTRODUCTION

TEACHER INDUCTION POLICY IN GLOBAL CONTEXTS

An Introduction

Jian Wang
Texas Tech University

Welcome to *Teacher Induction Policy in Global Contexts: Intentions, Implementations, and Influences,* the first book in the Teacher Induction Research, Policy, and Practice series. As both the book and series editor, I feel so excited to see the series' first book become a reality after a long and challenging journey.

This book started with a proposed series on teacher induction by Mr. George F. Johnson, president and publisher of Information Age Publishing, in the middle of 2018, considering my work on teacher induction and mentoring. After several months of serious consideration, I accepted the offer. Then, I passionately moved to conceptualize the book series and its first book, complete the book and series' calls, and distribute them through various channels. By mid-2019, I identified all the authors from various countries who would contribute a chapter on teacher induction policy development in their country to the book. The following year, I started engaging them in developing initial ideas, outlines, and first drafts for the book chapters.

As we entered into writing and editing the first draft chapters, the journey to the book editing and publishing process became anything but challenging. First, my wife became sick, which slowed down my feedback on first draft chapters from all the authors. Then, the pandemic hit, which changed the normal working rhythms of all the authors and me, ultimately delaying the submission of some draft full chapters and my feedback and editorial suggestions. During the pandemic, I was diagnosed with colon cancer, went through an emergent surgery followed by chemo for a year, and then on the road to recovery, which consequently slowed down my feedback to the final drafts of all the chapters and final editorial process. I have recovered and feel great the journey is over with the expected result.

BOOK INTENTIONS

This book included eleven chapters devoted to analyzing a country's teacher induction policy, focusing on its intentions, contexts, development, implementation, assumptions, challenges, and consequences. It also raised crucial research questions for further development and implementation of teacher induction policy in these countries emerging from their analysis. The focus of the book was motivated by two related assumptions.

First, teacher induction is becoming an increasingly important focus of education policy in many developed countries to help beginning teachers acquire professional teaching knowledge and practices and stay in teaching (Kutsyuruba et al., 2019). Such teacher induction policies are often shaped by economic and social transformation needs for teaching quality and student learning (Courtney et al., 2023). However, the focus and processes of teacher induction policy development in different countries are situated in the intricate and dedicated relationships between the tradition of teaching and teacher preparation, the social, political, economic, and education contexts, and the needs of beginning teachers, teaching profession, and student learning (Bush, 2018). A careful analysis of teacher induction policy development and implementation in these relationships would offer a great opportunity to understand unique and creative ways of teacher induction policy development and implementation and the competing needs and contexts shaping such policy development and implementation (Afdal, 2019; Courtney et al., 2023). This book contributes to a careful policy analysis of teacher induction policy development and implementation in various national contexts to help scholars, policymakers, and practitioners understand unique and creative ways of teacher induction policy development and implementation and their influential contextual factors.

Second, policy borrowing across different countries is a common practice in education that allows policymakers in particular countries to access different options and choices in their policy development instead of trial and error (Phillips & Ochs, 2003). Policy borrowing is also common in teacher induction policy and program development (Howe, 2006). However, such policy borrowing is often done without careful policy analysis as a base (Auld & Morris, 2014). These analyses include ones focusing on the differences in (a) specific problems the borrowed policy initially intends to solve; (b) social, political, and educational contexts in which the policy problems develop in the two different countries; (c) the explicit and implicit conceptual assumptions underlying the different policy initiatives; and (d) the implementation and associated challenges, and its intended and unintended impacts (Steiner-Khamsi, 2016). Without such an analysis as its base, implementing education policy borrowed from other countries can cause unnecessary financial, human resource, and emotional costs in the new countries (Burdett & O'Donnell, 2016). Consequently, this book assists scholars, policymakers, and practitioners in developing the above analysis central to teacher induction policy borrowing by mapping teacher induction policy intentions, contexts, assumptions, implementation, challenges, consequences, and crucial research questions in eleven countries.

BOOK STRUCTURE

The book is organized into four sections. Each includes several chapters. The first section analyzed national teacher induction policy development, implementation, and impacts in four countries with established centralized school systems. These countries are Bruner, Israel, Malaysia, and Singapore.

Shahrill, Jawawi, and Bolkiah identified the contexts in which Brunei's teacher induction policy initiative, the *Perantis Program*, was developed in 2019. These contexts included the revised national goal for school education, newly developed qualifications for recruiting beginning teachers, challenges they faced in teaching without induction support, and the potential of teacher induction policy to help address these issues, as informed by international reports. They then analyzed the policy's mandates, implementations, strengths, and limitations. In addition, they described a case study on the beginning teachers' experiences in the master program following the induction policy mandates. They discussed the program's role in improving new teachers' teaching performances and its implementation challenges. They concluded the chapter by discussing the implications of their analysis for future teacher induction policy and proposing the possible research necessary to improve Brunei's teacher induction program and practices.

Dali and Tubin analyzed the development and implementation of the 2-year compulsory teacher induction policy at the national level in Israel over the past decade. This teacher induction policy was initiated to attract quality teachers to the profession, improve teaching quality, and reduce novice teacher attrition. They examined the historical, social, and political contexts in which the teacher induction policy was developed. Then, they described its process, mandates, underlying assumptions, and effectiveness in responding to the needs. Additionally, they presented two cases of beginning teachers to demonstrate how the induction policy implementation affects their learning to teach in the school context. The chapter concluded with the challenges that teacher induction policymakers and practitioners face and the research questions worthy of further exploration in further developing and improving the policy and its effects in Israel.

In their chapter, Ishak and Jamil analyzed the teacher induction policy, the *New Teacher Development Program*, developed and implemented in Malaysia. They first discussed several contextual factors that motivated the teacher induction policy, such as the increase in student enrollment and, thus, the demands for the quality of teachers. They also described the policy goal as developing beginning teachers' pedagogical knowledge through professional development and teacher induction, thus improving students' intellectual quality as the country's human capital. Then, the authors introduced the policy mandates, relevant conceptions, and literature bases and specified the range of teacher induction demands from the central government to the schools in the school system. Consequently, with the above analysis as a base, they proposed the challenges the teacher induction policy faces in its further development and implementation and associated research questions.

In the last chapter of this section, Fang, Goh, and Loon analyzed Singapore's teacher induction and mentoring policy development and implementation since 2006. They started with an overview of three distinctive phases of teacher induction policy development, identified the national and international contexts motivating each phase, and discussed the issues and challenges the policy was developed to address. Then, the authors outlined teacher induction policy mandates, program specifics, and implementation processes in each phase. Additionally, they used two case studies to illustrate policy implementation at the school level and discuss the effects and issues related to teacher induction and mentoring policy implementation. They concluded the chapter by synthesizing the teacher induction policy's characteristics, effects, and challenges, discussing further teacher induction and mentoring policy development, and proposing research necessary to improve teacher induction policy and practices in Singapore.

The second section analyzed the development, implementation, and impacts of emergent national teacher induction policies developed in three countries where decentralized school systems have been traditionally developed. These countries include Australia, Chile, and Germany.

Kearney described the various contexts shaping teacher induction needs, leading to the first Australian national policy guideline, *Quality Initiative Teacher Education*, in 2016. These contexts included the national review of the teaching quality of beginning teachers central to shaping students' achievements and their needs for professional development, the increased role of the national government in funding schools over the years, and the development of social and economic policies in addressing the challenges through quality school education that Australia faced.. Then, the author analyzed the extent to which overall changes occurred in teacher induction practices since the national teacher induction policy implementation. Using a case study, he illustrated how the teacher induction policy was implemented in a specific school context and analyzed beginning teachers' experiences in the program. Finally, Kearney critiqued the teacher induction policy implementation as lacking policy and regulators' oversight and offered several implications for developing and implementing future Australian teacher induction policy.

In their chapter, Ávalos and Castillo described the contexts shaping the teacher induction policy development at the national level in Chile, including secondary students' protsest against the poor quality of public schools, leading to the awareness about beginning teachers' needs for professional development and poor working conditions. They discussed its mandates, current state, and strengths as the teacher induction policy was implemented. Then, the authors examined the effects of the second-year induction policy implementation in a university, drawing on interview data from mentors and beginning teachers in the program. Finally, they concluded the chapter by synthesizing what they learned about the Chilean teacher induction policy development, discussing its implementation challenges, and proposing research necessary to build the knowledge base for addressing these challenges.

Kotthoff and Hellmann described the social, educational, and historical tradition of teacher education in which Germany's induction policy, *Quality Initiative of Teacher Education*, was initiated in 2013. These contexts included the increased immigration leading to a diverse student population and integrating special education students into regular classrooms. New teachers fresh from teacher education programs could not teach as expected for the changing student population. The secondary school tracking system created various needs from different teaching professions. Then, the authors described the mandates and assumptions of the teacher induction policy and how its implementation was funded, implemented, and evaluated. Additionally, they analyzed the development and implementation of two university-based induction programs funded by the policy initiative and their intended and unintended effects. Finally, they discussed the challenges in developing and implementing the teacher induction policy and relevant questions worth further examination in Germany.

The third section analyzed teacher induction policy development, implementation, and impacts at the provincial and state levels in two countries where decentralized school systems have been the tradition. These countries are Canada and the United States.

In their chapter, Kutsyuruba, Godden, and Walker described the pan-Canadian contexts shaping the development, implementation, and impacts of the new teacher induction policy, *Ontario's New Teacher Induction Program*, developed in Ontario, Canada. They then explained the teacher induction policy's mandates and the connection between the initial teacher education in university programs, job-embedded professional development for new teachers during induction, and continuous teacher learning in the learning and leadership program throughout their careers. Additionally, the authors identified its literature-based assumptions and detailed its implementation process at the provincial, school board, and school levels. The chapter concluded by analyzing the teacher induction policy's impact and challenges and the implications for further induction policy development, implementation, and practices in Ontario, Canada

Youngs, Elmore, and Aswegen described contexts in which teacher induction and instructional coaching practices were developed and implemented at the district and state levels in the United States over the past 2 decades. They analyzed how teacher induction policies and programs were developed to support beginning teachers' retention using formally assigned mentors, orientation activities, professional development, and formative teacher assessment. In contrast, instructional coaching policies and programs were developed to support teachers in learning to teach effectively using activities in that content-based coaches observed their instruction, modeled lessons, met with teacher teams, and coordinated their professional development. Then, they analyzed a case of a beginning teacher induction policy and program developed in Connecticut and an instructional coaching program developed in a school district in Indiana. The authors identified the theoretical assumptions underlying the two programs, reviewed the research literature on their initiatives, and analyzed the strengths and limitations of each. Finally, they proposed an integrated approach to teacher induction by considering the relevant theoretical assumptions and discussed the implications of the integrated approach for teacher induction practice and research.

The last section analyzed teacher induction policy development, implementation, and impacts at the local level in two countries with decentralized school systems. These countries are Brazil and Finland.

In their chapter, Reali, Souza, and Anunciato analyzed contextual factors shaping the need for teacher induction in Brazil, such as the ethnic and regional social and economic equalities, the decentralized school system, and the characteristics of initial teacher preparation. Then, the authors described how the school education and teacher education policies developed and enacted in the last 35 years in a decentralized manner by municipal government and in the university context. They introduced teacher induction programs and practices at the municipal and university levels and discussed their characteristics. Additionally, they presented three mentoring programs developed in the university context for mentor and beginning teachers and analyzed their program characteristics, mandates, data, and results. They concluded the chapter by summarizing beginning teacher induction programs' contributions and challenges and proposing relevant research to advance its beginning teacher induction policy and practices in Brazil.

Harju and Niemi discussed the key characteristics of the Finnish educational system and the contexts in which new teachers taught after graduation. Then, they explained how the induction practices supported early-career teachers in Finland at the local school level. These teacher induction practices included mandatory job orientation for newly hired teachers and career-long teacher professional development in which newly hired teachers were also involved. Then, the authors analyzed two cases of teacher induction practices, one focused on peer-group mentoring and the other on mentors' training piloted to facilitate new teachers' professional development. They showed the positive impacts of both programs on beginning teachers' well-being and agency in teaching and learning to teach. The chapter concluded by considering the factors shaping successful teacher induction and highlighting further research for teacher induction development and implementation in Finland.

I hope this book will inspire thinking and enrich the understanding of scholars and researchers about teacher induction policy development, implementation, and effects in various national contexts. I also hope it will offer policymakers working to develop teacher induction policies and programs at national, state, provincial, and local school levels with various cases of induction policy development, implementation, and influential contexts as references. Finally, this book will allow practitioners working in the teacher induction programs at the school and university levels access the knowledge, skills, and process of mentoring and mentor training and understand different issues, needs, and processes of beginning teachers' learning to teach situated in various policy, program, and school contexts. As a collective, the chapters in the book will help advance the understanding of teacher induction policy and program development in various national contexts conceptually, methodologically, and practically and demonstrate how far we need to go to address the issues raised by different chapters.

As I put the final touch on this book introduction, I would like to acknowledge Mr. Johnson for his understanding, encouragement, and persistent support for me to finish this book project. I also want to acknowledge all the contributors for their quality contribution to understanding teacher induction policy development in 11 countries, for their patience, and for staying with me through the project. Finally, without the care, love, and support from my wife, Xiaoqing Yang; my son, Yang Wang; and my daughter, Lily Wang, I do not think I would have fully recovered from my cancer struggle and pulled this book project off.

REFERENCES

Afdal, H. W. (2019). The promises and limitations of international comparative research on teacher education. *European Journal of Teacher Education, 42*(2), 258–275.

Auld, E., & Morris, P. (2014). Comparative education, the 'new paradigm' and policy borrowing: Constructing knowledge for educational reform. *Comparative Education, 50*(2), 129–155.

Burdett, N., & O'Donnell, S. (2016). Lost in translation? The challenges of educational policy borrowing, *58*(2), 113–120.

Bush, T. (2018). Preparation and induction for school principals: Global perspectives. *Management in Education, 32*(2), 66–71.

Courtney, S. A., Austin, C. K., & Zolfaghari, M. (2023). International perspectives on teacher induction: A systematic review. *Teaching and Teacher Education, 125*, 104047.

Howe, E. R. (2006). Exemplary teacher induction: An international review. *Educational Philosophy and Theory, 38*(3), 287–297.

Kutsyuruba, B., Walker, K. D., & Godden, L. (2019). Contextual factors in early career teaching: A systematic review of international research on teacher induction and mentoring programs. *Journal of Global Education and Research, 3*(2), 85–123.

Phillips, D., & Ochs, K. (2003). Processes of policy borrowing in education: Some explanatory and analytical devices. *Comparative Education, 39*(4), 451–461.

Steiner-Khamsi, G. (2016). New directions in policy borrowing research. *Asia Pacific Education Review, 17*, 381–390.

PART I

NATIONAL INDUCTION POLICY DEVELOPMENT IN CENTRALIZED SYSTEM

CHAPTER 1

THE EVOLUTION OF TEACHER INDUCTION POLICY IN BRUNEI DARUSSALAM

Masitah Shahrill
Universiti Brunei Darussalam

Rosmawijah Jawawi
Universiti Brunei Darussalam

Shamsiah Zuraini Kanchanawati Tajuddin
Ministry of Education

ABSTRACT

One of the essential aspects of enhancing the (school) education quality in Brunei Darussalam is improving the quality of its teachers. The current teacher induction policy is meant to address this urgent demand. This chapter starts with a brief review of the contexts in which the teacher induction policy was developed. It then elaborates on the teacher induction initiative, the *Perantis* program, introduced in 2019, including its mandates, implementations, and strengths and limitations. Next, the chapter describes the first

---

Teacher Induction Policy in Global Contexts, pages 3–22
Copyright © 2024 by Information Age Publishing
www.infoagepub.com
All rights of reproduction in any form reserved.

case of beginning teachers' experiences in the Master of Teaching (MTeach) program following the induction policy mandates, analyzes its role in improving new teachers' teaching performances, and identifies the implementation challenges. The chapter ends with a discussion of the implications of this teacher induction policy analysis and possible research that can be developed out of this analysis to improve the teacher induction program and practices.

Teacher induction policy was developed to solve the problem of teacher turnover that disrupted the overall student school experience and affected their achievements in the United States (Glazerman et al., 2006). This policy defines the process for beginner teachers to learn to teach professionally (Wong, 2004), including learning how to manage classrooms, develop student motivation, deal with student differences, and conduct assessments on student learning (Anthony et al., 2011). It has also been useful in helping beginning teachers' socialization and full integration into a school professional community and school environments (Feiman-Nemser, 2010; Kearney, 2013).

This chapter presents the contexts in which the Ministry of Education of Brunei Darussalam (henceforth, Brunei) developed the teacher induction policy in the country in 2019. A description of the policy development, mandates and implementation, and identification of the benefits and challenges in the policy implementation follows it. The analysis will focus on the role of the policy in improving beginning teachers' teaching and experience, and challenges faced. The discussion will address future research directions in this area, and the implications on policy development.

CONTEXTS INFLUENCING TEACHER INDUCTION POLICY IN BRUNEI

Brunei is a country with less than half a million people located on the northwest coast of Borneo Island in the Southeast Asian region. It adopts the national philosophy concept of Malay Islamic Monarchy, a fusion of the Brunei-Malay culture, the teachings of Islamic principles, and monarchic administration system. The country is divided into Brunei-Muara, Tutong, Belait, and Temburong districts. The capital city, Bandar Seri Begawan, in the Brunei-Muara district, also has the largest concentration of population in the nation. While its official language is Malay, English is commonly used in social settings and the instructional medium in most schools and higher education institutions, for example, mathematics and science are taught in the English Language in primary and secondary schools (Goode, 2020; Haji-Othman et al., 2016; Ho & Deterding, 2021; Ishamina & Deterding, 2017; Sharbawi, 2020; Sharbawi & Jaidin, 2019).

Brunei has 14 pre-primary, 178 primary, and 35 secondary schools, five sixth-form centers (pre-university), twelve vocational and technical institutions, and seven higher education institutions, including one Polytechnic (Ministry of Education, 2020a), which all are government and nongovernment educational institutions under the purview of the Ministry of Education. The Ministry of Religious Affairs manages the government educational institutions relevant to Islamic religious education, and the Ministry of Education regulates all the government and private education institutions. One of the responsibilities of the Ministry of Education is developing and implementing the strategic, comprehensive, and dynamic planning of human resources (teachers), including 11,500 employees with more than 6,000 teaching staff at primary and secondary levels.

Newly Developed Education Goal and Teacher Induction Policy

One of the contexts shaping the development of teacher induction policy in Brunei is that the country established the goal to develop and reform its school education system to produce a well-educated, highly skilled, and accomplished workforce in January 2009, as iterated in the "Brunei Vision 2035" (Wawasan Brunei 2035, n.d.). The Ministry of Education officially launched the reform, National Education System for the 21st Century, better known as its Malay acronym "SPN21" for Sistem Pendidikan Negara Abad ke-21, to address the national educational goal by transforming its school education structure, curriculum, assessment, and technical education (Ministry of Education, 2013). Later, it proposed the *Strategic Plan 2018–2022* to address the national goal by improving human resources' (including teachers') knowledge, skills, and competencies, including teachers (Ministry of Education, 2018). This plan developed three specific strategic objectives: (a) transform the organization's human resource including teachers, towards a performance-driven culture, (b) provide equal and equitable access to quality education, and (c) enhance shared accountability with stakeholders in the development of teaching and learning (Ministry of Education, 2018).

Underlying these school education transformations are several assumptions. The goal of the school education system is presumably to produce a well-educated, highly skilled, and accomplished workforce. Teachers with the appropriate knowledge, skills, and competencies are central to producing such a workforce, in line with Vision 2035. These teachers need to learn to teach effectively in a performance-driven environment and be held accountable for their students' performances as expected. Consequently, the newly developed education goal and associated assumptions affected the goal and mandates of teacher induction policy in Brunei.

Teacher Preparation and Employment Changes and Teacher Induction Policy

The development of the teacher induction policy was also associated with the policy changes of teacher training and employment. Before 2009, Sultan Hassanal Bolkiah Institute of Education (SHBIE) was the sole provider for all initial teacher preparation through undergraduate teaching credential programs. It started as a teacher-training center in 1956, became Sultan Hassanal Bolkiah Teachers' College in 1972, upgraded to SHBIE in 1984. Eventually, it was integrated into the Faculty of Education, Universiti Brunei Darussalam, in 1988 (Ministry of Education, 2013).

The Ministry of Education would recruit graduates with bachelors' degrees in teacher education mostly from SHBIE as beginning teachers regardless of their major disciplines or their levels of degree classification, such as first, second lower, second upper, or third class with or without honors. Then, it would assign them to schools for 3 years of probation with daily-rated salaries before confirming them as official teachers (also known as education officers in the context of Brunei) with monthly-rated salaries. To become education officers, they had to pass the teaching observation-based assessment by the Ministry's school inspectors. Meanwhile, those who graduated without a bachelor's degree had to enroll and complete the postgraduate or graduate certificate program in education or technical education that SHBIE offered.

In 2009, a Master of Teaching (MTeach) program became the entry qualification for beginning teachers in the nation as required explicitly in meeting with the master-level competencies standard by the Brunei Darussalam Qualification Framework (Jawawi et al., 2014; Ministry of Education, 2014; Mundia, 2012; Shahrill et al., 2014). In this way, teachers would become highly calibrated professionals necessary to prepare the desired well-educated, highly skilled, and accomplished workforce. The MTeach is equivalent to Level 7 of the United Kingdom's Quality Assurance Agency and Level 9 of the Australian Qualifications Framework (Australian Qualifications Framework Council, 2013; Ministry of Education, 2014; Quality Assurance Agency for Higher Education, 2008).

By January 2020, SHBIE's MTeach Program has produced 849 graduates majoring in five areas of specialization, as shown in Figure 1.1. They include early childhood education and care, primary education, secondary education, vocational and technical education, and higher education. The sixth specialization, the inclusive and special education, was only newly introduced in January 2020 with expected graduates the following year.

The above changes in the beginning teacher recruitment policy helped create the need to develop a teacher induction curriculum and process before becoming education officers. This need was intensified as more and

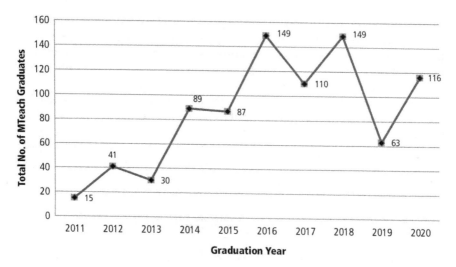

Figure 1.1 MTeach beginning teacher graduates from 2011–2020.

more beginning teachers graduated from the MTeach program with specialized knowledge for teaching in different disciplines and fields.

Issues Relevant to Teacher Induction Policy

Brunei had no official national-level policy governing teacher induction (Moskowitz & Stephens, 1997). To a large extent, the issues of beginning teachers' learning to teach were outlined in internal documents of the Ministry of Education available only to its stakeholders. As Moskowitz and Stephens (1997) observed:

> Although some beginning teachers may carry slightly less time-consuming or less difficult administrative duties, they assume the same responsibilities as fully-fledged teachers and receive a uniform salary appropriate to their probationary stature. (p. 24)

In their study in Israel, this lack of teacher induction support led to the reports on how beginning teachers struggled to cope with the school environment (Shayshon & Popper-Giveon, 2017), and in Malaysia and Australia, beginning teachers encountered the challenges in learning to teach effectively (Paronjodi et al., 2017). This reporting line helped create the need to support beginning teachers' policy-wise in Brunei.

Then, two international reports involving Brunei brought examples of policy solutions to the issues of beginning teachers from the 12 Asia-Pacific Economic

Cooperation member countries, including Brunei. The first report focused on how different Asia-Pacific Economic Cooperation member countries address the needs of teacher preparation and professional development (Darling-Hammond & Cobb, 1995). The second report focused on teacher induction, specifically in the Pacific Rim countries (Moskowitz & Stephens, 1997).

In summary, several conditions have led to the development of a teacher induction policy in Brunei in 2019. These contexts include the revised national goal for school education, new qualifications for recruiting beginning teachers, challenges they faced in teaching without induction support, and the potential of teacher induction policy in helping address these issues as informed by the international reports.

NEW TEACHER INDUCTION POLICY

Development of Teacher Induction Policy

His Majesty, the Sultan of Brunei, made a royal address at the 28th Teachers' Day Celebration in 2018, in which he specifically stressed the need for making the teaching profession effective in preparing children with creative thinking and cultural sensitivity for the era of globalization and rapid technology. These include: (a) the need to make the teaching career one of the top choices in the country; (b) the need to nurture the well-being of teachers by establishing the teaching ecosystem, that is, preparing pathways of teachers' career during their entire service; and (c) the need to re-visit the criteria for the recruitment of teachers.

The newly formed *Department of Educators Management* responded to the royal address and initiated the transformations of the teaching workforce in Brunei in 2019. These transformations were in four areas: (a) selection and recruitment of teachers, (b) deployment and redeployment of their teaching competencies, (c) their career development, and (d) their retirement and exit. The transformation of beginning teacher recruitment became the basis for the newly initiated teacher induction policy, *Perantis* program (Ministry of Education, 2018). Here, the Malay word, Perantis, means apprenticeship in English. This program was designed specifically for beginning teachers who obtained bachelor's degrees from local and overseas universities and were recruited as beginning teachers but not yet attained the official teacher status or formally known as "education officer" status.

Mandates and Rationales of Teacher Induction Policy

Four specific mandates are central to Perantis. The first mandate requires that all beginning teachers are recruited by successfully passing rigorous evaluations. These evaluations include a psychometric test, a teaching demonstration, an assessment of leadership and teamwork, and an initial interview assessment.

The rationale behind these mandates is that only those with strong dedication and commitment to teaching can impart knowledge to students effectively or meaningfully (Ministry of Education, 2018). It was developed by emulating the relevant policies in Finland and Singapore so that only the top 10% of their university graduates could enter the teaching profession (Darling-Hammond & Rothman, 2011) and then enroll in the Perantis.

The second mandate pertains to placing beginning teachers in several government schools for three to 12 months. During this stage, they are assigned an experienced mentor teacher at the respective schools who will guide, motivate, and advise the beginning teachers on teaching. In addition, the beginning teachers must pass the classroom observation assessment conducted by the school management team and the Ministry's Inspectorate Department inspector using Teacher Performance Appraisal (TPA; Department of Schools Inspectorate, 2020). They have to obtain at least a passing assessment point, Level 3 or higher in TPA based on Table 1.1, which means the good ranking with 51–70 out of 100 points in the assessment.

This mandate is consistent with the literature in teacher induction, in which a mentor is defined as a veteran teacher who plays a role in "increasing teacher satisfaction" which allows the school to see "the benefit of increased teacher retention, and in turn, student performance" (Hunter, 2016, p. 83). These mentors can help beginning teachers understand the school procedures and design a curriculum addressing student learning needs (Carver & Feiman-Nemser, 2009). They can also regulate their time to observe and coach their beginning teachers on improving their teaching (Bartlett & Johnson 2010). As shown in a study (Ingvarson et al., 2007), 84% of beginning teachers in Australia have significantly improved their teaching in the classroom due to mentors' guidance and critical feedback.

The third mandate requires beginning teachers who passed the TPA Level evaluation to enroll in the MTeach Program offered by SHBIE for 18 months while continuing teaching in the schools they were initially placed

TABLE 1.1 TPA Level, Grade Equivalent, and Percentage Range

TPA Level	Grade	Percentage (%) Range
1	1 (Not Satisfactory)	Below 40
2	2 (Satisfactory)	40–50
3	3 (Good)	51–70
4	4 (Very Good)	71–90
5	5 (Excellent)	91 and above

Note: Adapted from Department of Schools Inspectorate (2020, p. 87).

at the start of the Perantis. They need to achieve at least a grade of C+ and above for each course and a cumulative grade point average (GPA) of minimum 3.0 to graduate. In the MTeach program, beginning teachers are expected to understand the national education reform initiatives to advance the quality of teaching. They are also offered the chance to be familiar with the teaching and learning environment in schools and experience the teaching profession deeply to realize teaching is the primary choice for their professional career. The mandate is designed to resemble the apprentice-style system of the programs offered by Germany and France in which beginning teachers are offered the chance to learn the theories and practices of teaching at the same time (Howe, 2006; Kearney, 2014; Kotthoff & Terhart, 2013; Wong et al., 2005).

The fourth mandate requires beginning teachers to pass a final interview assessment by the Ministry's Department of Educators Management to become education officers and then be placed for teaching in schools based on their subject expertise. This mandate is developed to ensure the education officers will have the relevant tools to embark on a teaching profession with appropriate support and training.

All the teacher induction policy mandates address the challenges that beginning teachers have faced. They are developed to help beginning teachers cope with the same amount of teaching work, as experienced teachers would have (Paronjodi et al., 2017; Wong et al., 2005). They are also designed to address beginning teachers' isolation (Bacon, 2020; Hunter, 2016) resulting from their unfamiliar with the school system and the way it works (Shayshon & Popper-Giveon, 2017). Hopefully, they will stay in teaching, and thus, the cost for training and hiring new teachers can be reduced (Bacon, 2020; Glazerman et al., 2006; Hunter, 2016; Ronfeldt et al., 2013). Further, they are designed to support beginning teachers to develop teaching expertise that they often lack (Paronjodi et al., 2017) so that they become the more experienced and committed teachers (Glazerman et al., 2006) and more effectively impact students' performance and learning experience (Carroll, 2005; Long et al., 2012).

Implementation of Teacher Induction Mandates

The teacher induction policy has been implemented through several phases. The first cohort of beginning teachers in the Perantis started in September 2019, and the second and third cohorts began in January 2020 and 2021, respectively. The sequential cohorts are planned until 2023, as shown in Figure 1.2. For each cohort, beginning teachers were required to pass the evaluation assessments first, then placed in several schools to reach

The Evolution of Teacher Induction Policy in Brunei Darussalam • 11

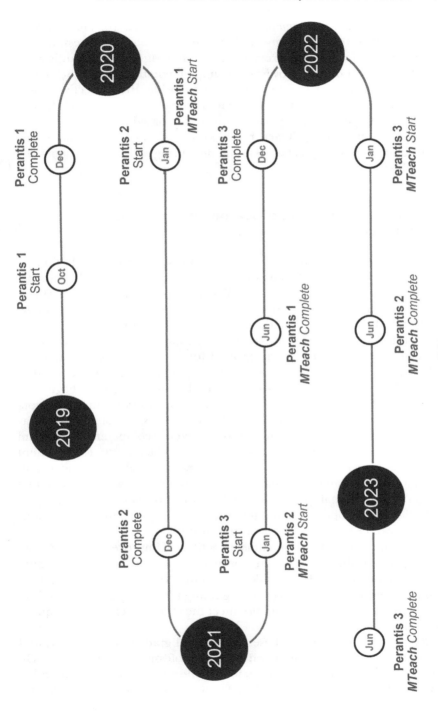

Figure 1.2 The chronology of the Perantis program from 2019–2023.

a good level in classroom teaching assessments, finally, enroll and complete the 18-month MTeach program, and pass the final interview assessment.

The Brunei government provides all the funding for the Perantis while the Ministry of Education oversaw its implementation. When beginning teachers are placed in selected schools nationwide, the respective school leaders and the appointed school mentors are responsible for evaluating their teaching performances using observation-based assessment. During their enrolment in the MTeach program, the evaluation includes assignments and classroom practice assessments during school practicums and research reports.

Benefits and Challenges of Teacher Induction Policy Implementation

The teacher induction policy has made two significant contributions to teacher development in Brunei with the support of the Brunei Darussalam Leadership and Teachers Academy (BDLTA; Ministry of Education, 2018), the arm for the Ministry of Education that looks after the training of all the teachers and school leaders in the country. First, Perantis have been carefully selecting beginning teachers based on the expected qualifications including candidates with science background for science teachers, candidates with English language and literature for English language teachers and so forth (Ministry of Education, 2018). Second, it also supported beginning teachers in the Program in their teaching career progression, professional development. For example, through the Ministry's "Teaching Pathway Program" novice teachers will undergo the teacher competencies program that will assist them to meet the "Brunei Teachers Standards" (Department of Schools Inspectorate, 2020). After 3 years of teaching experience, an education officer can pursue pathways of becoming master teacher, school leaders or educational specialists. Teachers are also given opportunities for professional development training in the different pathways of their choices, which can be short courses or advanced studies.

However, despite these observable benefits and improvements to the system in general, the teacher induction policy also faces several challenges in its implementation. First, while the Perantis did well in selecting only qualified university graduates to be beginning teachers, it has unintentionally left many graduates who did not meet the stricter recruitment requirements unemployed.

Concerning this, most of these unsuccessful graduates were sponsored by the government and intended to join professions other than teaching. Still, historically before the new induction program, they would become teachers as a last resort. Their failure to find a job now becomes a government welfare issue. However, alternative teaching employment may be sought with applying to private schools rather than relying on government vacancies alone.

Furthermore, due to the stricter current induction policy, the number of candidates admitted into SHBIE's MTeach program has reduced significantly. It implies the "critical mass" of students taking the different MTeach specializations and learning areas, which might be at a minimum thus limiting interactions and discussions during lectures. Thus, the meaningfulness of the MTeach experience on its own may not be maximized.

Finally, the teacher induction policy offers mentoring support for beginning teachers in their placement schools before MTeach. Teaching observation-based assessments are used to ensure they meet the requirements of a qualified teacher. However, not all the teacher candidates could pass these assessments to qualify for the MTeach program. And even, though there is an exit point at this stage, the policy might need to consider providing options to these unsuccessful candidates once they leave the program.

In short, the teacher induction policy in Brunei developed several mandates consistent with the ideas in the field of teacher induction and emulated some prominent international examples.

A CASE STUDY OF THE MTEACH PROGRAM

This section presents the case of the first cohort of beginning teachers' experiences in the MTeach program related to the third mandate of the teacher induction policy. Using this case as an example, we discuss the effects of the MTeach program on beginning teachers. We analyzed the challenges in implementing the MTeach program compared to the findings of other studies in teacher induction (Bacon, 2020; Hunter, 2016; Ingersoll & Strong, 2011; Wang et al., 2008).

Participants and Contexts

This case involved 44 first cohort beginning teachers in four specializations in the MTeach program, as shown in Table 1.2. All of these participants had completed the second mandate of teacher induction policy.

These participants came from the assigned schools of all four districts in Brunei associated with the program Perantis. They conducted their practicum in their assigned schools closest to their home, except three placed in two schools different from their initial placement. The participants were initially informed that they would have their practicum in different school environments for both semesters. Due to the COVID-19 pandemic and the

TABLE 1.2 Number of Beginning Teachers in Areas of Specialization of MTeach Program

MTeach Areas of Specialization	No. of Perantis Beginning Teachers
Early Childhood Education and Care	2
Primary Education	11
Secondary Education	30
Inclusive and Special Education	1

subsequential school closure from March to May 2020, they remained in the same school for their practicum for the two semesters (Ministry of Education, 2020b; Shahrill, Noorashid, & Keasberry, 2021; Shahrill, Petra, et al., 2021).

These participants were required to complete the first practicum module supplemented with fortnightly seminars in the first semester, and the second practicum module also accompanied the short seminars in the second semester. The practicum modules provide participants with practical teaching experiences in their placement classroom Monday to Thursday each week and 14 weeks per semester. Saturday is reserved for on-campus or online lectures for other modules within the MTeach program. In Brunei, workdays are Monday to Thursday and Saturday. During the program, a clinical specialist (typically a faculty member) and a school mentor appointed by the school leader were assigned to support each participant in completing the practicum modules, in each of which the seminar sessions were fortnightly embedded and held in the afternoon. The final grades for each practicum module were based on 70% of field performance moderated between the mentor and clinical specialist and 30% from the assignments in the seminar, which included reflective reports and seminar discussions based on video-recorded lessons. Data from the first and second semesters were used to analyze the program influences in this case study, as the participants were currently in the third and final semester.

In the final semester, they were only required to complete one methods module and one research module. The research module in the third semester in the MTeach program is worth 12 credits. Participants were expected to conduct site-based action research in their previous placement school and submit a 12,000-word study report as supervised by a faculty member before the end of the third semester.

Course and Teaching Performances

Our analysis of the performance data for the first two semesters led to two findings relevant to the participants' performance. First, all the participants,

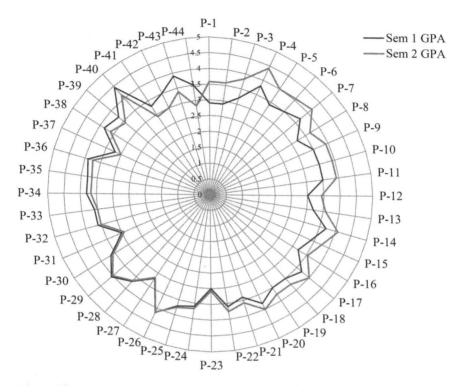

Figure 1.3 The GPA achieved by each Perantis beginning teacher during Semesters 1 and 2.

except one, performed above the required 3.0 GPA minimum in all their seminars based on the examination record. While three were borderline cases with a GPA below 3.1, four showed an excellent GPA of over 4.0. Figure 1.3 displays the GPA achieved by all the participants in each semester.

Second, as assessed by clinical specialists and mentors, most participants demonstrated increased ratings on their teaching performance for the practicum in their assigned schools. As indicated in Figure 1.4, of all the participants, only ten showed decreased ratings from their practicum in the second semester to the first semester, which could be explained by these participants teaching different subject areas in the two semesters. Consequently, they had to work with another subject mentor to teach a different content, which was difficult for them to build on what they learned from the first semester. In contrast, other participants were teaching the same or closely related subjects, such as general science and the pure science (biology, chemistry, or physics), for the first and second practicums respectively.

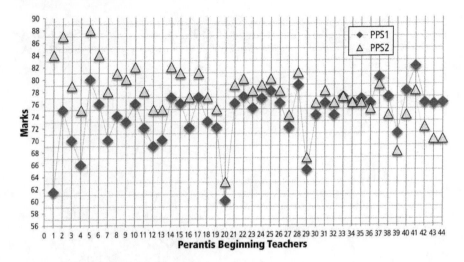

Figure 1.4 Ratings achieved by beginning teachers in two semesters.

They would have the opportunity to focus fully on the subject area without worrying to do any additional preparation for a different subject.

Beginning Teachers' Experiences in Induction Program

Nine participants were selected for group interviews to share their views and experiences in the MTeach program. They included three from the primary specialization representing three different primary schools and six from the secondary specializations representing two secondary schools. Among them, two started their teaching experiences in private schools that were observed and assessed by school inspectorates before joining the Perantis program. Our analysis of the group interview data with these participants led to the following findings.

First, while most participants were satisfied with their mentor support, a few shared negative experiences during several stages in their placements in the interviews. For example, they reported that some mentors were reluctant to take on the mentoring responsibility or even unaware of their appointment as mentors by school leaders. Other mentors lacked proper training on mentoring and offered insufficient or no feedback on participants' lessons. These situations were not consistent with the requirements of the Ministry of Education and those expectations of SHBIE for its MTeach program.

Second, most participants also showed their concerns about how they were observed and assessed during their placement in the school contexts. For example, the school inspectorates observed and assessed some participants by claiming that the inspectors were too strict regarding observations, although they gave constructive feedback to improve teaching. Those who were only observed and assessed by their school administrators were concerned about these observations, and assessments were often done on short notice. These concerns were reasonable considering these observations and assessments could impact if they could stay in teaching.

Overall, this case suggests that the MTeach program supported participants in developing academic and teaching performances as assessed using their course grades and performance rating by clinic specialists and school mentors. However, such performance was not consistent across all the participants. While participants felt supported by their placement schools, some were concerned about what their mentors did and how they were observed and assessed.

CONCLUSIONS AND FURTHER RESEARCH

This chapter focused on various aspects of teacher induction policy in Brunei, including its context, development, mandates, implementation, effects, and challenges shown through the case. Our analysis demonstrates the promising benefits of teacher induction policy with both support and pressure for beginning teachers to learn to be qualified teachers. Such support and pressure are essential as Darling-Hammond (2020) claimed, "Effective policies combine the right mixture of pressure and support for change in ways that increase the capacity for the good practice among the institutions that are the targets of the policy" (p. 7). This policy also shows the benefits of integrating careful selection and evaluation, academic training, and teaching practices through school–university partnerships. Such integration is also necessary to prepare teachers for effective teaching (Darling-Hammond, 2020).

Our policy analysis also indicates several challenges that the teacher induction policy had to face in its implementation within and beyond the goals of the policy. Within the policy's goals, the challenge is preparing mentor teachers to work effectively with beginning teachers and improving lesson observation-based assessments by the school inspector and administrators. Some points of concern beyond the policy goals can be identified:

- How can policymakers address the unintended consequence of the policy regarding the unemployment of unsuccessful candidates and, thus, reduce the cost of government scholarship on some of these students?
- How can policymakers make the multiple career paths for beginning teachers more efficient in their time and energy investments?

- How can policymakers help those beginning teachers who may not make their way through the teacher induction program?

The implications of our analysis for policymakers are several. Policymakers must engage beginning teachers in teacher induction programs with support and pressure to become a quality and highly educated teaching workforce. At the same time, it is also necessary for the policymakers to resolve the unemployment issue as an unintended consequence of the teacher induction policy implementations. They also need to figure out how to make the teaching profession attractive to talented students to pursue their careers through rigorous teacher induction processes. At the same time, they also need to consider minimizing the obstacles and challenges these processes could generate for the potential teacher candidates that may lead them to frustrations and burnout.

Based on our analysis, three recommendations can be offered to the university and school practitioners implementing teacher induction policy. Firstly, leaders and faculty members from SHBIE should work closely with school leadership and mentor teachers to ensure the course assessments reflected the understanding and practices central to helping produce a highly skilled workforce as policy expected. Secondly, school leadership and mentor teachers must also work closely with the leaders and faculty members from SHBIE to ensure the current research is used to inform their mentoring practices, observation-based assessments, and joint inquiry into their practices. Third, both parties need to pay more attention to developing formative assessments aligned with the needs of beginning teachers so they can be supported to go through the teacher induction successfully instead of facing pass or fail summative assessment alone.

This study has raised several questions worth further examination to improve teacher induction policy implementation:

- What are the *factors motivating beginning teachers* to choose to be teachers?
- How can the summative assessments be developed and aligned with each other in measuring beginning teachers' skills and understanding central to effectively teaching their students as expected?
- To what extent does the support for beginning teachers in the practicum field appropriately address their needs for learning to teach in different school contexts?
- What mentoring practices can be adapted to different contexts of beginning teachers' learning to teach?
- What does it take for a mentor teacher to learn to mentor effectively?

The newly reformed teacher induction policy was initiated in 2019 and the implementation may still be regarded at its infancy stage. Much of the focus has been on initial planning, development and implementation, and currently, at the implantation stage. The policy shows promise; indeed, there is still much work to be done for the policy to succeed. The above questions may add to a better understanding in the conceptualization and implementation in improving the teacher induction policy in Brunei.

DISCLAIMER

Some of the data and information used in this chapter are available upon formal request from the relevant departments at the Ministry of Education. In contrast, other data are available to the public and not confidential and limited. The views and opinions expressed in this chapter may not necessarily represent the Ministry of Education, Brunei Darussalam.

REFERENCES

Anthony, G., Haigh, M., & Kane, R. (2011). The power of the 'object' to influence teacher induction outcomes. *Teaching and Teacher Education, 27*(5), 861–870. https://doi.org/10.1016/j.tate.2011.01.010

Australian Qualifications Framework Council. (2013). *The Australian qualifications framework* (2nd ed.). Australian Qualifications Framework Council. https://www.aqf.edu.au/aqf-second-edition-january-2013

Bacon, W. J. (2020). *New teacher induction: Improving teacher self-efficacy* [Doctoral Dissertation]. University of Kentucky. https://uknowledge.uky.edu/cgi/viewcontent.cgi?article=1044&context=edl_etds

Bartlett, L., & Johnson, L. S. (2010). The evolution of new teacher induction policy: Support, specificity, and autonomy. *Educational Policy, 24*(6), 847–871. https://doi.org/10.1177/0895904809341466

Carroll, T. G. (2005). Induction of teachers into 21st-century learning communities: Creating the next generation of educational practice. *The New Educator, 1*(3), 199–204. https://doi.org/10.1080/15476880590966934

Carver, C. L., & Feiman-Nemser, S. (2009). Using policy to improve teacher induction: Critical elements and missing pieces. *Educational Policy, 23*(2), 295–328. https://doi.org/10.1177/0895904807310036

Darling-Hammond, L. (2020). Accountability in teacher education. *Action in Teacher Education, 42*(1), 60–71. https://doi.org/10.1080/01626620.2019.1704464

Darling-Hammond, L., & Cobb, V. L. (1995). *Teacher preparation and professional development in APEC members: A comparative study*. U.S. Department of Education. https://files.eric.ed.gov/fulltext/ED383683.pdf

Darling-Hammond, L., & Rothman, R. (2011). *Teacher and leader effectiveness in high-performing education systems.* Alliance for Excellent Education. https://edpolicy.stanford.edu/library/publications/150

Department of Schools Inspectorate. (2020). *Handbook for Brunei teachers' standards teacher performance appraisal 2.0.* Brunei Darussalam Ministry of Education.

Feiman-Nemser, S. (2010). Multiple meanings of new teacher induction. In J. Wang, S. J. Odell, & R. T. Clift (Eds.), *Past, present, and future research on teacher induction: An anthology for researcher, policymakers, and practitioners* (pp. 15–30). Rowman & Littlefield.

Glazerman, S., Senesky, S., Seftor, N., & Johnson, A. (2006). *Design of an impact evaluation of teacher induction programs.* Mathematica Policy Research, Inc. https://files.eric.ed.gov/fulltext/ED496290.pdf

Goode, C. (2020). English language in Brunei: Use, policy, and status in education—A review. *Indonesian JELT: Indonesian Journal of English Language Teaching, 15*(1), 21–46. https://doi.org/10.25170/ijelt.v15i1.1411

Haji-Othman, N. A., McLellan, J., & Deterding, D. (Eds.). (2016). *The use and status of language in Brunei Darussalam: A kingdom of unexpected linguistic diversity.* Springer. https://doi.org/10.1007/978-981-10-0853-5

Ho, H. M. Y., & Deterding, D. (Eds.). (2021). *Engaging modern Brunei: Research on language, literature, and culture.* Springer. https://doi.org/10.1007/978-981-33-4721-2

Howe, E. R. (2006). Exemplary teacher induction: An international review. *Educational Philosophy and Theory, 38*(3), 287–297. http://dx.doi.org/10.1111/j.1469-5812.2006.00195.x

Hunter, W. (2016). *New teacher induction: A program evaluation* [Doctoral dissertation]. The College of William and Mary. http://dx.doi.org/10.21220/W4TG6W

Ingersoll, R. M., & Strong, M. (2011). The impact of induction and mentoring programs for beginning teachers: A critical review of the research. *Review of Educational Research, 81*(2), 201–233. https://doi.org/10.3102/0034654311403323

Ingvarson, L., Kleinhenz, E., Khoo, S. T., & Wilkinson, J. (2007). *The VIT program for supporting provisionally registered teachers: Evaluation of implementation in 2005.* Victorian Institute for Teaching. https://research.acer.edu.au/teacher_education/2/

Ishamina, A., & Deterding, D. (2017). English-medium education in a university in Brunei Darussalam: Code-switching and intelligibility. In B. Fenton-Smith, P. Humphreys, & I. Walkinshaw (Eds.), *English medium instruction in higher education in Asia-Pacific: From policy to pedagogy* (pp. 281–298). Springer. https://doi.org/10.1007/978-3-319-51976-0_15

Jawawi, R., Jaidin, J. H., & Shahrill, M. (2014). Teacher education in Brunei Darussalam: Transforming tomorrow's generation through teacher education today. In Radjasa, M. N. Dalimin, M. M. Nor, S. Wichidit, & R. Jawawi (Eds.), *Education transformation toward excellent quality based on ASEAN community characteristics* (pp. 1–13). Faculty of Tarbiya and Teacher Training, Islamic State University Sunan Kalijaga. https://digilib.uin-suka.ac.id/id/eprint/19316/

Kearney, S. P. (2013). *New scheme teacher induction: Challenges and opportunities.* Scholar's Press.

Kearney, S. (2014). Understanding beginning teacher induction: A contextualized examination of best practice. *Cogent Education, 1*(1), Article 967477. https://doi.org/10.1080/2331186X.2014.967477

Kotthoff, H.-G., & Terhart, E. (2013). New solutions to old problems? Recent reforms in teacher education in Germany. *Revista Española de Educación Comparada, 22*(1), 73–92.

Long, J. S., McKenzie-Robblee, S., Lee Schaefer, L., Steeves, P., Wnuk, S., Pinnegar, E., & Clandinin, D. J. (2012). Literature review on induction and mentoring related to early career teacher attrition and retention. *Mentoring and tutoring: Partnership in learning, 20*(1), 7–26. http://dx.doi.org/10.1080/13611267.2012.645598

Ministry of Education. (2013). *The national education system for the 21st century: SPN21* (2nd ed.). Brunei Darussalam Ministry of Education. https://www.moe.gov.bn/spn21dl/SPN21%20ENG%20(2013)%20COMPLETE.pdf

Ministry of Education. (2014). *Brunei Darussalam qualification framework*. Brunei Darussalam Ministry of Education. https://bdnac.moe.gov.bn/wp-content/uploads/2020/11/Brunei-Darussalams-Qualification-Framework-November-2014.pdf

Ministry of Education. (2018). *2018–2022 Ministry of Education strategic plan*. Brunei Darussalam Ministry of Education. Retrieved August 31, 2020, from http://www.moe.gov.bn/DocumentDownloads/Strategic%20Plan%20Book%202018-2022/Strategic%20plan%202018-2022.pdf

Ministry of Education. (2020a). *Brunei Darussalam education statistics 2019*. Ministry of Education, Brunei Darussalam.

Ministry of Education. (2020b, March 10). *Surat pemberitahuan kementerian pendidikan bilangan: Perubahan tarikh cuti penggal pertama persekolahan* [Press release]. http://www.moe.gov.bn/SitePages/NewsArticle.aspx?AID=637

Moskowitz, J., & Stephens, M. (1997). *From students of teaching to teachers of students: Teacher induction around the Pacific Rim*. U.S. Department of Education. https://files.eric.ed.gov/fulltext/ED415194.pdf

Mundia, L. (2012). Policy changes in Brunei teacher education: Implications for the selection of trainee teachers. *The Education Forum, 76*(3), 326–342. https://doi.org/10.1080/00131725.2012.682489

Paronjodi, G. K., Jusoh, A. J., & Abdullah, M. H. (2017). A comparative study of beginning teacher induction in Malaysia and Victoria (Australia): A review of the literature. *Journal of Research, Policy & Practice of Teachers, and Teacher Education, 7*(1), 36–48. https://doi.org/10.37134/jrpptte.vol7.no1.5.2017

Quality Assurance Agency for Higher Education. (2008). *The framework for higher education qualifications in England, Wales, and Northern Ireland*. Southgate House.

Ronfeldt, M., Loeb, S., & Wyckoff, J. (2013). How teacher turnover harms student achievement. *American Educational Research Journal, 50*(1), 4–36. https://doi.org/10.3102/0002831212463813

Shahrill, M., Jaidin, J. H., Salleh, S. M., & Jawawi, R. (2014). Realising teacher quality at the M-Level. *European Conference on Education* (pp. 323–338). The International Academic Forum. http://papers.iafor.org/wp-content/uploads/papers/ece2014/ECE2014_02828.pdf

Shahrill, M., Noorashid, N., & Keasberry, C. (2021). COVID-19: Educational practices and responses in Brunei Darussalam. In L. H. Phan, A. Kumpoh, K. Wood, R. Jawawi, & H. Said (Eds.), *Globalisation, education, and reform in Brunei Darussalam* (pp. 325–354). Palgrave MacMillan. https://doi.org/10.1007/978-3-030-77119-5_16

Shahrill, M., Petra, M. I., Naing, L., Yacob, J., Santos, J. H., & Abdul Aziz, A. B. Z. (2021). New norms and opportunities from the COVID-19 pandemic crisis in a higher education setting: Perspectives from Universiti Brunei Darussalam. *International Journal of Educational Management, 35*(3), 700–712. https://doi.org/10.1108/IJEM-07-2020-0347

Sharbawi, S. (2020). An English-centric monolingual Brunei? Predictions and reality. *Asian Englishes, 22*(3), 257–281. https://doi.org/10.1080/13488678.2019.1709335

Sharbawi, S., & Jaidin, J. H. (2019). Brunei's SPN21 English language-in-education policy: A macro-to-micro evaluation. *Current Issues in Language Planning, 21*(2), 175–201. https://doi.org/10.1080/14664208.2019.1657267

Shayshon, B., & Popper-Giveon, A. (2017). 'These are not the realities I imagined': An inquiry into the lost hopes and aspirations of beginning teachers. *Cambridge Journal of Education, 47*(4), 1–17. https://doi.org/10.1080/0305764X.2016.1214238

Wang, J., Odell, S. J., & Schwille, S. A. (2008). Effects of teacher induction on beginning teachers' teaching: A critical review of the literature. *Journal of Teacher Education, 59*(2), 132–152. https://doi.org/10.1177/0022487107314002

Wawasan Brunei 2035. (n.d.). *Goal 1*. Prime Minister's Office. Retrieved September 7, 2020, from http://www.wawasanbrunei.gov.bn/SitePages/Goal%201.aspx

Wong, H. K. (2004). Induction programs that keep new teachers teaching and improving. *NASSP Bulletin, 88*(638), 41–58. https://doi.org/10.1177/019263650408863804

Wong, H. K., Britton, T., & Ganser, T. (2005). What the world can teach us about new teacher induction. *Phi Delta Kappan, 86*(5), 379–384. http://dx.doi.org/10.1177/003172170508600509

CHAPTER 2

TEACHER INDUCTION AND PROFESSIONAL DEVELOPMENT POLICY

The Case of Israel

Noy Dali
Ben-Gurion University of the Negev, Israel

Dorit Tubin
Ben-Gurion University of the Negev, Israel

ABSTRACT

One of the main problems in Israel's education system is novice teacher attrition. The research literature suggests that one of the reasons for teacher attrition traces back to the induction process. Over the past decade, the Ministry of Education has implemented policy initiatives to increase teacher status, reduce novice teacher attrition, and attract quality teachers. This chapter examines the development of teacher induction and professional development policy in Israel and its effectiveness in responding to these challenges. It begins with the historical, social, and political contexts in which the teacher

Teacher Induction Policy in Global Contexts, pages 23–41
Copyright © 2024 by Information Age Publishing
www.infoagepub.com
All rights of reproduction in any form reserved.

induction policy was developed and then analyzes its process, mandates, and underlying assumptions. In addition, it presents two cases to demonstrate how the implementation of the induction policy affects novice teachers. We conclude with the challenges that teacher induction policymakers and practitioners face and questions worthy of further exploration.

The State of Israel was established in 1948 and currently has a population of 9.1 million. In 2019, 1.82 million students studied at 5,163 schools, with 182,000 teachers (Israel Central Bureau of Statistics, 2019), and 11,000 new beginning teachers joined the education system from 2019 to 2020 (Ministry of Education, 2020). Israel's education system is centralized, with the Ministry of Education administering nine geographical and administrative districts and four education sectors. The Ministry of Education determines educational policy in all aspects, including the national curriculum, teacher employment, professional development, and school buildings. The districts and sectors implement the policy in collaboration with the municipalities and schools in their jurisdiction (Yogev, 1996).

The Ministry of Education develops the induction policy and general guidelines for teacher training and induction to promote quality and retention nationally. Thus, a certain degree of freedom is left for each academic institution, municipality, and school to implement this policy following their specific circumstances.

This chapter discusses the historical, social, and political contexts in which Israel's teacher induction policy was developed and implemented, followed by an analysis of the policy, its mandates, and underlying assumptions. Next, two cases are presented to demonstrate how the implementation of the induction policy affects novice teachers. The chapter concludes with the challenges facing teacher induction policymakers and practitioners and research questions meriting further exploration to address these challenges effectively.

HISTORICAL, SOCIAL, AND POLITICAL CONTEXTS OF THE INDUCTION POLICY

Israel's teacher induction policy is situated in several historical, social, and political contexts. *Historically,* Israel's population has grown from half a million to nine million residents over the last 70 years due to mass immigration of populations from different countries with different religions and ethnicities and children needing appropriate and egalitarian education (Yogev, 1996). It placed a heavy burden on the rapidly growing education system and necessitated the recruitment of many teachers, with little attention paid to their qualifications. For example, 19-year-old female soldiers, or immigrants who were partly fluent in Hebrew, could receive a teaching certificate and become teachers if they completed a 2-year preparation program at a teacher seminar without undergoing a formal induction process (Hofman & Niederland, 2012).

In the 1970s, given the students' complex backgrounds, growing educational gaps, constant teacher shortage, and dissatisfaction with the quality of teachers, the Ministry of Education introduced the Integration Reform. The goals of the reform were to postpone student screening for vocational and regular education, integrate students from different backgrounds, and increase the status of teachers. The reform included a restructuring of the school system into three schooling levels: elementary schools (1st–6th grades), junior high schools (7th–9th grades), and high schools (10th–12th grades). One of the reform results was that the teacher union split into elementary and junior high school teachers and secondary school teachers, who were trained in separate training institutions following unique curriculums. The diversification of the training institutions called for a national induction program (Lazovsky & Reichenberg, 2006).

From the late 1970s to the 1990s, the Ministry of Education promoted the academization of the teaching profession to improve teachers' salaries, professionalization, and social status (Hofman & Niederland, 2012). At the end of the process, the 2-year teacher seminars became 4-year academic colleges qualified to award their graduates a bachelor's degree and a teaching certificate. The academization reform led to the establishment of twelve new colleges that train elementary and junior high school teachers and the five university schools of education that train secondary school teachers (Hofman & Niederland, 2012; Yogev, 1996). While differently implemented, all the training institutions include an induction program that emphasizes teaching experience in the real context of an actual classroom, support of a personal mentor, and a group workshop (Lazovsky & Reichenberg, 2006). Despite the Ministry of Education's centralized governance, the social conditions of Israeli society affect the process.

Socially, Israeli society is divided into four sectors—secular, religious, Arab, and ultra-Orthodox—each with its education system governed by the Ministry of Education (Yogev, 1996). The students in each sector differ in ethnic origin, religion, and values, consequently holding different beliefs and needs. Therefore, national-level education policies, including the induction policy, are implemented differently in each sector (Yogev, 1996). The ultra-Orthodox sector, for example, can employ male teachers who study in nonacademic ultra-Orthodox institutions and female teachers who are trained in ultra-Orthodox seminaries without undergoing an induction process. In most cases, teachers receive training at an academic institution in the specific sector they will teach, characterized by unique curriculums, different acceptance criteria, and diverse induction processes. This chapter focuses on the largest education sector, the state-secular sector (about 45%

of the student population), where the national induction policy is more consistently developed and implemented.

Politically, the two teacher trade unions, the Israel Teachers Union for Elementary School Teachers and the Teachers Association for Secondary School Teachers, have also influenced the development and implementation of the induction policy, as they represent the teachers' different interests and working conditions (Hofman & Niederland, 2012). In 2010, motivated by teacher shortage and their low status, the two unions and the Ministry of Education initiated an extensive reform that impacted teachers' salaries, working conditions, and professional development processes throughout the teacher population (Avidov-Ungar & Herscu, 2020). Based on the assumption that teacher quality and retention depend on lifelong learning throughout a teacher's career (Ministry of Education, 2010), the reform defines three main professional development periods: entry-level, advanced, and expert. At the entry level, the induction process was expanded to include internship, personal mentoring, workshops, and seminars associated with aspects of classroom management, as well as greater autonomy for principals to adapt the induction process to their school's context (Avidov-Ungar & Herscu, 2020).

Influenced by the above historical, social, and political contexts, constant teacher shortage, attrition, and dissatisfaction with teacher quality (Donitsa-Schmidt & Zuzovsky, 2016; Lazovsky & Reichenberg, 2006; Ministry of Education, 2020; Weinberger & Donitsa-Schmidt, 2016), the 2-year induction process and policy has become a central issue.

TEACHER INDUCTION POLICY

This section presents the teacher induction policy's structure, process, and implementation. It then details the policy's mandates, including improving teacher quality, reducing teacher turnover, and enhancing teacher retention, and concludes with an analysis of the assumptions underlying the induction policy.

Induction Policy Processes and Implementation

In 2020, the Ministry of Education developed a compulsory 2-year induction policy to improve the quality of teacher training, ease beginning teachers' survival in teaching, and reduce teacher turnover (Ministry of Education, 2020). According to this policy, teacher induction is structured as a 2-year process.

The first year of teacher induction begins in the fourth and final year of the teacher preparation programs and is defined as the "internship year." The aim of the first year is for teacher interns to gain practical experience by working part-time in a training school and practicing teaching their subject at the relevant educational level (elementary or high school). They also practice entering a school during their preparation program since they are required to look for a part-time position at a training school on their own while the Ministry of Education pays their salary.

The teacher interns are assigned a personal mentor for the year in the training school, as in most induction policies worldwide (Alles et al., 2019). The mentors must participate in training programs offered at the teacher preparation institutions and learn how to treat beginning teachers as ongoing learners who need help, guidance, and role models for teaching (Feiman-Nemser et al., 1999). In their weekly meetings, the mentors observe the teacher interns in the classroom, discuss teaching practices, strengths, and weaknesses, and suggest ways to improve. The mentors also mediate abstract teaching models for the "here and now," translating the school's codes and norms into specific events.

At the same time, the teacher interns have to participate in an internship workshop offered at their teacher preparation institution or the training school, constituting personal and group support for their teaching practices. In the workshop, teacher interns learn how to adapt theoretical pedagogic models to particular situations. They also learn how to deal with the "praxis shock" that occurs when encountering school reality by sharing experiences with other teacher interns and workshop facilitators (Dicke et al., 2015). The mentors and school principals conduct formative and summative assessments during the internship year. The assessments address four areas: (a) the teacher's commitment to students, (b) expertise in teaching their discipline, (c) classroom management, and (d) the teacher as a learner. Teacher interns who pass the summative assessment successfully receive a teaching license and start the second year as beginning teachers. Those who encounter difficulties in passing their assessment must undergo an additional internship year.

In the second year, the beginning teachers choose the school where they wish to work as full-time teachers and become an integral part of the teaching staff, subject to the school's approval (Lazovsky & Reichenberg, 2006). They are also assigned a coach, typically a senior teacher, who has completed a mentor training program. At the end of the second year of induction, the beginning teachers undergo summative assessments by their coach and the school principal, following the four areas stated above. Those who pass the assessment successfully receive a permanent position at the school.

To sum up, the induction policy aims to strengthen the connection between the academic institution and the schools, help beginning teachers cope with difficulties in the first years of teaching and enable professional development while supporting socialization in the teaching profession and the school organization. This induction policy has been implemented in schools across the country. While compulsory components, such as formative and summative assessments and group workshops, are implemented, they do not necessarily lead to the policy's expected results. The lack of time and supervision over mentoring and coaching means that the personal meetings do not have a clear agenda and a pre-determined schedule. In addition, training programs for mentors and coaches are offered at teacher preparation institutions, but few mentors attend them (Lazovsky & Reichenberg, 2006). Some difficulties in the policy's implementation stem from its basic assumptions.

Policy Mandates and Assumptions

The induction policy has three mandates. The first is *to improve the quality of novice teachers* by offering them theoretical knowledge, conceptual models, and practical tools for everyday use in the classroom (Alles et al., 2019). This mandate reflects several ideas on novice teachers' development in the research literature. The first suggests that teaching quality can be improved by helping beginning teachers bridge the theory-practice gap and shortening their learning curve (Morrison, 2008). The second indicates the importance of novice teachers practicing teaching in a real-life classroom to deal with classroom management challenges, curriculum planning, teaching methods, and evaluation tools (Spalding et al., 2011). It further reflects the idea that university–school cooperation can help infuse school practice with new teaching models and enrich teacher preparation institutions with greater attention to novice teachers' emergent needs (Reynolds et al., 2002).

While this mandate helps to improve the quality of novice teachers by practicing teaching in a real-life classroom at the internship school (Lieberman, 1995), it does have some conceptual limitations. One is the assumption that effective teaching practice is generic across different subjects and school contexts (Danielson, 2007). In other words, if it is effective for one subject in one school, it will be useful for other subjects in other schools. However, this implicit assumption is not empirically sustainable since a universally effective teaching practice is yet to be identified (Lieberman, 1995). As Shulman (1986) suggests, practice should be content-specific and more relevant for supporting student learning in each discipline. It can be a problem, especially when beginning teachers are assigned to teach a different subject, grade, or school level to those they trained for in their preparation program. Another limitation of the generic assumption is the difficulty of entering a school following the two-phase induction process and changing schools after the internship year. Adjusting to a particular school and creating a network of contacts is an important part of job embeddedness (Ng & Feldman, 2007), and readjusting to a second school after one year might impact the novice teacher's involvement in the new school.

The second policy mandate is *to reduce teacher turnover* through personal mentoring and coaching during the induction years, as suggested in the literature (Ingersoll & Smith, 2004). This personal guidance promotes socialization in the school and familiarization with the teaching contexts. It enhances professional ties with teacher colleagues and supports the use of acquired expertise (Holtom & O'Neill, 2004; Ng & Feldman, 2007).

Underlying this mandate is the assumption that personal mentoring and coaching help novice teachers address challenges such as feeling overwhelmed, unclear expectations, role conflicts, and life-work balance, and feel at ease in the teaching profession (Beijaard et al., 2010; Howe, 2006; Wang & Odell, 2002). It also implicitly suggests that any mentoring or coaching is better than nothing. However, when the mentor or coach has not been trained for the task, or when they are not from the same discipline as the beginning teacher, or unavailable due to workload, they may not be effective in supporting novice teachers and may even impair their willingness to remain in the teaching profession (Beijaard et al., 2010; Ingersoll & Smith, 2004; Wang & Odell, 2002).

The third mandate is *to enhance novice teacher retention* by engaging them with colleagues to broaden their professional perspective, learning about their school context, and receiving observation-based feedback about their instruction practice. This mandate is consistent with the idea that teachers are more likely to stay in teaching when they can develop a professional identity, become acquainted with the teaching profession, and socialize in their specific school contexts (Feldman & Ng, 2007). It also echoes the idea that teachers are more likely to improve their teaching practices and stay in the school when they belong to a professional group of colleagues that engages with teaching practices, data-based feedback, and friendly criticism (Becher & Lefstein, 2021).

The power of professional learning communities is well documented (DuFour, 2004); however, under certain conditions, it may cause learning by imitation. Such learning presents a master-apprentice relationship in which the inexperienced practitioner strives to adopt and emulate an experienced practitioner's practices (Lochmiller, 2014). In addition, it creates a "pedagogical signature" (Shulman, 2005), which, if strongly present, shapes the novice teachers' patterns of conforming, performing, and thinking, as well as the conservative professional standards they expect from themselves and others.

In sum, the 2-year induction policy aims to strengthen the connection between the preparation programs and the schools, help novice teachers cope with difficulties in the first years, and support their socialization with the teaching profession and the school organization. It is designed to implement three mandates in particular. First, to bridge the theory-practice gap based on beginning teachers' abilities, interests, and occupational requirements and help them learn to teach effectively. Second, to form professional ties with colleagues, using mentoring and coaching that presumably offer novice teachers emotional support, task assistance, and the necessary information to stay in teaching. Third, developing their professional identity through ongoing professional development supports their retention and continuous professional growth (Holtom & O'Neill, 2004; Ng & Feldman, 2007).

TWO CASES OF POLICY IMPLEMENTATION AND EFFECTS

This section uses the experiences of two beginning teachers in a school context to demonstrate the teacher induction policy's implementation, strengths, and weaknesses. The first case presents the experiences of the first author of this chapter, Noy, as a novice teacher in an elementary school, based on her personal diary written during this period in 2020. The second case reflects the experiences of a beginning teacher, Larry, who came to education from a high-tech company. Larry's case is part of a larger study focusing on the induction routine in a successful high school in Israel (Dali, 2022).

The Case of Noy

Noy had just completed her BA in social science at university and started working as a substitute teacher to decide whether to choose teaching as her career. The school recruited Noy as a part-time teacher due to the teacher shortage in her geographical region, especially in the required disciplines. Following regulations, school principals can recruit teachers who do not yet have a teaching certificate as part-time teachers for three years until they complete all their formal requirements (Ministry of Education, 2019). To acquaint her with the school's culture and teaching contexts, the school assigned her a mentor from the same discipline, the vice principal, to guide her throughout the school year. As Noy relates:

> The principal handed me the "school file" at the beginning of the year, which included the organizational chart, school vision, curriculum, and other documents. I had no idea what to do, but I was happy I had a mentor to help me. The meetings with my mentor, the vice principal, who taught the same fourth grade I was teaching, began in the first week of the school year.

Noy's mentor scheduled weekly meetings with her to discuss various issues. However, as Noy describes, some meetings were canceled: "We were supposed to meet once a week for one hour, scheduled in advance, but sometimes the meetings were canceled due to her workload. We spent most of the time discussing classroom management issues and communication with parents."

When the need to interact with students' parents arose, her mentor often hastened to interact with them directly instead of letting Noy handle the situation, as Noy explains:

> Usually, she dictated answers to messages from the students' parents, and, in some cases, she talked to them herself. She explained that due to her experience, she's better able to deal with the parents, which spares me from clashing with them.

The mentor also involved teachers from other grade levels or subjects in observing and giving feedback on Noy's teaching. However, these observations were often not scheduled in advance and mainly focused on her weaknesses in class management. Such activities frequently undermined Noy's confidence instead of supporting her, as she relates:

> My mentor asked teachers from other grades or disciplines to observe me when I was teaching, but no one informed me in advance who would come and observe. Their presence and interference during the lesson prevented me from managing the class as I wanted to. Their feedback was mostly about the students' behavior and chatting. These situations humiliated me, and I felt inexperienced in front of the students.

Her part-time status and the administrative focus of the staff meetings also limited Noy's chances to learn from her colleagues and receive a response to her growing needs. She describes her relationship with her colleagues:

> Due to my part-time teaching position, I couldn't attend department meetings regularly. When I did, the meetings usually dealt with administrative issues and didn't provide professional help with pedagogical questions. Although the teachers were supportive and willing to help, we rarely met, and my general feeling was that I was left alone to sink or swim.

Consequently, after one year as a part-time teacher, Noy decided to leave teaching, mainly because of her negative induction experiences. She explains: "I decided to leave the teaching profession altogether. The negative experience of the induction process wasn't the only factor influencing my decision, but it did leave its mark."

Noy's case suggests that implementation of the induction components following the national teacher induction policy is insufficient to lead to the expected outcomes. For example, Noy's school ostensibly implemented all the induction practices, including assigning a teacher from the same discipline as a mentor, having fellow teachers observe her teaching and give feedback, and involving her in department meetings. Nevertheless, without quality time and the necessary expertise in each induction process, the novice teacher's learning is not as expected by the induction policy. There are several reasons for this.

First, the mentor's effectiveness may be compromised due to the mentor's position as vice principal, a limited understanding of a novice teacher's needs, and how to meet those needs. It led to irregular mentoring meetings, narrow focuses on classroom management and parent relations, and limited opportunities for the new teacher to learn how to interact with parents.

Additionally, the random observations of Noy's classroom teaching by teachers from different grade levels and subjects often limited their feedback to students' behaviors. Such observations and feedback often impacted Noy's professional self-confidence rather than functioning as a formative assessment to answer her needs and improve her teaching practices (Holtom & O'Neill, 2004; Ng & Feldman, 2007).

Finally, the staff meetings were often structured around a general administrative function rather than diagnosis, intervention, and inference about teaching and student learning (Becher & Lefstein, 2021). Consequently, these meetings rarely served as opportunities to develop Noy's professional identity and often impaired her job embeddedness due to weak collegial ties and emphasis on issues unrelated to teaching. All these reasons contributed to Noy's decision to leave the teaching profession.

The Case of Larry

After working as a developer in a high-tech company, Larry changed to become an English teacher. He completed the teacher education program and started his internship year at an elementary school, which he describes as a negative experience.

> I worked in an education program at the school before, so I already knew most of the teachers, and no one saw me as a novice teacher. No one observed me teach. I didn't get the assessment or guidance I needed as a novice teacher. The school principal was my mentor, but we didn't meet at all. The internship workshop was held at the college and wasn't connected to the school context and didn't help me deal with my specific challenges of school life.

As a consequence of this situation, Larry decided to leave the elementary school and try another internship year in a high school, which led to a better experience in several ways. First, the internship workshop was offered in the school context and, thus, was much more suitable for him, as he relates:

> I decided to do an internship at a high school. The department heads introduced us to the school staff and curriculum at the beginning of the year and gave us a tour of the school. I also participated in an internship workshop at the school. It was much better [than the previous out-of-school workshop] practically and technically because it was with teachers from the same school who had the same experiences as mine. College studies lack practical experience. Everything seems good in theory, but when the classroom door closes, you're on your own, and it's different.

Second, he had "a senior teacher from the English staff" as his mentor and a supportive department head. They supported his need to learn how to teach by focusing their interactions on "professional issues" and "offering solutions for problems and answers to questions." They made him feel "more confident" about teaching English. He explains:

> In meetings with my mentor, I learned to write a lesson plan and a class curriculum. I also learned how to check students' tests. In staff meetings, each teacher shared their progress, and I was able to understand my status in relation to other teachers.

Larry's case suggests that several factors shaped his positive experience in the second internship period compared to the negative experience at the elementary school. First, the internship workshop was offered at the internship school, which allowed Larry to interact with other teacher interns from the school and learn about teaching practices in a specific context (Tamir et al., 2017). He also received professional support for teaching English from his mentor, a senior English teacher, and his department head, who was experienced in teaching the subject and resourceful in addressing specific problems. Finally, his positive relationships and collaborations with other teachers and the group support in the school context helped him position himself as a learner of teaching and provided opportunities for developing professional knowledge (Ng & Feldman, 2007).

In summary, while the two cases do not represent Israel's entire induction policy implementation, they illustrate some strengths and lacunas in this policy's implementation. They suggest that teacher induction policy should go beyond surface forms and processes to focus on quality time and opportunities for beginning teachers to learn to teach. As shown directly in Larry's case and indirectly in Noy's case, this support includes: (a) mentors specializing in teaching the same subject and at the same grade levels and understanding their needs when learning to teach; (b) sufficient time to interact with other novice teachers in the school; (c) colleagues offering observations and feedback on their teaching practices; and (d) department meetings structured around their needs when learning to teach.

Policy Impacts on Teacher Induction

Implementing the teacher induction policy in Israel is a complicated process, which, as with other policy implementations, has intended and unintended impacts and results (Pressman & Wildavsky, 1984). In the case of beginning teachers learning to teach, these intended and unintended impacts include the following:

First, the teacher induction policy offers interns a paid part-time teaching position for their first year in a school. This position enables them to practice teaching in a real class, familiarize themselves with teaching duties and the school's organization, and thus reduce the theory-practice gap (Feiman-Nemser et al., 1999). While teacher interns learn to teach with their mentor, their part-time position prevents them from establishing professional ties with their subject team. It delays their adjustment to the organization's values and norms (Ng & Feldman, 2007), as demonstrated in Noy's case. In addition, the workshops can produce both intended and unintended impacts.

For example, when the internship workshop takes place in a teacher preparation institution, it can create an unintended situation whereby teacher interns feel detached from the school context because they have limited opportunities to interact with their peers who have similar teaching experiences in the school. In this situation, the theory-practice gap widens rather than narrows, resulting in frustration, as shown in Larry's first-year internship experience. In contrast, when the workshop is offered in the school context, it can help teacher interns develop a positive experience, as anticipated in the policy and as shown in Larry's second internship.

Second, the mentoring and coaching during the induction process provide the support needed for beginning teachers in their transition into the teaching profession by mediating the initial difficulties they encounter and helping with professional identity development, as anticipated in the policy. However, it can also lead to unintended impacts (Lazovsky & Reichenberg, 2006; Weinberger & Donitsa-Schmidt, 2016).

For example, assigning a mentor from a different discipline to a teacher intern can focus on classroom management issues rather than on pedagogical issues, promoting each student's learning and supporting professional development (Ingersoll & Smith, 2004; Wayne et al., 2008). As demonstrated in the case of Noy, this also prevented her from receiving observation-based feedback on her teaching practices in her subject. The fit between a beginning teacher's subject and that of their coach is even more crucial because when beginning teachers choose a school (that accepts them) for the second year of their induction process, they are assigned a new coach from the school staff for fewer hours.

In addition, the policy's focus on pushing beginning teachers to rely on their coaches' experience and directions as sources of learning in teaching can also lead to an unintended situation. For example, a beginning teacher's dependence on their coach's summative assessment creates an environment wherein following the coach's experience and directions is the best strategy for surviving the second year and earning a permanent position. It may result in beginning teachers teaching by conforming to existing rules, bureaucratic demands, and the school's hierarchy rather than following their students' learning needs (Rennert-Ariev, 2008; Wang & Odell, 2002). Thus, it could prevent them from teaching creatively and developing innovative strategies central to transforming student learning (Lochmiller, 2014).

Third, the teacher induction policy supports beginning teachers adapting to full-time teachers' teaching requirements, cultural norms, and codes. This focus can lead to intended and unintended impacts on beginning teachers' teaching and professional development.

For example, as shown in the case of Larry's second-year induction experience, this policy focus can help beginning teachers learn to teach effectively by adjusting to the expectations and teaching requirements in their school contexts, with support from their coaches who teach the same subject. It also provides opportunities for beginning teachers to form social connections and access professional support through interactions with teachers from the same subject team. As suggested in the literature (Jäppinen et al., 2015), when beginning teachers work in subject teams of teachers who meet regularly and function as a professional learning community, they are exposed to discussions and analyses of classroom events and students' learning problems (Abbott, 2014; Berliner, 2001). Collaboration and continuous communication with colleagues, subject team members, and administrative staff help beginning teachers feel part of the school and increase their commitment, sense of belonging, and satisfaction with teaching (Shapira-Lishchinsky et al., 2019).

However, in most cases, although the beginning teachers join the subject team, they do not receive special attention, as evidenced in the case of Larry's first-year induction experience. As shown in Noy's case, it can limit beginning teachers' chances to interact with teachers from the same subject team around teaching issues during staff meetings. Furthermore, it can weaken their professional networks and interpersonal relationships with other teachers, counselors, middle leaders, and principals, who can provide novice teachers with emotional and professional support

(Shapira-Lishchinsky & Ben-Amram, 2018; Schechter, 2015) and even reduce attrition and turnover.

While Israel's teacher induction policy has the best intentions, its flexible implementation can lead to contradictory results. For example, an internship workshop may provide opportunities to interact with peers and reduce the theory-practice gap; however, when an academic institution offers the workshop, it reduces beginning teachers' opportunities to interact with peers from the same school and connect theory to practice. In addition, mentoring and coaching may promote professional identity development. They may also encourage beginning teachers to model themselves on their coaches and conform to existing practices and school contexts, which might increase their compliance and discourage them from questioning current teaching practices and learning. Lastly, mentoring and coaching may promote socialization in the teaching profession and the school organization. Still, the schools' flexible choice of mentors and coaches may also limit the discourse about novice teachers' needs when learning to teach. Consequently, this may delay the development of professional skills and socialization to their subject team.

POLICY CHALLENGES AND RESEARCH QUESTIONS FOR TEACHER INDUCTION

Our analysis of the development and implementation of the teacher induction policy in Israel highlighted several challenges that this policy faces at the macro and micro levels. These challenges are discussed from the theoretical perspective of organizational learning (Argyris, 1997), along with further research directions that can clarify these challenges.

Macro-Level Challenges and Research Focuses

Developing and implementing a uniform and quality teacher induction policy is challenging (Alles et al., 2019). It is especially difficult when different districts, sectors, and schools enjoy autonomy in their implementation, as in the Israeli case (Weinberger & Donitsa-Schmidt, 2016). The main challenges are a lack of information exchange, organizational inquiry, and cumulative knowledge. Further research is required to determine how schools and districts establish effective induction processes to promote mutual learning.

It is also challenging to develop and implement a coherent induction process split into two stages, each governed by different actors with different goals. Personal mentoring and coaching, for example, take place in the school context and are provided by senior teachers from the school, while internship workshops are provided by the teacher preparation institutions (Bickmore & Bickmore, 2010; Tamir et al., 2017). Moreover, during the first year of induction, the teacher interns work as part-time teachers, while in the second year, they can choose any school they wish and usually start as full-time, autonomous teachers. There is little coherence between the two years since they usually occur in different schools, with different actors, different mentoring practices, and the novice teachers' different statuses and career stages. Thus, it is necessary to understand how teacher preparation programs and schools can collaborate to generate coherent professional support for beginning teachers at the various learning stages (Beijaard et al., 2010).

Micro-Level Challenges and Research Focuses

There are also micro-level challenges in the personal mentoring and workshop. Regarding personal guidance, it is challenging for schools to select the right person from the limited number of suitable teachers since they usually already fill midlevel leadership positions. It is also unclear what is the best training model for mentors and coaches, given the absence of a consensus on their role definition, professional knowledge, and required expertise (Lazovsky & Reichenberg, 2006; Shapira-Lishchinsky et al., 2019). Israel's induction policy assumes that mentor training is generally beneficial (Maynard, 2000) and offers a general guideline for programs and schools to train mentors and coaches (Ministry of Education, 2015). However, its effectiveness is as yet unclear.

Consequently, the schools are left alone to select mentors and coaches for novice teachers based on their perspectives, needs, approaches, and priorities (McCann et al., 2005). In addition, mentors have neither the time nor the motivation to share their experiences and learn from each other. Therefore, it is important to develop and study mentor training models and to create workshops for the mentors' and coaches' ongoing learning and professional development.

It is also challenging to develop effective organizational routines for the induction process, given the school principals' autonomy to implement it as best fits their school's conditions. Different leadership styles, management approaches, and educational priorities affect school principals' abilities to improve novice teachers' experiences, learning to teach, and retention (McCann et al., 2005). It also affects the assignment of mentors, time allocation, meeting scheduling, and socialization of the entire educational staff. The primary role of a principal who wishes to improve the induction process is to create an organizational climate that encourages peer learning, partnership, collaboration, and trust between the beginning teacher, school management, and the entire school staff. To achieve this, the principal must develop effective organizational routines for the teacher induction process.

Organizational routines are "repetitive, recognizable patterns of interdependent actions carried out by multiple actors" (Feldman & Pentland, 2003, p. 95). In teacher induction, these routines reflect the call to view teacher induction and professional development as a single process (Alles et al., 2019). It can be achieved by assigning the beginning teachers to a subject team from the beginning, with the department head as their mentor responsible for their induction and integration with subject team members, and the subject team members function as a professional learning community (DuFour, 2004). Such a community engages in collaborative inquiry (Little, 2012) to diagnose learning problems, plan an intervention, monitor its implementation, and assess the results (Abbott, 2014). In this context, the beginning teachers develop their professional knowledge and teaching skills (Huffman & Kalnin, 2003), bridge the theory-practice gap, form a professional identity (Beijaard et al., 2004), and learn how to contend with the challenges, changes, and crises in teaching (Middlewood et al., 2005).

Such challenges, crises, and changes became even more real during the COVID-19 pandemic and its aftermath (Dvir & Schatz-Oppenheimer, 2020). However, the current policy guidelines do not provide a clear vision for developing novice teachers within the regular and ongoing school routine. Further study to explore ways to integrate novice teachers into the subject team's regularities and classroom teaching practices and immerse them into the school's culture will help to complete and further develop the teacher induction policy.

REFERENCES

Abbott, A. (2014). *The system of professions: An essay on the division of expert labor*. University of Chicago Press.

Alles, M., Apel, J., Seidel, T., & Stürmer, K. (2019). How candidate teachers experience coherence in university education and teacher induction: The influence of perceived professional preparation at university and support during teacher induction. *Vocations and Learning, 12*(1), 87–112. https://doi.org/10.1007/s12186-018-9211-5

Argyris, C. (1997). Learning and teaching: A theory of action perspective. *Journal of Management Education, 21*(1), 9–26.

Avidov-Ungar, O., & Herscu, O. (2020). Formal professional development as perceived by teachers in different professional life periods. *Professional Development in Education, 46*(5), 833–844. https://doi.org/10.1080/19415257.2019.1647271

Becher, A., & Lefstein, A. (2021). Teaching as a clinical profession: Adapting the medical model. *Journal of Teacher Education, 72*(4), 477–488. http://doi.org/10.1177/0022487120972633

Beijaard, D., Buitink, J., & Kessels, C. (2010). Teacher induction. *International Encyclopedia of Education, 3*(7), 563–568.

Beijaard, D., Meijer, P. C., & Verloop, N. (2004). Reconsidering research on teachers' professional identity. *Teaching and Teacher Education, 20*(2), 107–128. https://doi.org/10.1016/j.tate.2003.07.001

Berliner, D. C. (2001). Learning about and learning from expert teachers. *International Journal of Educational Research, 35*(5), 463–482. https://doi.org/10.1016/S0883-0355(02)00004-6

Bickmore, D. L., & Bickmore, S. T. (2010). A multifaceted approach to teacher induction. *Teaching and Teacher Education, 26*(4), 1006–1014. https://doi.org/10.1016/j.tate.2009.10.043

Dali, N. (2022). Teacher induction routines—Structure, characteristic, and implications [Thesis submitted in partial fulfillment of the requirements for the Master of Arts, Ben Gurion University of the Negev, Israel]. (Hebrew)

Danielson, C. (2007). *Enhancing professional practice: A framework for teaching.* ASCD.

Dicke, T., Elling, J., Schmeck, A., & Leutner, D. (2015). Reducing reality shock: Classroom management skills training effects on beginning teachers. *Teaching and Teacher Education, 48*, 1–12. https://doi.org/10.1016/j.tate.2015.01.013

Donitsa-Schmidt, S., & Zuzovsky, R. (2016). Quantitative and qualitative teacher shortage and the turnover phenomenon. *International Journal of Educational Research, 77*, 83–91. https://doi.org/10.1016/j.ijer.2016.03.005

DuFour, R. (2004). What is a "professional learning community"? *Educational Leadership, 61*(8), 6–11.

Dvir, N., & Schatz-Oppenheimer, O. (2020). Novice teachers in a changing reality. *European Journal of Teacher Education, 43*(4), 639–656. https://doi.org/10.1080/02619768.2020.1821360

Feiman-Nemser, S., Schwille, S., Carver, C., & Yusko, B. (1999). *A conceptual review of literature on new teacher induction.* National Partnership for Excellence and Accountability in Teaching.

Feldman, D. C., & Ng, T. W. (2007). Careers: Mobility, embeddedness, and success. *Journal of Management, 33*(3), 350–377. https://psycnet.apa.org/doi/10.1177/0149206307300815

Feldman, M. S., & Pentland, B. T. (2003). Reconceptualizing organizational routines as a source of flexibility and change. *Administrative Science Quarterly, 48*(1), 94–118.

Hofman, A., & Niederland, D. (2012). Is teacher education higher education? The politics of teacher education in Israel, 1970–2010. *Higher Education Policy, 25*(1), 87–106. https://doi.org/10.1057/hep.2011.24

Holtom, B. C., & O'Neill, B. S. (2004). Job embeddedness: A theoretical foundation for developing a comprehensive nurse retention plan. *Journal of Nursing Administration, 34*(5), 216–227.

Howe, E. R. (2006). Exemplary teacher induction: An international review. *Educational Philosophy and Theory, 38*(3), 287–297. https://doi.org/10.1111/j.1469-5812.2006.00195.x

Huffman, D., & Kalnin, J. (2003). Collaborative inquiry to make data-based decisions in schools. *Teaching and teacher education, 19*(6), 569–580. https://doi.org/10.1016/S0742-051X(03)00054

Ingersoll, R. M., & Smith, T. M. (2004). Do teacher induction and mentoring matter? *NASSP Bulletin, 88*(638), 28–40.

Israel Central Bureau of Statistics. (2019). *Internal mobility and leaving the system among teaching staff, 2000–2018.* Jerusalem, Israel. (Hebrew)

Jäppinen, A. K., Leclerc, M., & Tubin, D. (2015). Collaborativeness as the core of professional learning communities beyond culture and context: evidence from Canada, Finland, and Israel. *School Effectiveness and School Improvement, 27*(3), 315–332. https://doi.org/10.1080/09243453.2015.1067235

Lazovsky, R., & Reichenberg, R. (2006). The new mandatory induction program for all beginning teachers in Israel: Perceptions of inductees in five study tracks. *Journal of Education for Teaching, 32*(1), 53–70. https://doi.org/10.1080/02607470500510977

Lieberman, A. (1995). Practices that support teacher development: Transforming conceptions of professional learning. *Innovating and Evaluating Science Education, 95*(64), 67–78.

Little, J. W. (2012). Professional community and professional development in the learning-centered school. In M. Kooy & K. Van Veen (Eds.), *Teacher learning that matters: International perspectives* (pp. 22–46). Routledge.

Lochmiller, C. R. (2014). Leadership coaching in an induction program for novice principals: A 3-year study. *Journal of Research on Leadership Education, 9*(1), 59–84. https://doi.org/10.1177%2F1942775113502020

Maynard, T. (2000). Learning to teach or learning to manage mentors? Experiences of school-based teacher training. *Mentoring and Tutoring, 8*(1), 17–30. https://doi.org/10.1080/713685510

McCann, T. M., Johannessen, L. R., & Ricca, B. (2005). Responding to new teachers' concerns. *Educational Leadership, 62*(8), 30–34.

Middlewood, D., Parker, R., & Beere, J. (2005). *Creating a learning school.* Paul Chapman Publishing.

Ministry of Education. (2010). *Professional development of teaching staff: "Ofek Hadash" policy.* Ministry of Education. (Hebrew)

Ministry of Education. (2015). *Internship and induction into teaching.* Ministry of Education. (Hebrew)

Ministry of Education. (2019). *Regulation for recruitment candidates and induction of teaching staff for the 2019–2020 school year.* Ministry of Education. (Hebrew)

Ministry of Education. (2020). *The education system for 2020–2021 school year.* Ministry of Education. (Hebrew)

Morrison, J. B. (2008). Putting the learning curve in context. *Journal of Business Research, 61*(11), 1182–1190.

Ng, T. W., & Feldman, D. C. (2007). Organizational embeddedness and occupational embeddedness across career stages. *Journal of Vocational Behavior, 70*(2), 336–351. https://doi.org/10.1016/j.jvb.2006.10.002

Pressman, J. L., & Wildavsky, A. (1984). *Implementation: How great expectations in Washington are dashed in Oakland; Or, why it's amazing that federal programs work at all, this being a saga of the economic development administration as told by two sympathetic observers who seek to build morals on a foundation* (Vol. 708). University of California Press.

Rennert-Ariev, P. (2008). The hidden curriculum of performance-based teacher education. *Teachers College Record, 110*(1), 105–138.

Reynolds, A., Ross, S. M., & Rakow, J. H. (2002). Teacher retention, teaching effectiveness, and professional preparation: A comparison of professional development school and non-professional development school graduates. *Teaching and Teacher Education, 18*(3), 289–303. https://doi.org/10.1016/S0742-051X(01)00070-1

Schechter, C. (2015). Toward collective learning in schools: Exploring U.S.A. and Israeli teachers' perceptions of collective learning from success. *International Journal of Educational Reform, 24*(2), 160–184.

Shapira-Lishchinsky, O., & Ben-Amram, M. (2018). Exploring the social ecological model based on national student achievements: Extracting educational leaders' role. *International Journal of Leadership in Education, 21*(3), 380–398. https://doi.org/10.1080/13603124.2017.1318956

Shapira-Lishchinsky, O., Benoliel, P., Schechter, C., & Klein, J. (2019). *Integrated research to develop index for examining the ecological school culture for new teachers' retention: Scientific summary report.* Bar-Ilan University. (Hebrew)

Shulman, L. S. (1986). Those who understand: Knowledge growth in teaching. *Educational researcher, 15*(2), 4–14.

Shulman, L. S. (2005). Signature pedagogies in the professions. *Daedalus, 134*(3), 52–59.

Spalding, E., Klecka, C. L., Lin, E., Wang, J., & Odell, S. J. (2011). Learning to teach: It's complicated but it's not magic. *Journal of Teacher Education, 62*(1) 3–7. https://doi.org/10.1177/0022487110384196

Tamir, E., Pearlmutter, N., & Feiman-Nemser, S. (2017). How day school teachers perceive their working conditions: A national study. *Journal of Jewish Education, 82*(2), 92–108. https://doi.org/10.1080/15244113.2017.1307054

Wang, J., & Odell, S. J. (2002). Mentored learning to teach according to standards-based reform: A critical review. *Review of Educational Research, 72*(3), 481–546.

Wayne, A. J., Yoon, K. S., Zhu, P., Cronen, S., & Garet, M. S. (2008). Experimenting with teacher professional development: Motives and methods. *Educational Researcher, 37*(8), 469–479. https://doi.org/10.3102%2F0013189X08327154

Weinberger, Y., & Donitsa-Schmidt, S. (2016). A longitudinal comparative study of alternative and traditional teacher education programs in Israel: Initial training, induction period, school placement, and retention rates. *Educational Studies, 52*(6), 552–572. https://doi.org/10.1080/00131946.2016.1231679

Yogev, A. (1996). Practice without policy: Pluralist teacher education in Israel. In M. Craft (Ed.), *Teacher education in plural societies: An international review* (pp. 57–71). Palmer Press.

CHAPTER 3

ECONOMIC, SOCIAL, AND EDUCATIONAL CONTEXTS AND DEVELOPMENT OF TEACHER INDUCTION POLICY IN MALAYSIA

Enhancing Novice Teachers' Intellectual Capitals

Nor Asniza Ishak
Universiti Sains Malaysia

Hazri Jamil
Universiti Sains Malaysia

ABSTRACT

Teacher induction policies have improved teachers' professional development in Malaysia. Motivated by the growth of student enrollment and the demands for the quality of teachers, they cover a vast range of actions from the central government to the schools in the education system. The New Teacher Development program becomes a prime component of these policy initiatives to develop novice teachers' pedagogical knowledge through professional development or teacher induction and, thus, improve students' intellectual quality as the country's human capital. Consequently, several questions need to be asked: To what extent is this program effective? Is the program implemented comprehensively and holistically, involving all new teachers? Will the ministry always support new teachers through teacher induction? In this chapter, we answer these questions by analyzing the policy documents, relevant conceptions, and research in teacher induction. With this analysis as a base, we discuss the halogens that the program faces in its further development and implementation and associated research questions.

Raising education quality and standards through teacher professional development has become an important focus of educational reform policy initiatives covering various actions and discourses from the central government to the locals in Malaysia (Petras et al., 2012). The changing social, economic, and educational contexts have shaped such a focus.

CONTEXTUAL INFLUENCES ON TEACHER INDUCTION POLICY

Socio-Economic Transformations and Changed Visions for Teaching

Entering the 21st century, Malaysia experienced rapid socioeconomic and cultural transformation and challenges in development, including education (Ministry of Education, 2004; Siddiqui, 2012). They include the changes in the education system, which focus on enhancing the quality of education and also cover the quality of teachers in the Malaysian education system (Ministry of Education, 2013). These transformations call for its new citizens to develop intellectually, spiritually, emotionally, and physically and become knowledgeable and competent citizens who can contribute to the harmony and betterment of the family, society, and nation (Ministry of Education, 2013). They demand that the teaching profession develop the quality necessary to provide a world-class education for its citizens to compete globally and effectively (Ministry of Education, 2013).

Consequently, the National Education Philosophy for Malaysia initiated in 1988 was revised in 1996 to enshrine a vision of education to address these needs for its citizens (Al-Hudawi et al., 2014). As it states:

> Education in Malaysia is an ongoing effort toward further developing the potential of individuals in a holistic and integrated manner to produce intellectually, spiritually, emotionally, and physically balanced and harmonious individuals based on a firm belief in and devotion to God. This effort is designed to produce Malaysian citizens who are knowledgeable and competent, possess high moral standards, are responsible and capable of achieving elevated levels of personal well-being, and can contribute to the harmony and betterment of the family, the society, and the nation at large. (Ministry of Education, 2023, para. 1)

The newly developed vision led to several policy efforts to redefine what and how students need to learn and, thus, relevant teaching benchmarks. The Malaysia Teacher Standard (SGM) was established in 2009 to provide all teachers with a benchmark standard to achieve in their classrooms (Ministry of Education, 2013). Of these benchmarks, using effective pedagogical approaches to help students develop high order thinking skills becomes the important benchmark for teachers.

Teaching has long been viewed as a highly respected profession with a stable and long career path in Malaysia (Paronjodi et al., 2017). It has contributed to youth literacy rates from 88% in 1980 to near-universal literacy of 99% today. It has also improved the secondary education completion rate from around 7% in 1950 to almost 75% today (Paronjodi et al., 2017). Consequently, it increased the adult literacy rate from less than 70% in 1950 to over 92% in 2010 and lowered the no-schooling rate of the population aged 15 and above from 60% to less than 10% during the same time.

However, research showed that the existing teacher pedagogical practices in *Malaysia* do not help students engage in higher-order thinking (Ishak et al., 2021). For example, by analyzing the assessment data from 384 lower secondary students, Kiong et al. (2012) found that students demonstrated low thinking skills as measured by the high order thinking test. This situation is explained by the fact that teachers always present information to students to memorize while offering them few chances to question or debate because they have to complete teaching content in a limited time (Jamil, 2009). It can be further explained based on high order thinking skills situated in teachers' knowledge, skills, and attitudes toward the content they teach (Rajendran, 2000). However, teachers who do not practice higher-order thinking are less confident (Hashim & Hamzah, 2003) and, thus, have difficulty developing a pedagogy to teach these skills (Rajendran, 2008).

This line of research motivated the Ministry of Education to launch a comprehensive review in October 2011 to see how the Malaysian educational system aligns with rising international education standards to build public and parental support for preparing students for the 21st century (Ishak et al., 2021). Growing from this review was the Malaysian Education Blueprint 2013–2025 (Blueprint), which gathered the ideas and perspectives from various experts and agencies on their assessments of Malaysia's education system (Ministry of Education, 2013). These experts and agencies included the World Bank, the United Nations Educational, Scientific, and Cultural Organisation (UNESCO), the Organisation for Economic Co-operation and Development (OECD), and six local universities (Ministry of Education, 2013).

The Blueprint proposed three directions for Malaysia's education reforms: *Understand the challenges* facing the Malaysian education system, including improving access to education, raising teaching standards, closing students' achievement gaps, fostering unity amongst students, and maximizing system efficiency. The Ministry established an unobstructed vision and aspirations for individual students and the education system over the next 13 years. It proposed six education system transformations, including meeting new demands, raising expectations, and initiating and supporting overall civil service transformation.

Then, the Ministry engaged various stakeholders in developing responses and feedback to the reform initiatives proposed in the Blueprint. For example, during the development of Malaysia Education Blueprint, over 55,000 Ministry officials, teachers, school leaders, parents, students, and members of public institutions across Malaysia were engaged in interviews, focus groups, surveys, National Dialogue town halls, Open Days, and roundtable discussions on proposed reform (Ministry of Education, 2013). Consequently, over 200 memorandums were generated for the Ministry, and over 3,000 articles and blog posts were developed on the issues raised in the Blueprint (Malaysia Education Blueprint, 2013–2025, Ministry of Education, 2013). The Ministry appointed a 12-member national panel and a 4-member international panel of experts to provide independent input into the Blueprint report (Samsudin, 2021).

Additionally, the Ministry started aligning the transformations outlined in the Blueprint with other public policies. For example, it worked closely with the Performance Management and Delivery Unit to develop the Government Transformation Programme 2.0 initiatives on education to prioritize the reforms suggested in the Blueprint.

The above studies, reviews, and public discussion of Malaysia's existing teaching and education system fertilize the soil where the policy initiatives to transform teacher preparation and development, including the teacher induction policy, were initiated and implemented. They ensure these policy initiatives receive public support and align with the changed vision of students learning and teaching benchmarks.

Increased Student Enrollments and Teacher Education Reform

Since independence, the huge growth of student enrolment in the school also generates the issue of sufficient qualified teachers in Malaysia. Thus, it motivates the transformation of teacher education and professional development policy efforts, including teacher induction (Jamil, 2014).

For example, only about half the population in Malaysia received formal schooling, with 6% of children having secondary level and 1% receiving post-secondary level education when Malaysia became independent in 1957 (Ministry of Education, 2013). By 2011, Malaysia achieved near-universal enrolment of 94% at the primary level, with just 0.2% dropping out. The enrolment rates at the lower secondary level rose to 87%, and that at the upper secondary level reached 78% (Hanewald, 2016). These enrolment rates are even higher once private schools are factored in. For instance, they are 96% at primary, 91% at lower secondary, and 82% at the upper secondary consequently. In parallel, there has been a rapid expansion in preschool education, with 77% of students enrolled in some form of either public or private preschool (Hanewald, 2016).

The growth of the student population produced two issues regarding the teaching profession. For one, it causes the need to prepare teachers with quality. For example, only half of the new teachers received formal teacher preparation from public higher institutions (Ismail & Awang, 2017). In addition, about 93% of applicants for the university-based undergraduate teacher education program scored below the minimum academic requirement, with only 1% receiving seven distinctions in 2010. Finally, only 7% of post-graduate students achieved high academic performances in the Post-Graduate Teaching Course 2010 (Hanewald, 2016). Additionally, there were insufficient qualified teachers in science and mathematics subject areas in rural areas such as Sabah and Sarawak of Malaysia (Jamil et al., 2011; Perman, 2021).

Development of Teacher Preparation and Development Policies

The above contextual changes drove the Ministry of Education to explore ways to attract high-performing candidates from a broader range of backgrounds into the teaching profession (Ismail & Awang, 2017). Thus, the teaching profession can become highly selective, like those in top-performing countries like Finland, Singapore, and South Korea, with only the top 10%–30% of applicants accepted into teacher education programs (Ismail & Awang, 2017).

First, the Ministry upgraded teacher preparation institutions to raise their status. It raises the requirements to enter teacher preparation programs to make teaching a more incredible and respectful profession. For example, the Ministry raised the minimum preservice training qualification from a diploma to a bachelor's degree for primary teachers as the existing requirements for secondary school teachers (Jamil et al., 2011). It started the policy of selecting and prioritizing applicants into teacher preparation programs based on seven distinctions in the Malaysia Education Certificate (Jamil et al., 2011).

Second, accordingly, it changed the teacher training colleges that only offered diplomas to the institutes of teacher education to offer bachelor's degrees to their graduates following the Education Development Master Plan 2006–2010 developed in tandem with the economic development policy of the Ninth Malaysia Plan (Prime Minister Department, 2006). Consequently, the Higher Education Institutions and the Institute of Teacher Education were designated to offer teacher training programs in Malaysia.

Third, the Matriculation Department under the Ministry of Education, responsible for pre-university education, offers alternative routes for students from Malaysia pre-university education to become teachers (Ministry of Education, 2013). These students are academically talented secondary school students who are carefully screened and selected for the pre-university education programs to be prepared to study abroad later in countries like the United Kingdom, Australia, and New Zealand. When graduating from the universities abroad, these students were offered the opportunity to become teachers through 40 programs designed following the New Teacher Development Program for beginning teachers developed by the Ministry of Education, which we will describe later. The pre-university programs received funding support from the Malaysian government.

The above reforms on teacher education requirements and institutions led to several promising results. They helped improve the quality of applicants for teacher education programs. For example, by 2010, 31% of primary school teachers had received a bachelor's degree (Ministry of Education, 2013). The ratio between the applicant and admitted trainee also increased from 3% in 2010 to 65% in 2012 based on their scores in their academic performance assessment in seven distinctions (Ministry of Education, 2013). The percentage of teacher education applicants with high academic performances in the post-graduate teaching course also rose from 7% in 2010 to 13% in 2012 (Ministry of Education, 2013). In some teacher training programs, applicants per program have been residing 38 to 1, surpassing

Singapore, South Korea, and Finland (Ministry of Education, 2013). These contextual changes also drove the reform of teacher education curricula, practices, and field experience based on the newly developed vision and teaching benchmarks in several ways (Ministry of Education, 2013). For instance, the goals of teacher education have changed over the years according to the pressing needs of the education system (Lee, 2004). Consequently, several teacher education programs have been developed to cater to the following priorities at different times. These priorities are to ensure that enough teachers of the various levels needed by the schools are recruited and trained, raise the quality of teachers, train enough teachers in specialized subjects like English, science, and mathematics, provide sufficiently trained teachers for vocational and technical schools, offer in-service training and professional development to practicing teachers and all kinds of education practitioners including school counselors, schooler educators, curriculum developers, and others.

Second, it required teacher preparation programs to increase and intensify field experiences for preservice teachers to practice their teaching skills in schools under the guidance and supervision of experienced teachers (Lee, 2004). For example, teaching practices in Malaysia's preservice teacher preparation programs were traditionally limited to 10 weeks (Lee, 2004). The Ministry now requires approximately 20% of the total credit hours for the practice part of teacher preparation programs (Ministry of Education, 2013). This reform was inspired by top-performing teacher education programs at the National Institute of Education in Singapore and the Melbourne Graduate School of Education in Australia, which allocate around 40% of the course time to preservice teachers' teaching practices in school contexts.

Finally, the Ministry further supports teachers in developing new teaching competencies. For example, it developed a compulsory training program with various modules to help teachers develop competencies central to nurturing students' higher order thinking in the school contexts, as inspired by the research on effective teacher professional development (Ministry of Education, 2013). In the program, teachers must participate in any program modules to develop their competencies based on their strengths and interests or the areas for improvement (Ministry of Education, 2013). It also developed an e-Guru video library of exemplary teaching to support teachers in visualizing how effective teaching can be implemented in their classrooms (Ministry of Education, 2013). These videos also became important sources for pedagogical skills training and coaching sessions (Ministry of Education, 2013). In addition, it transformed the school improvement specialist coach program by employing experienced teachers to coach their colleagues in learning to teach in the school context (Ministry of Education, 2013). Now the full-time program positions were offered to experienced teachers to coach more teachers with greater frequency, focusing on curriculum, assessment, pedagogy, and their relationship specifically, especially in supporting teachers in lower band schools, such as Bands 5, 6, and 7 (Ministry of Education, 2013). In Malaysia, public schools are divided into 7 performance Bands, from Band 1 (the highest performance) to Band 7 (the lowest performance; Ayob, 2012).

Teacher quality is the most recognized measure of student achievement and school success (Goh & Blake, 2015). Teacher actions, knowledge, and creativity for effective teaching are widely accepted and will continually expand and change (Goh & Blake, 2015). The policy initiatives in teacher preparation and professional development are showing promising results. In terms of teacher professional development, over 90% of teachers report spending approximately ten days each year on professional development, which is more than the Ministry-mandated requirement of seven days per year based on the Teaching and Learning International Survey (TALIS; Harris et al., 2018). This professional development covers self-study and off-site workshops to school-based coaching activities, such as classroom observations and lesson planning.

In sum, the new teacher induction policy emerged from Malaysia's social, economic, and educational transformations as the country entered the 21st century. The social and economic transformations called for its education system to equip citizens with the knowledge and skills necessary to compete in a globalized world and contribute to the harmony and betterment of the family, society, and nation. This emerging need for citizens demands teaching quality and effectiveness transformation, thus, education system transformations.

The substantial increase in student population at the various levels also calls for attracting, preparing, and retaining sufficient and qualified teachers who can teach as expected by the newly developed benchmarks for education. These emerging needs motivated the changes in the requirement for becoming teachers, teacher preparation program curriculum and practical experience, and teacher professional development programs.

The new teacher development policy, the *New Teacher Development Program*, emerged in 2010 as part of the government's efforts to prepare, retain, and develop teachers to address the educational needs and issues of the tram orations under the influences of social and economic transformations and teacher preparation and development policies. Mandated for all beginning teachers in Malaysia in 2015, this program *was* developed to enhance quality among new teachers throughout their first year as teachers (Ministry of Education, 2015).

NEW TEACHER DEVELOPMENT POLICY: ITS INTENTIONS, MANDATES, AND IMPLEMENTATION

Developed by the Ministry, the *New Teacher Development Program* (NTDP) is a school-based and structured learning program designed to improve professional development and, thus, new teacher quality (Ministry of Education, 2015). This initiative to continue building teacher capacity throughout their careers is among the important National Key Result Areas (NKRA), which focuses on teacher quality. NTDP is one of the fifteen initiatives under the NKRA to ensure excellence in teaching (Kamaruddin & Boon, 2020). The NTDP is designed for continuous new teacher professional development in the school context through various phases. Experienced teachers will mentor new teachers to understand their school environment, culture, system, and national educational aspirations. As a bridge from their initial preparations to continuing professional development in the school context, it is also to help new teachers apply their knowledge, instruction procedures, teaching strategies, and classroom management skills learned from their teacher preparation programs to school contexts.

Challenges New Teacher Development Program Aims to Address

The new teacher development program is developed to support the changed learning vision and teaching benchmarks like other educational policy efforts. It is also developed to address several challenges that new teachers often face in learning to teach in classroom contexts (Zakaria et al., 2016).

One of these challenges is that new teachers often lack a commitment to teaching compared to their experienced colleagues (Mavroulis, 2012). The assumption is that new teachers' commitment to teaching is part of their emotional intelligence, and the lack of such commitment makes it difficult to manage their stress in teaching (Goh, 2012; Goh & Blake, 2015). Thus, improving new teachers' commitment to teaching could help them manage their stress in teaching efficiently, especially those stressed by dynamic changes in the teaching profession (Goh & Blake, 2015).

Another challenge is that new teachers are often unprepared for the changes in the teaching profession at both organizational and individual levels. However, teachers are the main drivers and actors in implementing teaching transformation (İnandi & Giliç, 2016). Consequently, the expected goals of national education reform will be interrupted and cannot be actualized when new teachers are not ready to transform their classrooms (Goh & Blake, 2015; Gallant & Riley, 2014). The assumption is that new teachers' readiness for change at the individual level could be improved when they can actively make their teaching decisions as professionals (Cheng et al., 2004). However, their readiness to change could be weakened when working in an accountable school culture and bureaucratic school organization (Cheng et al., 2004).

Like what has already been implemented in the teaching profession in developed countries to improve teacher quality, the new teacher development program is seen as useful to change schools, teachers, and pupils into an excellent work culture for new teachers to perform tasks and responsibilities more systematically (Harris et al., 2018; Ministry of Education, 2015). Guided by mentor teachers and supported by experienced teachers and school administrators, the program will help new teachers learn to teach professionally and implement reformed teaching effectively. Thus, it will help improve the country's teaching profession continuously (Goh, 2012; Goh & Blake, 2015).

Structure and Mandates of the New Teacher Development Program

This new teacher development program is designed for new teachers in the first year of teaching with three sequential phases of induction experiences (Ministry of Education, 2015). The first is the orientation phase, structured in the first 3 months of a new teacher's career. This phase is developed following what suggestion or assumption is in the literature. In this phase, the new teachers are expected to learn how to adapt to their schools' environment and working culture, for example, being exposed to day-to-day tasks, understanding file management, teaching responsibilities, and so on.

To support their learning to teach in the phase, they are assigned mentor teachers who are typically experienced teachers in the same subject area (Ministry of Education, 2015). They are required to interact with their mentors weekly in official mentoring meetings for at least two teaching periods. In these meetings, mentor teachers assist beginning teachers in socializing into the school culture and developing self-confidence in teaching. They also coach and guide beginning teachers to develop professional conduct and teacher competency.

The second phase is the teaching phase, structured as 1 year starting from the first day the new teacher reports to school. However, the period can be extended if the new teacher does not increase skills and competence based on the professional competence dimensions (knowledge, skills, and professional values). This phase provides professional guidance, support, and assistance to new teachers until they achieve the level of professional competence desired (Ministry of Education, 2015). In particular, it cultivates new teachers' positive teaching attitude and professional values, increases their adaptability, resilience, competitiveness, and creativity, and improves their observation skills, concern about, and sensitivity to students. It also supports them in integrating theory into teaching and learning practice, mastering teaching strategies, and identifying and solving teaching and learning problems. The mentor will conduct their mentoring using description, discussion, observations, observation notes, collected information, guidance, lectures, and workshops. New teachers in this phase will be evaluated formally and informally by the mentor teacher using the portfolio created by the new teacher (Ministry of Education, 2015).

The third phase is the professional development structured when the new teacher reports to school and continues throughout their teaching career. This phase's objective is to guide and develop the professionalism competencies among new teachers in improving knowledge, skills, and relevant professional values to meet 21st-century education requirements. This phase will be implemented by the New Teacher formally via self-initiative (individual and school-based) and formally via an initiative of the Malaysian Ministry of Education. This phase will be evaluated by the mentor teacher using the portfolio created by the New Teacher (Ministry of Education, 2015)

Implementation of New Teacher Development Program

The new teacher development program (PPGB) is one program that supports continuous new teacher professional development starting when they enter education services and are placed in schools. This school-based or work-based program covers orientation, mentoring, and professional development Phases. The implementation period of this program is between 1 to 3 years.

New teachers are placed under the guidance of experienced mentor teachers to learn about the school's work environment and culture and to get deeper knowledge related to the country's education system and aspirations. The new teachers will also delve into the field of teaching and learning based on existing knowledge and skills, learning subject management and school administration management through interaction, tutoring, and working together with other teachers such as senior assistants, heads of fields, heads of committees, teacher counselors and teacher's co-curricular advisor, sports, and associations/clubs at school (Ministry of Education, 2015).

In particular, PPGB aims to help new teachers adapt to the environment, community, and school culture to make them role in a real situation. It also develops their potential for positive attitude practice, increased adaptability, resilience, competitiveness, creativity, observation skills, concern, and sensitivity toward students. It also develops their skills to integrate theory with teaching and learning practice and effectively use teaching strategies and skills to solve teaching and learning problems. Finally, it improves new teachers' professional competence, knowledge, and professional values to meet the educational needs of the 21st century.

Overall, the new teacher development program is implemented to enable new teachers to produce knowledgeable, high-minded students, skilled in leading, able to communicate in various languages and have an ethical and national identity. The Ministry of Education will provide funding for the program implementation and will be monitored by the school's principal.

EFFECTS AND ISSUES OF NEW TEACHER DEVELOPMENT PROGRAM

Research has been developed to examine the effects of new teacher development programs on beginning teachers' learning to teach and explore the issues with the program's implementation. In this section, we reviewed the relevant research on the effects of the new teacher development program on beginning teachers' learning to teach as expected by the teaching benchmarks and the issues in its implementation.

Effects of New Teacher Development Program

Several studies examined the effects of new teacher development programs on beginning teachers' learning to teach. Teachers are an important workforce for achieving Malaysian educational aims in enhancing education quality and developing the nation's human capital.

Research by Jamil (2014) and followed by Salleh and Hatta (2019) mentioned that a program for the development of continuous professionalism of new teachers is implemented on a school basis through structured guidance through various phases of developing the new teachers in the school in Malaysia. In this program, experienced teachers will mentor new teachers to understand the school's environment, culture, system, and national educational aspirations. It helps new teachers learn to teach during induction and increase their teaching professionalism later.

Issues of New Teacher Development Program

Another key issue observed in studies done on novice teachers is professional development among them. Zakaria et al. (2016) and Kamaruddin and Boon (2020) studies explored the issues and problems of implementing the new teacher development program. They identified several features of the new teacher development program implemented in their schools. It supported beginning teachers to enhance their commitment and readiness to teaching transformation. It engaged them in collective teamwork, focusing on their ethics and personal development. It further guided them to improve student achievement by developing their knowledge, classroom management, problem-solving, and communication skills. The study found that the program was not developed based on a proper understanding of beginning teachers' commitment and readiness to teaching and teaching transformation. Beginning teachers are a professional group different from experienced teachers. Thus, different methodologies are needed to understand their experience and commitment to the profession.

Zakaria et al. (2016) also divided this issue into two categories: novice teachers' personal quality and professional identity. This issue was investigated in studies done by Ismail et al. (2012), Senom et al. (2013), and Kabilan and Veratharaju (2013). Kabilan and Veratharaju (2013) showed that novice English language teachers were not given professional development courses in their first three years despite their readiness to attend such courses. Meanwhile, Senom et al. (2013) noted recent educational changes in teacher professional development for novice English as a second language teachers in Malaysia, including attending programs such as seminars, workshops, and courses. Novice teachers are also expected to undergo a more structured professional development program like narrative inquiry, lesson study groups, and peer coaching (Zakaria et al., 2016).

CONCLUSIONS, CHALLENGES, AND FUTURE RESEARCH

This chapter first analyzed two contexts where teacher induction policy was situated and developed carefully. For one, Malaysia's social and economic transformations motivated the change of its vision for student learning in school contexts, which led to the establishment of new teaching benchmarks. On the other, the substantial increase in the student population in schools helped create the need to select, prepare, and further sufficient yet qualified teaching forces for Malaysian classrooms, as expected by the changed teaching benchmarks.

Under the influence of these contexts, the Ministry intimated several reforms to produce sufficient and qualified teachers as expected by the new teaching benchmarks. These reforms include broadening the entry for talented students to the teaching profession, upgrading the requirements for entry into teaching, transforming the teacher preparation curriculum and practical experiences, and enhancing teacher professional development. The teacher induction policy was developed as part of these reform initiatives.

Second, we analyzed the major teacher induction policy, *New Teacher Development Program*. In this analysis, we attended to the specific issues particular to beginning teachers in learning to teach that the program was developed to address and their needs to learn to teach as expected by the newly developed teaching benchmark. These issues are their weak commitment to teaching and readiness to teach transformation. We also analyzed specific mandates, including experienced teachers who will be mentors who guide new teachers to understand the school's environment and culture, system, and national educational aspirations, and the extent to which each of these mandates reflects the ideas of teacher induction literature. In addition, we analyze the program implementation with a focus on the implementation process and funding related to the implementation.

Finally, drawing on the relevant research, we analyzed the effects and issues of implementing the new teacher development program. This analysis led to the following effects of the program on beginning teachers' learning to teach. These effects help new teachers learn to teach in the teacher induction period and later increase their teaching professionalism through their career based on the help of the mentor teacher. The analysis also led to several issues regarding the program implementation. These issues are novice teachers were not given any professional development courses in their first three years despite their readiness to attend such courses. It is also noted that there were recent educational changes in the structure of teacher professional development.

REFERENCES

Al-Hudawi, S. H. V , Fong, R. L. S , Musah, M. B., & Tahir, L. M. (2014). The actualization of the Malaysian national education philosophy in secondary schools: Student and teacher Perspectives. *International Education Studies, 7*(4), 57–68.

Ayob, A. (2012). Education administrators' professional standards The Malaysian perspective. *Journal of Research, Policy, & Practice of Teachers & Teacher Education, 2*(1), 60–74.

Cheng, Y. C., Chow, K. W., & Mok, M. M. C. (2004). Reform of teacher education amid paradigm shift in school education. In Y. C. Cheng, K. W. Chow, & M. M. C. Mok (Eds.), *Reform of teacher education in the Asia-Pacific in the new millennium* (pp. 1–19). Dordrecht.

Gallant, A., & Riley, P. (2014). Early career teacher attrition as arrested development: New thoughts on an intractable problem. *Teacher Development, 18*(4), 562–580.

Goh, P. S. C., & Blake, D. (2015). Teacher preparation in Malaysia: Needed changes. *Teaching in Higher Education, 20*(5), 469–480.

Goh, P. S. C. (2012). The Malaysian teacher standards: A look at the challenges and implications for teacher educators. *Educational Research for Policy and Practice, 11*(2), 73–87.

Hanewald, R. (2016). The impact of English on educational policies and practices in Malaysia. In R. Kirkpatrick (Ed.), *English language education policy in Asia*. Springer.

Harris, A., Jones, M., Ismail, N., Adams, D., & Sumintono, B. (2018). Leading turnaround and improvement in low performing schools in Malaysia and Indonesia. In C. Meyers & M. Darwin (Eds.), *International perspectives on leading low-performing schools: Contemporary perspectives on school turnaround and reform* (pp. 267–287). Information Age Publishing.

Hashim, R., & Hamzah, S. (2003). *The teaching of thinking in Malaysia*. Research Centre, International Islamic University Malaysia.

İnandi, Y., & Giliç, F. (2016). Relationship of teachers' readiness for change with their participation in decision. making and school culture. *Educational Research and Reviews, 11*(8), 823–833.

Ishak, N. A, Jamil, H., & Abd Razak, N. (2001). *Amalan pedagogi produktif dalam meningkatkan kualiti intelektual pelajar* [Productive pedagogical practices in improving the intellectual quality of students]. USM Press.

Ismail, R., & Awang, M. (2017). Quality of Malaysian teachers based on education and training: A benefit and earnings returns analysis using human capital theory. *Quality Assurance in Education, 25*(3), 303–316.

Ismail, A., Haron, N., & Kaneson, A. G. (2012). *Amalan pembangunan profesionalisme dalam kalangan guru-guru novis* [The practice of developing professionalism among novice teachers]. Retrieved from http://www.medc.com.my/medc/journals/volume%204/Amalan%20Pembangunan%20Profesionalisme%20Dalam%20Kalangan%20Guru-guru%20Novis

Jamil, H. (2009). Education policy matters. In F. A. Rahman, F. Piee@Shafiee, & H. Elias (Eds.), *Teachers' learning, curriculum innovations and knowledge applications* (pp. 47–62). Universiti Putra Malaysia Press.

Jamil, H. (2014). Teacher is matter for education quality: A transformation of policy for enhancing the teaching profession in Malaysia. *Journal of International Cooperation in Education, 16*(2), 181–196.

Jamil, H., Razak, N. A., Raju, R., & Mohamed, A. R. (2011, March). Teacher professional development in Malaysia: Issues and challenges. In *Africa-Asia university dialogue for educational development report of the International Experience Sharing Seminar: Actual status and issues of teacher professional development* (pp. 85–102). Hiroshima University: Center for the Study of International Cooperation in Education.

Kabilan, M. K., & Veratharaju, K. (2013). Professional development needs of primary school English-language teachers in Malaysia. *Professional Development in Education, 39*(3), 330–351.

Kamaruddin, Z., & Boon, Y., (2020). Challenges in integrating New Teacher Development Program in schools: A systematic literature review. *Universal Journal of Educational Research, 8*(5A), 81–88. https://doi.org/10.13189/ujer.2020.081912

Kiong, T. T., Yunos, J. M., Heong, Y. M., Hussein, A. H., & Mohamad, M. M. (2012). Thinking skills for secondary school students in Malaysia. *Journal of Research, Policy & Practice of Teachers and Teacher Education, 2*(2), 12–23.

Lee, M. N. (2004). Malaysian teacher education into the new century. In Y. C. Cheng, K. W. Chow, & M. Mo. C. Mok (Eds.), *Reform of teacher education in the Asia-Pacific in the new millennium* (pp. 81–91). Springer.

Mavroulis, G. J. (2012). *The impact of mentor conversations on the classroom performance of novice teachers* [PhD Thesis, University of Wisconsin-Madison]

Ministry of Education. (2004). *The development of education: National report of Malaysia.* Ministry of Education Malaysia.

Ministry of Education. (2013). *Malaysia education blueprint 2013–2025: Preschool to post-secondary education.* Ministry of Education Malaysia.

Ministry of Education. (2015). *New teacher development policy.* Retrieved from https://www.moe.gov.my/muat-turun/penerbitan-dan-jurnal/terbitan/buku-panduan-1/1603-panduan-pelaksanaan-program-pembangunan-guru-baharu-ppgb-2015/file

Ministry of Education. (2023). *Falsafah Pendidikan Kebangsaan.* https://www.moe.gov.my/falsafah-pendidikan-kebangsaan, paragraph 1.

Paronjodi, G. K, Jusoh, A. J., & Abdullah, M. H. (2017). A comparative study of beginning teacher induction in Malaysia and Victoria (Australia): A review of the literature. *Journal of Research, Policy & Practice of Teachers & Teacher Education, 7*(1), 36–48.

Perman, A. A. (2021). *Teaching science and mathematics in rural area: A case study of Sk Sabur, Sabah, Malaysia.* E-Proceeding of International Conference on Language, Education, Humanities & Social Sciences.

Petras, Y., Jamil, H., & Mohamed, A. R. (2012). How do teachers learn? A study on the policy and practice of teacher professional development in Malaysia. *KEDI Journal of Educational Policy, 9*(1), 51–70.

Prime Minister Department. (2006). *The ninth Malaysian plan* (9MP). Putrajaya: The Economic Planning Unit, Prime Minister's Department .

Rahman, N. A., & Ibrahim, M. N. (2013). *Pemikiran kritis dan kreatif: Konsep pendekatan dan aplikasi dalam pengajaran dan pembelajaran* [Critical and creative thinking: Conceptual approaches and applications in teaching and learning]. Penerbit Universiti Pendidikan Sultan Idris.

Rajendran, N. S. (2000, October). Kesusasteraan sebagai wahana mengajar kemahiran berfikir aras tinggi [Literature as a vehicle for teaching high-level thinking skills]. In *Prosiding Seminar Kebangsaan Penyelidikan dan Pembangunan Dalam Pendidikan* [Proceedings of the National Seminar on Research and Development in Education] (pp. 201–210).

Rajendran, N. S. (2008). *Teaching and acquiring: Higher-order thinking skills, theory & practice.* Penerbitan Universiti Sultan Idris.

Salleh, M., & Hatta, M. (2019). Best practices for promoting teachers' professional development in Malaysia. *UMT Education Review, 2,* 1–26. https://doi.org/10.32350/uer.22.01

Samsudin, M. A. (2021). Digital learning landscape in Malaysia during the Covid-19 pandemic: The perspective of ecological techno-subsystem theory. *Journal of International Cooperation in Education, 24*(2), 131–151.

Senom, F., Zakaria, A. R., & Ahmad Shah, S. S. (2013). Novice teachers' challenges and survival: Where do Malaysian ESL teachers stand? *American Journal of Educational Research, 1*(4), 119–125.

Siddiqui, K. (2012). Malaysia's socioeconomic transformation in historical perspective. *International Journal of Business and General Management, 1*(2), 20–50.

Zakaria, S., Saidin, K., & Mohamad, R. (2016). Issues among novice teachers in Malaysia. *Proceeding of ICECRS, 1*(2016), 855–862. Malaysia: Universiti Utara Malaysia.

CHAPTER 4

TEACHER INDUCTION POLICIES AND PRACTICES IN SINGAPORE

Yanping Fang
*National Institute of Education,
Nanyang Technological University*

Rachel Goh
*English Language Institute of Singapore,
Ministry of Education*

Kenneth Kang Neng Loon
*Catholic High School,
Ministry of Education*

ABSTRACT

This chapter reviews the research literature, policy documents, and research studies on developing and implementing Singapore's induction and mentoring policies since 2006 in three distinctive parts. First, it provides an overview of three phases of policy development, focusing on the national and international contexts that motivated the policy, discusses the issues and challenges it was developed to address, and outlines each phase's policy mandates, program specifics, and implementation processes. Second, it includes two studies illustrating policy implementation at the school level and discusses the effects and issues related to the induction and mentoring policy implementation. Third, it synthesizes the characteristics, effects, and challenges facing teacher induction policy development and implementation. It also offers directions for induction and mentoring policy development and the necessary research to improve the policy and practices in Singapore.

Singapore students consistently demonstrated high performances in various international comparisons, such as the Programme for International Student Assessment (PISA) and the Trends in International Mathematics and Science Study (TIMSS). Its education system has presumably contributed to such students' performance (Simonds, 2018), especially through the alignment of its central policy, school practices, and student assessments (Bautista et al., 2015; Tan, C. Y., & Dimmock, 2014). This chapter examines how its teacher induction policies and practices developed to support beginning teachers over the years could help explain such students' performance.

Beginning teachers are teachers in the first two years of their teaching career in Singapore, according to the country brief of the National Center on Education and the Economy (NCEE, 2016). They typically graduated from the university teacher preparation program and had at least one year of working experience in other sectors (Davie, 2015). These teachers must participate in the 2-year Structured Mentoring Programme initiated in 2006, which has been developed and modified to this day (Chong & Tan, Y. K., 2006; NCEE, 2016).

In this chapter, we review the policy documents, program requirements, and relevant research literature to trace the trajectory of the Structured Mentoring Programme development over the past 15 years in three phases. We start with a broad overview of the social and historical contexts driving the development of teacher induction policies and the issues these policies were developed to address in each of the three phases. We also examine the induction policy mandates, underlying design rationales, implementation processes, and evaluation in the different phases. Then, we review two research studies to show the impacts and issues of induction policy implementation on beginning teachers' learning to teach and its intended and unintended consequences. We end the chapter by synthesizing our macro and micro analysis of teacher induction policy development, implementation, effects, and issues. With the synthesis as a base, we discuss the directions for future induction policy development and the relevant research necessary to understand and improve induction policies and practices.

SOCIAL, ECONOMIC, AND EDUCATION CONTEXTS AND NEEDS OF TEACHER INDUCTION

From its independence in 1965 to 1978, Singapore underwent a 13-year survival period. The need for social cohesion, political unity, and skilled workers for a post-colonial economy drove the bilingual policies in its education system (Ho & Gopinathan, 1999). Such a policy stresses English as the medium of all content-area education from the start of schooling, with students' mother tongue languages (Chinese, Malay, and Tamil) required each as a single subject. The ramification of the policy was that in-service teachers had to develop their language proficiency for teaching within a short period, including beginning teachers, to use English for instruction.

From 1979 to1996, Singapore entered an efficiency-driven era characterized by rapid industrialization and relevant social development, which motivated (the) policies aimed at enhancing school retention and establishing a streamed school system (Tan et al., 2016). During these periods, teacher induction attracted little attention to education policy development.

Then, the national policy, *Thinking Schools, Learning Nation*, was launched in 1997, which positioned schools as important places for innovation and learning under the global knowledge-economy impetus (Ho & Gopinathan, 1999). Consequently, teachers were expected to develop students as "thinking and committed citizens, capable of making good decisions to keep Singapore vibrant and successful in future" and life-long learners to "make learning a national culture" (Goh, C. T., 1997, pp. 5–6). The education system was decentralized into cluster and independent schools to achieve these ambitious goals, and critical thinking and information technology were infused into all subject areas (Ho & Gopinathan,1999). In 2004, the policy, *Teach Less and Learn More*, was launched to decentralize the national curriculum to encourage school-based components stressing "inquiry, experimentation, exploration and application" to meet the needs of individual schools and pedagogical development (Gopinathan & Mardiana, 2013, p. 26). The design and implementation of teacher induction were also decentralized to schools. While mentoring in Singapore was used as a primary teacher induction strategy, "the practices tend[ed] to vary more widely, as they [were] tailored to the needs of individual teachers and schools" (Moskowitz & Stephens, 1997, p. 12).

Central to these monumental education reforms was the role of teachers in offering quality teaching. Thus, teachers must shift examination-based teaching to holistic classroom instruction (Tharman, 2004). In these classrooms, students could have more choices and multiple pathways to success while enjoying learning. Consequently, it was important to support beginning teachers in learning how to teach as advocated by the reforms (Chong & Tan, Y. K., 2006). The need to support beginning teachers' learning to teach intensified since many teachers were nearing retirement age, and schools were experiencing a huge influx of new teachers (Fang et al., 2009). Currently, Singapore has the youngest teaching force among the OECD countries, with an average age of 38 compared to the OECD mean of 44 years (OECD, 2019).

Singapore's first formal induction policy emerged from these broad social and economic contexts in 2006, focusing on school-based induction and mentoring support for beginning teachers (Chong & Tan, Y. K., 2006). This policy was informed by international research (Darling-Hammond, 1988; Huling-Austin, 1990), especially the seminal work on teacher induction in China, Japan, France, New Zealand, and Switzerland (Britton et al., 2003). This body of international research advocated for effective school-based support systems for beginning teachers to develop their teaching skills, which served as a foundation for Singapore's teacher induction policy initiative (Chong & Tan, Y. K., 2006; Tan, O. S., 2015).

DEVELOPMENT OF TEACHER INDUCTION POLICY IN SINGAPORE

Established in 2006, Singapore's first formal induction program had been developed and transformed into three distinctive phases over the past 15 years. Each phase lasted about 5 years with adapted focuses, mandates, and responses to align with the paradigm shift in educational policies, preparing students for a changing and increasingly uncertain world.

First Phase of Induction Policy Development

Policy Focuses

During its initial phase from 2006 to 2010, Singapore's induction policy focused on establishing a school-based collaborative infrastructure crucial for supporting teacher induction. Specifically, three core platforms were introduced.

First, in 2009, nationwide Professional Learning Communities (PLCs) were implemented across all schools, providing a platform for beginning teachers to integrate into the school culture (Ng, E. H., 2009). These PLCs could presumably foster a culture of collaboration and reduce overreliance on one-on-one mentoring. These policy initiatives demonstrated the Singapore government's determination to empower and encourage teachers to have ownership of their learning to teach (Hairon & Dimmock, 2012; Wong, K. Y., 2013).

Second, the Academy of Singapore Teachers (AST) was established in 2010 to oversee the implementation of PLCs at the school level (Lee & Lee, 2013). It guided the selection of master teachers and specialists to help create networks of teachers across schools, grade levels, and content areas so that teachers could develop their teaching knowledge through bottom–up initiatives (Hairon & Dimmock, 2012). It also offered training courses for beginning teachers, mentor teachers, and colleagues (Bautista et al., 2015).

Third, in 2010, a cornerstone tripartite system was established between the Ministry of Education (MOE) initiating the induction policy, the National Institute of Education (NIE) responsible for teacher education, teacher training, and research, and the schools where the induction policy was implemented (Bautista et al., 2015). Through the partnership, "the Singapore education system ensures clarity of purpose, confluence, congruence, and alignment of purposes across stakeholders and other educational champions" for teacher induction (Tan, O. S., 2015, p. 198).

Policy Mandates

During this phase, policy mandates were coherently reflected in the 2-year Structured Mentoring Program (SMP), weaving together induction, school-based mentoring, and outside-school formal training (Chong & Tan, Y. K., 2006; NCEE, 2016). The SMP toolkit, introduced in 2006, was designed to support beginning teachers to develop their knowledge of teaching, understand their roles as teachers, and enhance their teaching competencies within a community of practice with the support of more experienced peers "through the realization of their personal and professional aspirations" (Tan, O. S., 2019, p. 2).

The program developed several mandates to achieve these policy goals (Bautista et al., 2015). First, each beginning teacher was matched with a mentor, usually a senior teacher partly released from teaching duty. Second, beginning teachers' teaching load was reduced to two-thirds as that of more experienced teachers to help them transition smoothly from preservice training to school practice. Third, at least 1 hour per week was required for all teachers to be involved in inquiry-based professional development in the PLCs at the school level. Finally, a simplified version of the lesson study became the focus of inquiry-based professional development in the PLCs of 51 pilot schools. In the lesson study, peer lesson observations and post-lesson conferences were developed to engage teachers in exchanging ideas and practices (Ng, E. H., 2009).

These mandates were initiated to reinforce beginning teachers' smooth transition through the tripartite system (Wong, J., & Bautista, 2016), with MOE, NIE, and the schools playing different roles in their implementation. MOE developed initiatives for schools nationwide to develop professional development and networking opportunities. NIE offered initial teacher preparation and training courses for beginning teachers and the newly established AST. At the same time, schools with MOE's support developed professional development programs and teacher networking in alignment with the policy initiatives.

Effects and Issues of Policy Implementation

The first phase of induction policy implementation led to several effects and issues. First, the professional communities initiated by the AST, the training programs offered through NIE, and the training workshops initiated at the school level contributed to teachers' preparation, including beginning teachers, for the reforms toward holistic assessment proposed by the Primary Education Review and Implementation Committee (MOE, 2009).

Second, there was a shortage of quality mentors and, thus, limited the nation's aspiration for teaching innovation through better-prepared teachers, including beginning teachers (Curdt-Christiansen & Silver, 2011).

Third, the policy of matching beginning teachers with designated mentors contributed to the perception among teachers that the responsibilities for inducting beginning teachers resided with only certain individuals in schools, such as senior teachers. This perception could limit the role of PLCs in supporting beginning teachers' induction. It would be an impetus for broadening the concept of inducting teachers in schools in the later phase of the development of the induction policy (MOE, 2018a).

Finally, as observed in an earlier study on teacher induction, the issue with the schools' autonomy in initiating their induction program and teachers' networking contributed to cross-school variation in the quality of induction programs and mentoring practices (Moskowitz & Stephens, 1997). Consequently, these variations would affect the quality of beginning teachers' learning to teach as the teacher induction policy intended.

Second Phase of Induction Policy Development

Policy Focuses

Singapore's second 5-year induction policy development from 2011 to 2015 aimed to support ability-driven education reform (Heng, 2012; Tan, O. S., 2019). Motivated by the 21st Century Competencies movement, this reform was developed to shift teaching towards a student-centered and values-driven approach unique to the contexts of Singapore (Tan, O. S., 2015). Specifically, the induction policy was developed to improve mentor teacher preparation with clearer expectations and broaden school PLC initiatives to help beginning teachers understand reformed teaching approaches, school culture, school expectations, and ethos (Heng, 2012).

Policy Mandates

The policy mandates of this phase are specifically reflected in two programs. The first was the Skillful Teaching and Enhanced Mentoring (STEM) program, initiated in 2011 (NCEE, 2016). It was developed to train school leaders, senior teachers, master teachers, and instructional mentors to support beginning teachers in aligning their teaching with education reform (Heng, 2012, 2013).

More specifically, it offered mentors training on providing more targeted and personalized mentoring to address beginning teachers' needs, motivation, and lifelong goals (Sim, 2012). It required mentors to help beginning teachers master the craft of teaching, model learning to teach, share their expertise, and motivate them to become better teachers (Heng, 2014). It also measured how well schools provide more time for mentors to interact with mentees, integrate preservice education with in-service mentoring, and structure mentoring developments through the updated induction policy (Bautista et al., 2015).

The second was the Mentor Preparation Program, under STEM, developed in partnership with the New Teacher Center in California (NCEE, 2016). It was designed to align school induction and mentoring practices with the values-based teacher education framework stressing student-centered teaching, teacher identity, and service (Goodwin et al., 2017). It required schools to redefine the roles of mentors in offering development support and formative appraisal for beginning teachers' learning to teach while leaving the role of a summative evaluation of their performance to the reporting officers at the school levels (Ng, P. T., 2012). In 2015, the Instructional Mentoring Program (IMP) was introduced to accelerate efforts to equip schools with competent Instructional Mentors (MOE, 2015). It would replace STEM by 2017, as elaborated in the next section on the third phase of induction policy development.

Effects and Issues of Policy Implementation

The second phase of induction policy implementation led to several effects and issues. First, it led to a much higher percentage of current experienced teachers (39%) serving as mentors to beginning teachers in Singapore compared to the global average of 14% (OECD, 2014). Second, the number of STEM schools increased from 30 to 120, covering one-third of all government schools by 2015 (NCEE, 2016). Finally, the cross-school variation in implementing the induction program, specifically IMP, remained an issue. Officers from AST who visited schools participating in IMP noticed school variations in the implementation of beginning teacher induction and mentoring, affecting the quality specified by the policy intent (Low et al., 2019).

Third Phase of Induction Policy Development

Policy Focuses

The third phase of induction policy development started in 2016 and continues. It continued emphasizing teacher induction as a support for the assessment reform in the first phase and the student-centered and values-based education reform in the second (MOE, 2018b). It further stressed the role of teacher induction in supporting beginning teachers' well-being and addressing their needs to attend to students' well-being in teaching by breaking the confines of exam-driven practices (Hung, 2017).

Policy Mandates

The induction policy mandates in the third phase were reflected in three programs. The first was the instructional mentoring program (IMP) for senior teachers, replacing STEM in 2017, to help beginning teachers develop teaching and assessment practices that promote the "Joy for Learning" (2017) and "Learn for Life" (2018) initiatives that aimed to enable students to excel beyond exams and be curious and eager to learn for all their lives and be resilient, adaptable, and global in their outlook (MOE, 2018b).

IMP required mentor teachers to attend an 8-day training program focusing on two areas. It focused on developing mentors' skills in understanding beginning teachers' needs and developing mentoring relationships with them. For example, understanding beginning teachers' aspirations and concerns using active listening and creating a safe and trusting relationship with them by sharing professional challenges and identifying growth areas with them for their quality learning to teach (AST, n.d.-a). It also focused on using effective mentoring to support their learning to teach by attending to the Singapore Teaching Practice (STP) in mentor–novice conversations (MOE, 2022). Developed based on the belief that every child wants to and can learn, the STP covers 24 teaching areas central to teachers' decisions regarding the design and implementation of curriculum, including developing positive classroom culture, lesson preparation and enactment, and assessment and feedback (MOE, 2022).

The second was the Inducting Teachers in Our Schools (ITOS) guide, developed in 2018 as "a revision of the Structured Mentoring Program (SMP) toolkit" (MOE, 2018a, p. 1). It expanded teacher induction and mentoring to cater to the needs of the increasing number of second-career and redeployed teachers due to a range of school mergers since 2017 by stressing teacher mentoring across the whole teaching fraternity (MOE, 2018a). That means that every teacher leader can be an instructional mentor when equipped with shared beliefs, a common language, skill sets, and protocols.

It described induction implemented in two distinct but related phases. In the orientation stage, system-wide learning platforms in the MOE Teacher Induction Framework and school-based programs were provided to beginning teachers to familiarize them with their new school contexts. The school's PLCs offered school-based mentoring and collaboration opportunities in the support phase with more experienced teachers. The ITOS guide expanded the scope of induction beyond inducting beginning teachers to "meet[ing] the needs of different segments of teachers" (MOE, 2018a, p. 1). It also reinforced the important role of PLCs in teacher induction and mentoring.

The third was the National Digital Learning Program, launched in 2020 during the unforeseen COVID-19 pandemic (MOE, 2020a; Siti, 2020). It was initiated to enable students to develop the necessary skills in this digital age, and to enhance classroom learning experiences. Consequently, the program required all teachers to be familiar with ICT tools and strategies and, in particular, the use of technology for conducting virtual lessons during the nationwide school closures and subsequently during home-based learning set as a regular part of schooling post-COVID-19 (Davie, 2020). MOE (2020b, 2020c; Ong, 2020) identified teachers' need for support in the e-Pedagogy as part of the 6 areas of professional development under the "SkillsFuture for Educators" aligned with the policy of "Learn for Life" (OPAL, 2021; Teng, 2020).

This roadmap that spells out the proficiency levels in the six practice areas, including assessment literacy and inquiry-based learning, helps meet mentoring needs to support beginning teachers (AST, n.d.-b; MOE, 2020b, 2020c). It empowers teacher mentors to work with beginning teachers to identify their learning needs and to recommend suitable resources in One Portal All Learners (OPAL2.0) for their professional development (OPAL, 2021). Teacher mentors can help beginning teachers curate appropriate micro-learning units designed for self-directed learning in the OPAL 2.0 repository and recommend suitable professional development courses in the OPAL2.0 learning management system. Access to the curated resources, specifically those in e-Pedagogy, helps beginning teachers develop their capacity to leverage digital technology effectively to sustain students' learning synchronously and asynchronously in the new normal.

Effects and Issues of Policy Implementation

Several effects and issues observed in the earlier phases of induction policy developments remain a concern, particularly the gaps in program implementation. First, while various programs in the MOE teacher induction framework are in place at the systemic level, such as the Beginning Teachers' Orientation Programme (BTOP) and Beginning Teachers' Symposium, only "85% of teachers report[ed] having participated in some kind of formal or informal induction when they joined their current school" (OECD, 2019, p. 3). In addition, only 54% of beginning teachers indicated they were assigned a mentor (OECD, 2019). The cross-school variation in teacher induction practices is an issue that warrants further research.

Our overview of Singapore's three induction and mentoring policy development phases suggests several patterns. First, teacher induction policies addressed the needs of different education reforms and beginning teachers at different times. For example, the first phase focused on the support of mentors and colleagues to beginning teachers in developing ownership of teaching strategies that help students learn how to inquire, experiment, explore, and apply the important knowledge and skills expected by the reformed curriculum. The second phase emphasized mentors' support for beginning teachers in learning to teach using a student-centered and values-based approach promoted by the teaching reform. The third phase stressed the role of mentors in attending to beginning teachers' psychological needs and well-being to develop teaching and assessment skills that nurture students' well-being as self-motivated and lifelong learners.

Second, the later induction and mentoring programs were developed by consolidating the earlier ones. For instance, although focusing on different aspects, all three phases consistently focused on training mentors to support beginning teachers in developing effective teaching strategies and assessment skills.

Third, the induction and mentoring programs developed in the second and third phases relied heavily on the infrastructures developed in the first phase to situate their initiatives. These infrastructures include the school-based PLCs, teacher mentoring program, and the partnership between MOE, NIE, and schools.

INFLUENCES AND ISSUES OF SCHOOL-LEVEL INDUCTION POLICY IMPLEMENTATION

In this section, we introduce two studies examining school-level teacher induction practices and the influences of such practices at the school level to understand policy implementation. The first one (Goh, R., 2016; Goh, R., & Fang, 2017) examines the teacher induction practices during the second policy phase by comparing beginning teachers' experiences in two elementary schools, drawing on observation and interview data. The second (Low et al., 2019) investigates the affordances and challenges of teacher induction and mentoring under one-to-one mentor-mentee support structures by analyzing survey and interview data from beginning teachers.

Study 1: Contexts Matter for Induction and Mentoring

Contexts, Participants, and Data Sources

The first study (Goh, R., 2016; Goh, R., & Fang, 2017) was conducted with teachers in two elementary schools. New Vision Elementary School (pseudonym) was built less than a decade ago, while Ningxia Elementary School (pseudonym) was established with a long history. Both implemented learning circles and action research for teacher collaboration and developed lesson study as the focus of their PLCs in 2009. Both had an influx of beginning teachers when the study started in 2014.

The study participants involved 11 first-grade teachers including three beginning teachers from each of the two elementary schools. Teachers in both schools conducted lesson study cycles by planning, observing, and discussing research lessons facilitated by the team leaders. The lesson study cycles were developed to help beginning teachers align their thinking with the longer-term student literacy development goals and enhance their disposition and knowledge using student-centered pedagogies. After two lesson study cycles, they were interviewed about their first-hand learning-to-teach experience in the lesson study activities. The research lessons were taught by two experienced teachers at New Vision Elementary School, while each of the three beginning teachers at Ningxia Elementary School taught the research lessons.

Study Findings

The analysis of interview data led to several findings. First, all the beginning teachers from both schools valued the opportunities to either teach the research lessons or observe the more experienced teachers enacting the research lessons and discussing the research lessons during the planning and post-lesson discussions. Second, they valued their chances to understand the insights regarding the research lesson development and implementation from the more experienced teachers. Third, the more experienced teachers valued their learning opportunities from the beginning teachers' fresh insights.

However, the beginning teachers from the two schools developed different experiences in learning to teach from the lesson study cycles. Those in New Vision Elementary School expressed that they learned most of the student-centered teaching approaches and received support for their inquiry into teaching through mentoring and induction from all the team members. They also had opportunities to identify the conflicting views of teaching and debate over alternative teaching perspectives. Additionally, they felt more empowered seeing students' thinking and other teachers' classroom practice through the lesson study cycles.

In contrast, the beginning teachers from Ningxia Elementary School felt they had fewer chances to examine conflicting teaching ideas in planning and discussing their research lessons and develop alternative perspectives and practices. Thus, they often ended up maintaining the status quo of established practices without questioning. They also expressed feeling less empowered due to receiving vague ideas and suggestions from experienced teachers. In addition, although they wished to observe how experienced teachers would teach the research lessons, they hesitated to ask the more experienced teachers to do so.

The study suggests that the more open exploration nature of the New Vision Elementary School PLC and the experienced teachers' leading in teaching the research lessons contributed to the beginning teachers' learning to teach from their induction experiences. However, the examination-driven teaching practice and beginning teachers-focused research lessons in Ningxia Elementary School limited the novices' learning-to-teach experiences.

Study 2: Promises and Challenges in Induction Programs

Participants, Data Sources, and Contexts

The second study (Low et al., 2019) involved a survey with 896 teachers and interviews with 17 of them from four schools on the influences and challenges facing the induction policy, *Inducting Teachers in Our Schools* (ITOS), as mentioned earlier.

In the four interview schools, mentors were required to observe beginning teachers' teaching and conduct weekly pre- and post-lesson discussions based on the new Singapore Teaching Practice (STP) areas. Such a mentoring practice reflects a cognitive apprenticeship (Collins et al., 1991) in an "authentic domain activity" (Brown et al., 1989, p. 39). Mentors and beginning teachers were paired across departments and subject areas to ensure the confidentiality of beginning teachers' teaching from their colleagues and reporting officers from the same content area in the same school.

Study Findings

The analysis of survey and interview data revealed several findings. From the beginning teachers' perspective, they benefited most from the structured mentoring sessions in learning to teach during their induction. These mentoring sessions made them more confident in teaching along with their mentors.

From the perspective of mentor teachers, they valued the trust and support received from school leaders for their mentoring practices to support beginning teachers' learning to teach. The structured mentoring sessions also enabled them to focus on their mentoring duties, created a sharing culture among all teachers, and made them more conscious of their mentoring language use and confidence in mentoring. Additionally, they could use various data sources to assess beginning teachers' practices, although the data use was less uniform across schools. These data included lesson observations, feedback from beginning teachers, general views of the beginning teachers held by their reporting officers, and assessment models shared and communicated in the schools. Finally, mentor teachers further indicated that beginning teachers should improve their classroom management and instruction strategies.

The study suggests that the teacher induction program lacked a standard assessment system for mentor teachers to rely on to develop valid judgments of beginning teachers' baseline competencies demonstrated in teaching. Such a situation positions the development of beginning teachers' learning to teach and becoming experienced in teaching as competencies developed over time rather than as a measure of observable indicators. In addition, matching beginning teachers with mentors across departments and content areas could also prevent beginning teachers from developing content and specialized content knowledge necessary for effective content-based teaching practices with the support of mentors.

In summary, in the first study, the New Vision and Ningxia cases illustrate that school contexts mattered for the characteristics and quality of beginning teachers' induction and mentoring, shaping the role of lesson study in supporting beginning teachers' learning to teach. These contexts include those related to school-level factors and team-level factors. The second study showed that the structured mentoring practices developed under the ITOS induction policy influenced beginning teachers' learning to teach and mentors' mentoring practices. At the same time, it posed challenges to developing effective mentoring practices because of unarticulated standards for assessing beginning teachers' teaching practices and mismatching mentors with beginning teachers in their teaching subjects.

DISCUSSION AND CONCLUSION

We evaluated the development, influences, and adequacy of teacher induction and mentoring provisions in Singapore based on the macro policy analysis and micro research studies on the effects of policy implementation. This evaluation led us to the following understandings, conclusions, and implications for Singapore's induction policy development and implementation.

Singapore Teacher Induction Policy, Program, and Practices

Our analytical review of the 15-year trajectory of Singapore's induction and mentoring policy shows that teacher induction and mentoring have become a coherent system of policies and practices built over time. On the one hand, this system was developed to meet the needs of education reforms resulting from increasing and changing social, cultural, and political demands. On the other hand, it was developed to support beginning teachers to learn to teach and assess effectively in ways aligned with education reforms. The coherence of these policy developments occurred based on the infrastructure of PLCs, mentoring programs, and the partnership between MOE, NIE, and schools established in the first phase.

The system started against the international backdrop of an increasing reliance on induction support for beginning teachers to stay in teaching (Moskowitz & Stephens, 1997). Then, it has evolved from exposing beginning teachers to one-on-one mentoring and formal training courses to broadening their access to PLCs and learning to teach effectively alongside experienced practitioners with training for mentoring (MOE, 2018a).

A series of programs was central to the system's development and implementation to meet the changing social, cultural, and political demands over different phases. These programs included the Structured Mentoring Program (SMP) initiated in 2006, the Skillful Teaching and Enhanced Mentoring (STEM) initiated in 2011, the Instructional Mentoring Program (IMP) in 2017, and Inducting Teachers in Our Schools (ITOS) in 2018. Through these continuously updated programs, a new teaching force has been satisfactorily supported to teach students effectively for the future of Singapore.

However, despite their successes, two issues exist in developing and implementing teacher induction programs. First, like the induction systems in other countries, the funding and growth of these programs have been based on "a kind of act of faith" in their effectiveness (Britton et al., 2003, p. 300) instead of being subjected to proper evaluation and research. Thus, it is necessary to develop research that evaluates the effectiveness of induction and mentoring programs and practices, which is central to developing evidence-based teacher induction and mentoring programs.

Second, the focus of the induction programs has been evolving from the system-wide effort to enhance beginning teachers' teaching by moving them away from teaching for exams to teaching for children's holistic development and joy of learning. Such an evolution of teaching induction and mentoring programs with changing focuses also poses a challenge to developing research to examine the effects of these programs.

Lessons Drawn From Two Studies

Our review of the two studies on the influences and challenges of school-level teacher induction and mentoring programs led to several conclusions and implications. These studies suggest that the effectiveness of teacher induction programs on the quality of beginning teachers' learning to teach may not solely rely on theoretically sound and carefully designed mentoring cycles (Fang et al., 2009). Although useful, the effectiveness of these cycles could be compromised by the existing teaching culture and practices in the school contexts in which these cycles are implemented. Thus, it is necessary to understand the influence of school contexts in shaping the effects of induction program inventions. Such an understanding constitutes a necessary knowledge for developing effective induction practices adaptable to various teaching contexts.

The two studies also indicate that a standard evaluation system assessing the quality of beginning teachers' teaching is central to developing mentoring practices useful to support beginning teachers' learning to teach. Consequently, it is necessary to understand what makes a good mentoring assessment system possible.

Additionally, these studies show that mismatching mentors and beginning teachers in content areas and fields can be problematic in improving beginning teachers' knowledge and practice of content-based teaching. Therefore, examining what makes content-based mentoring relationships effective for beginning teachers' learning to teach and the other factors facilitating or limiting the effectiveness of such mentoring relationships is essential. Such an examination will help develop the knowledge base necessary for identifying and training mentors effectively to develop a nurturing environment that supports beginning teachers in learning to teach.

Ushering Teacher Induction in the Post-Pandemic Era

Undoubtedly, COVID-19 has affected schooling globally, and Singapore is not spared. It shapes deliberation on what is important for students to learn, how they need to learn, and what will influence their learning. It makes it central for teachers to use technology effectively in teaching in the changing educational environment. It is important to understand how technology can effectively shape what students are expected to learn and how they learn in the dynamic and evolving educational context.

Thus, mentors can focus their mentoring on supporting beginning teachers' capacity for teaching with technology, as envisioned in the SkillsFuture for Educators policy (MOE, 2020c). In turn, students' experiences can be enhanced by teachers with such proficiencies as they promote the new National Digital Literacy Program (Aisyah, 2022). To develop teacher mentoring with the above focus, it is important to understand what mentors need to do in shaping beginning teachers' learning to use technology in teaching. Such an understanding would bring the necessary insight into the development of induction and mentoring programs and practices in the post-pandemic era.

REFERENCES

Academy of Singapore Teachers. (n.d.-a). *Instructional mentoring.* https://academyof singaporeteachers.moe.edu.sg/programmes-publications/professional-development-programmes/instructional-mentoring-programme

Academy of Singapore Teachers. (n.d.-b). *Skills future for educators.* https://academyof singaporeteachers.moe.edu.sg/professional-excellence/skillsfuture-for-educators-(sfed)

Aisyah, K. (2022). *Singapore's national digital literacy programme.* https://opengovasia.com/national-digital-literacy-programme-in-singapore/

Bautista, A., Wong, J., & Gopinathan, S. (2015). Teacher professional development in Singapore: Depicting the landscape. *Psychology, Society and Education, 7*(3), 311–326.

Britton, E., Paine, L., Pimm, D., & Raizen, S. (Eds.). (2003). *Comprehensive teacher induction: Systems for early career learning.* Kluwer Academic Publishers.

Brown, J. S., Collins, A., & Duguid, P. (1989). Situated cognition and the culture of learning. *Educational Researcher, 18*(1), 32–42.

Chong, S., & Tan, Y. K. (2006, November 28–30). *Supporting the beginning teacher in Singapore schools—The structured mentoring programme* [Conference presentation]. APERA Conference 2006, Hong Kong. http://edisdat.ied.edu.hk/pubarch/b15907314/full_paper/1226593489.pdf

Collins, A., Brown, J. S., & Holum, A. (1991). Cognitive apprenticeship: Making thinking visible. *American Educator, 15*(3), 6–11.

Curdt-Christiansen, X. L., & Silver, R. E. (2011). Learning environments: The enactment of educational policies in Singapore. In C. Ward (Ed.), *Language education: An essential for a global economy* (pp. 2–24). SEAMEO Regional Language Centre.

Darling-Hammond, L. (1988). Policy and professionalism. In A. Lieberman (Ed.), *Building a professional culture in schools* (pp. 55–77). Teachers College Press.

Davie, S. (2015, November 19). Singapore Education ministry cuts back on hiring teachers. *The Straits Times.* https://www.straitstimes.com/singapore/education/singapore-education-ministry-cuts-back-on-hiring-teachers

Davie, S. (2020, June 28). Home-based learning set to be regular part of schooling post Covid-19, says Education Minister Ong Ye Kung. *The Straits Times.* https://www.straitstimes.com/singapore/education/home-based-learning-set-to-be-regular-part-of-schooling-post-covid-19-says

Fang Y. P., Lee, K-E. C., & Haron, S. T. (2009). Lesson study in mathematics: Three cases from Singapore. In K. Y. Wong, P. Y. Lee, B. Kaur, P. Y. Foong, & S. F. Ng (Eds.), *Mathematics education: The Singapore journey* (pp. 104–129). World Scientific.

Goh, C. T. (1997, June 2). *Shaping our future: Thinking schools, learning nation.* 7th International Conference on Thinking, Singapore. https://www.nas.gov.sg/archivesonline/speeches/record-details/6d6bdccf-d5d7-11e8-ab1b-001a4a5ba61b

Goh, R. (2016). *A tale of two schools: teacher learning through lesson study* [Unpublished doctoral thesis]. Nanyang Technological University. https://repository.nie.edu.sg/handle/10497/18555

Goh, R., & Fang, Y. (2017). Improving English language teaching through lesson study: Case study of teacher learning in a Singapore primary school grade level team. *International Journal for Lesson and Learning Studies, 6*(2), 135–150. https://www.emerald.com/insight/content/doi/10.1108/IJLLS-11-2015-0037/full/html

Goodwin, A. L., Low, E. L., & Darling-Hammond, L. (2017). *Empowered educators in Singapore: How high-performing systems shape teaching quality.* Jossey-Bass.

Gopinathan, S., & Mardiana, A. B. (2013). Globalization, the state and curriculum reform. In Z. Deng, S. Gopinathan, & C. K.-E., Lee (Eds.). *Globalization and the Singapore curriculum* (pp. 15–32). Springer.

Hairon, S., & Dimmock, C. (2012). Singapore schools and professional learning communities: Teacher professional development and school leadership in an Asian hierarchical system. *Educational Review, 64*(4), 405–424.

Heng, S. K. (2012, September 12). *Keynote address by Mr. Heng Swee Keat, Minister for Education* [Keynote address]. Ministry of Education Work Plan Seminar 2012, Singapore. https://www.moe.gov.sg/news/speeches/keynote-address-by-mr-heng-swee-keat—minister-for-education—at-the-ministry-of-education-work-plan-seminar—on-wednesday—12-september-2012-at-920-am-at-ngee-ann-polytechnic-convention-centre

Heng, S. K. (2013, September 25). *Keynote address by Mr. Heng Swee Keat, Minister for Education.* Ministry of Education Work Plan Seminar 2013, Singapore. https://www.moe.gov.sg/news/speeches/keynote-address-by-mr-heng-swee-keat—minister-for-education—at-the-ministry-of-education-work-plan-seminar-2013—on-wednesday—25-september-2013-at-915am-at-ngee-ann-polytechnic-convention-centre

Heng, S. K. (2014, April 9). *Opening address by Mr. Heng Swee Keat, minister for education.* International Conference of Teaching and Learning with Technology (iCTLT), Singapore. https://www.moe.gov.sg/news/speeches/opening-address-by-mr-heng-swee-keat—minister-for-education—at-the-international-conference-of-teaching-and-learning-with-technology-ictlt-at-the-suntec-international-convention-and-exhibition-centre—at-900am-on-wednesday—9-april-2014

Ho, W. K., & Gopinathan, S. (1999). Recent developments in education in Singapore. *School Effectiveness and School Improvement, 10*(1), 99–117.

Huling-Austin, L. (1990). Teacher induction programs and internships. In W. R. Houston, R. Howsam, & J. Sikula (Eds.), *Handbook of research on teacher education* (pp. 535–548). Macmillan.

Hung, D. (2017, March 4). School's all drill? That won't explain how Singapore topped PISA. *The Straits Times.* https://www.straitstimes.com/opinion/schools-all-drill-that-wont-explain-how-spore-topped-pisa

Lee, D., & Lee, W. O. (2013). A professional learning community for the new teacher professionalism: The case of a state-led initiative in Singapore schools. *British Journal of Educational Studies, 61*(4), 435–451.

Low, E. L., Ng, P. T., Goodwin, L. A., Liu, W. C., Goh, S.-E., Yeung, A. S. S., Chua-Lim, Y. C., Syed Mahmood, S. N. A., Pandian, S. P. J., Cai, L., Hui, C., & Cheong, B. C. (2019). *Supporting factors to effective beginning teacher mentoring: An exploratory study of teacher mentoring practices in Singapore* (OER Research Report). National Institute of Education.

Ministry of Education. (2009). *Report of the primary education review and implementation committee*. http://www.moe.gov.sg/media/press/files/2009 /04/peri -report.pdf

Ministry of Education. (2015). *Instructional mentoring in schools: An update paper from the mentor coach team* (Paper presented to chairman and members of Professional Directors' Meeting), Singapore, Ministry of Education.

Ministry of Education. (2018a). *Inducting teachers in our schools: Guide*. Academy of Singapore Teachers, Ministry of Education.

Ministry of Education. (2018b, September 28). *Learn for life—Preparing our students to excel beyond exam results* [Press release]. https://www.moe.gov.sg/news/press -releases/20180928-learn-for-life-preparing-our-students-to-excel-beyond -exam-results

Ministry of Education. (2020a). *The Singapore teaching practice*. https://www.moe.gov .sg/news/press-releases/20200304-learn-for-life-ready-for-the-future-refreshing -our-curriculum-and-skillsfuture-for-educators

Ministry of Education. (2020b). *Six areas of practice*. https://www.moe.gov.sg/micro sites/cos2020/skillfuture-for-educators.html

Ministry of Education. (2020c). *Learn for life—Ready for the future: Refreshing our curriculum and SkillsFuture for educators* https://www.moe.gov.sg/news/press-releases/ 20200304-learn-for-life-ready-for-the-future-refreshing-our-curriculum-and -skillsfuture-for-educators

Ministry of Education. (2022). *The Singapore teaching practice*. https://www.moe.gov .sg/education-in-sg/our-teachers

Moskowitz, J., & Stephens, M. (1997). *From students of teaching to teachers of students: Teacher induction around the Pacific Rim*. APEC.

National Center on Education and the Economy. (2016). *Empowered educators: How high-performing systems shape teaching quality around the world. Country Brief—Singapore: A teaching model for the 21st century*. National Center on Education and the Economy. http://ncee.org/wpcontent/uploads/2017/02/Singapore CountryBrief.pdf

Ng, E. H. (2009, September 17). *Speech by Dr. Ng Eng Hen, Minister for Education and Second Minister for Defense* [Speech]. MOE Work Plan Seminar 2009, Singapore. http://www.moe.gov.sg/media/speeches/2009/09/17/work-plan-seminar .php

Ng, P. T. (2012). Mentoring and coaching educators in the Singapore education system. *International Journal of Mentoring and Coaching in Education, 1*(1), 24–35.

One Portal All Learners 2.0. (2021). *SkillsFuture for educators—A one-stop portal to provide information on SkillsFuture for Educators*. https://www.opal2.moe.edu.sg/ csl/s/skillsfuture-for-educators-sfed/wiki/page/view?title=Overview

Ong, Y. K. (2020, June 28). *Opening address by Mr Ong Ye Kung, minister for education*. 2020 Schools and Institutes of Higher Learning Combined Workplan Seminar, Singapore. https://www.moe.gov.sg/news/speeches/20200628-opening -address-by-mr-ong-ye-kung-minister-for-education-at-the-2020-schools-and -institutes-of-higher-learning-combined-workplan-seminar

Organisation for Economic Co-operation and Development. (2014). *Results from TALIS 2013: Country note, Singapore*. OECD Publishing. https://www.oecd .org/education/school/TALIS-2013-country-note-Singapore.pdf

Organisation for Economic Co-operation and Development. (2019). *TALIS 2018 results (Volume I): Teachers and school leaders as lifelong learners*. OECD Publishing. https://doi.org/10.1787/1d0bc92a-en

Sim, A. (2012, July 11). *Speech by Ms. Sim Ann, Senior Parliamentary Secretary, Ministry of Education and Ministry of Law*. NIE Teachers' Investiture Ceremony, Singapore. https://www.moe.gov.sg/news/speeches/speech-by-ms-sim-ann—senior-parliamentary-secretary—ministry-of-education-and-ministry-of-law-at-the-nie-teachers—investiture-ceremony-at-930am-on-wednesday—11-july-2012—at-the-nanyang-auditorium—nanyang-technological-university

Simonds, D. (2018). What other countries can learn from Singapore's schools. *The Economist*. https://www.economist.com/leaders/2018/08/30/what-other-countries-can-learn-from-singapores-schools

Siti, S. (2020, January 25). President Halimah given tour of Pasir Ris Secondary School's digital initiatives. *The Straits Times*. https://www.straitstimes.com/singapore/president-halimah-given-tour-of-pasir-ris-secondary-schools-digital-initiatives

Tan, C. Y., & Dimmock, C. (2014). How a 'top-performing' Asian school system formulates and implements policy: The case of Singapore. *Educational Management Administration & Leadership*, *42*(5), 743–763.

Tan, C., Koh, K., & Choy, W. (2016). The education system in Singapore. In S. Juszczyk (Ed.), *Asian education systems* (pp. 129–148). Adam Marszalek Publishing House.

Tan, O. S. (2015). Innovating teacher education in a complex era. *Educational Research for Policy and Practice*, *14*(3), 193–200.

Tan, O. S. (2019). Teacher's professional development. In W. Striełkowski & J. Cheng (Eds.), *Advances in social science, education, and humanities research, Proceedings of the 3rd International Conference on Current Issues in Education*. Atlantis Press. https://doi.org/10.2991/iccie-18.2019.1

Teng, A. (2020). The new road map offers more training for teachers. *The Straits Times*. https://tnp.straitstimes.com/news/singapore/new-road-map-offers-more-training-teachers

Tharman, S. (2004, September 29). *Speech by Mr. Tharman Shanmugaratnam, Minister for Education*. MOE Work Plan Seminar 2004, Singapore. http://www.moe.gov.sg/speeches/2004/sp20040929.htm

Wong, J., & Bautista, A. (2016, April). *Features of most and least helpful professional development experiences: A study with primary music specialists* [Conference presentation]. Annual Meeting of AERA, Public Scholarship to Educate Diverse Democracies. Washington, DC. United States.

Wong, K. Y. (2013, January 17–20). *Diverse pathways for life-long teacher professional development* [Conference presentation]. International Science, Mathematics and Technology Education Conference (ISMTEC 2013), Bangkok, Thailand.

PART II

NATIONAL INDUCTION POLICY DEVELOPMENT
IN DECENTRALIZED SYSTEM

CHAPTER 5

BEGINNING TEACHER INDUCTION IN AUSTRALIA

Current Policy Trends and Future Challenges

Sean Kearney
University of Notre Dame Australia

ABSTRACT

Although the importance of beginning teacher induction has been recognized over two decades, variations and inconsistencies in teacher induction practices persist in Australia. The Commonwealth government released the first set of policy guidelines for implementing beginning teacher induction, *Graduate to Proficient: Australian Guidelines for Teacher Induction into the Profession*, in 2016. This chapter reviews the historical contexts that lead to the release of national guidelines and examines the recent research regarding beginning teacher induction to ascertain whether any significant changes occurred in teacher induction practices since the release of the guidelines. Then, through a case study of beginning teacher induction, this chapter illustrates how the guidelines are implemented in a specific school context, analyzes beginning teachers' experiences in the program, and discusses the policy implications of the case. The findings from the case indicate that a lack of policy and regulators' oversight of

Teacher Induction Policy in Global Contexts, pages 83–100
Copyright © 2024 by Information Age Publishing
www.infoagepub.com
All rights of reproduction in any form reserved.

teacher induction implementation following the release of the guidelines has led to little change in the teacher induction practices.

Like most industrial countries seeking to improve the performances of their school systems (Organisation for Economic Co-operation and Development [OECD], 2015), Australia has also been reforming teaching and learning in its school over the past 20 years. Australia established teaching quality as one of the factors, if not the most important, shaping student achievement in the early 2000s (Hattie, 2003; Rowe, 2003) following what happened in the United States in the 1990s (Darling-Hammond, 2000). Consequently, the past decade has seen increased state and federal interventions in the teaching profession throughout Australia. At the state level, these interventions include improving initial teacher education programs and attracting and retaining high-quality teachers (Bruniges et al., 2012). At the national level, they offer teacher professional development and enforce the formal registration and standardization of the teaching profession (Australian Institute for Teaching and School Leadership, 2015). For example, the Australian Institute for Teaching and School Leadership (AITSL), formed in 2005, has promoted teaching excellence through the development and implementation of the Australian Professional Standards for Teachers, which became the foundation for teacher accreditation and induction (AITSL, 2015).

Beginning Teacher Induction is one of Australia's latest movements to improve teaching and student outcomes. The publication of *The Australian Guidelines for Teacher Induction Into the Profession* in 2016 (I will use *the Guidelines* in the rest of this chapter) was the first national-level effort to standardize Australia's teacher induction practice (AITSL 2016a).

This chapter begins with an overview of the Australian educational landscape. It explains where and when Australia started its teacher quality movement and how it led to the *Guidelines* for teacher induction. The second section analyzes the *Guidelines* and their policy implications based on the research on the best practice of teacher induction. The following section reports the initial results of a case study on one teacher induction program and analyses those results against the *Guidelines*. Finally, the chapter concludes with an overall analysis of beginning teacher induction, policy implications of the *Guidelines*, and the future directions for teacher induction in Australia.

DEVELOPMENT OF NATIONAL GUIDELINES FOR TEACHER INDUCTION

Contexts of Policy Development

Teacher induction practices didn't become prevalent in Australia until the 1990s (Dinham, 1992; Ramsey, 2000). These practices were informally implemented in the late 1990s and more formally in the 2000s, which were handled at the school level involving basic familiarization of beginning teachers with policies and practices in a particular school context (Department of Education Science and Training, 2002; Khamis, 2000; McCormack & Thomas, 2003).

A motivation for teacher induction programs and practices came from the concern of declined quality teaching and, thus, students' achievements as shown in the international comparison (Organisation for Economic Cooperation and Development, 2018). This concern specifically reflected in the review by the New South Wales Department of Education and Training:

> Such (teacher induction) programs must be more sophisticated than introductory familiarization programs and may involve core packages developed cooperatively between the employers, universities, and others with appropriate expertise. Those responsible for their delivery would have detailed knowledge and training in these programs as part of professional practice. Indeed, such induction programs should be recognized in any system of teacher accreditation. (Ramsey, 2000, p. 66)

Although little resulted from this review regarding beginning teacher induction at the state levels. Australia's Department of Education Science and Training released two reports in the early 2000s focusing on teacher induction. The first report, *An Ethic of Care: Effective Programs for Beginning Teachers*, defined teacher induction as "support programs for beginning teachers" and a "critical phase within a continuum of professional learning" (Department of Education Science and Training, 2002, p. 11). It became the first genuine attempt to offer the national level support for teachers' professional development that would subsequently impact student achievement. The second report released in the following year, *Australia's Teachers: Australia's Future—Advancing Innovation, Science, Technology, and Mathematics* (Department of Education Science and Training, 2003), recognized the national provision of well-designed teacher induction as a key to support and guide beginning teachers to be successful as they transit from novice to professional in the early years of their careers.

These two reports illustrate the increased role of the national government in funding schools over the years in a state-based system where school funding traditionally came through a partnership between federal and state and territory systems (Gonski et al., 2011). For example, the total investment of the Australian government for schooling rose from $4.8 billion in 1999–2000 to $20 billion in 2009–2011 (The Treasury, 2000, 2008). This growth in federal funding has formed a foundation for the nationalization and standardization of education in the country. As Lingard (2000) suggests, the role of the Commonwealth government in Australian schooling was not obvious until the 1970s.

There was also the growing role of the national government in developing social and economic policies in addressing the challenges from the globalization of the world economy at the national level as part of a broader world trend since the late 1970s (Rizvi & Lingard, 2010). Consequently, Australia saw the emergence of several new national policy organizations. For example, AITSL was founded to develop national standards for the teaching profession. The Australian Curriculum, Assessment, and Reporting Authority was formed to develop the Australian Curriculum, the National Assessment Program, and the My School website. These national forces pushed the change of traditional roles of the state and federal governments in education policy.

Formation of National Teacher Induction Guidelines

The national policy that standardizes the teaching profession, including teacher induction, was developed through several stages in Australia. First, it is based on the Hobart Declaration on Schooling (1989) and the Adelaide Declaration on National Goals for Schooling (1999). The former was an agreement between the State, Territory, and Commonwealth Ministers of Education that declares the schooling of Australia's children central to building the nation's future. The latter superseded the former by proposing what students need to learn, the roles of schooling and teachers in their learning process, and the national-level needs to enhance the status and quality of the teaching profession at the national level. The Ministerial Council on Education, Employment, Training, and Youth Affairs officially adopted these ideas in 1999.

Second, the Teacher Quality and Educational Leadership Taskforce was established in 2001 to advise on the professional standards for teachers, which released a *National Framework for Standards for Teaching: A Consultation Paper* through a series of consultations with different parties (Ministerial Council on Education, Employment, Training, and Youth Affairs [MCEETYA], 2003). The National Framework "outlines core dimensions and attributes of standards that guided the development of generic, specialist, and subject-specific standards" for teaching (MCEETYA, 2003, p. 8). Endorsed by state, territory, and federal ministers, this framework became the base for national educational policies and guidelines.

The Melbourne Declaration on Educational Goals for Young Australians superseded the Adelaide Declaration (2008) proposed a 10-year plan for Australian schooling to develop a world-class curriculum and assessment. Its purpose was to improve the school learning outcomes of students with different backgrounds by developing collaboration, supports, accountability, and transparency at the national level. The Australian government initiated the Smarter Schools—Improving Teacher Quality National Partnership in 2009 to set up the national standards and teacher registration as the national priorities to improve the quality of teacher education in supporting the schooling reform.

Finally, under the auspices of the Ministerial Council for Education and Early Childhood Development and Youth Affairs, the Australian Institute for Teaching and School Leadership (AITSL) was charged to validate and finalize the development of the Australian Professional Standards for Teachers, begun in 2009, updated in 2011 and then finalized in 2015 (AITSL, 2011, 2015).

Under the Australian Professional Standards for Teachers, all teachers in Australia must have their registration/certification renewed throughout their careers in four stages (AITSL, 2018). These stages in the sequence include (a) graduate, (b) proficient, (c) highly accomplished, and (d) lead, with the first two as compulsory and the last two optional. Thus, teachers are registered at the graduate level, and most progress to proficient in a given timeframe and then maintain that level based on their professional knowledge, practice, and engagement. Teachers have 3 to 5 years to progress from their graduation in initial teacher education to proficient teachers when teacher induction would be implemented.

Summary

As the first national-level policy for teacher induction, the *Guidelines* were motivated by several forces over the years. First, the need to support beginning teachers to continue learning was recognized as a contributor to positively impacting students' learning in the early 2000s (Department of Education Science and Training, 2002, 2003). Second, the increased role of the national government in funding schools in a state-based system since the 2000s, in which the funding for schools traditionally came through a partnership between federal, state, and territory systems (Gonski et al., 2011). Third, the growing role of the national government in developing social and economic policies in addressing the challenges from globalization (Rizvi & Lingard, 2010).

The journey of developing national guidelines for beginning teacher induction is lengthy. It started with the agreement among state and territory governments on a national curriculum and the necessary national standards for teachers based on the recognition that teacher quality affects students' learning. Finally, the national level guidelines of teacher induction were developed as part of the efforts to improve teaching quality "having a material impact on learner outcomes" (AITSL, 2016a, p. 3).

THE GUIDELINES AND ITS IMPLEMENTATION

The *Guidelines* define the process of teacher induction as a period of moving beginning teachers from the graduate stage to the level of proficiency to reach full accreditation and remain in the teaching profession. Thus, it is helpful to unpack teacher induction and its relevant support as the *Guidelines* specify, evaluate its purposes for teacher development as the relevant research literature suggests, and examine how it was implemented to meet the purposes.

Australian Guidelines and Effective Teacher Induction in Literature

The etymology of "induction" comes from the Latin, "*inducer*" or "*to lead.*" Following the meaning of this term, beginning teachers should be thought of as the neophyte being led into a professional community of practice by more experienced colleagues (Kearney, 2015). Thus, teacher induction is "the primary phase in a continuum of professional development leading to the teacher's full integration into a professional community of practice and continuing professional learning throughout their career" (Kearney, 2014). In a similar vein, the *Guidelines* define teacher induction, accordingly, as shown below:

> A formal program and other support provided to assist early career teachers who have achieved the Graduate career stage in the Standards to move to the Proficient career stage—to learn, practice and refine the elements of the professional role that are best acquired while teaching. (AITSL, 2016a, p. 2)

To identify the extent to which the *Australian Guidelines* reflect characteristics of effective teacher induction, I reviewed ten articles published over the last decade based on their specific descriptions of the characteristics of effective teacher induction (Kearney, 2013). This body of literature includes international reports (Darling-Hammond et al., 2009; Moskowitz & Stephens, 1997; Organisation for Economic Co-operation and Development, 2005), national reports from the United States (Fulton et al., 2005), Australian national reports (Department of Education Science and Training, 2002, 2003), literature reviews in the international context (Howe, 2006) and in the United States (Serpell, 2000), two empirical studies (Smith & Ingersoll, 2004; Wood & Stanulis, 2009), and a report of state-level induction practices in New South Wales (New South Wales Department of Education and Training, 2004).

My review of this body of literature led to the following eight characteristics of effective teacher induction: (a) provision of a mentor, (b) opportunities for collaboration, (c) implementation of structured observations, (d) reduced teaching and time-release for working with beginning teachers, (e) evaluation of quality teaching, (f) opportunities for professional discussions and communication, (g) professional support and professional networking, and (h) continuing professional development (Kearney, 2014). I came to the results shown in Table 5.1 by comparing the policy initiatives

TABLE 5.1 Australian Guidelines Compared to Characteristics of Effective Induction

Guidelines Initiatives	Literature Suggestions	Match or Not
Practice-focused mentoring by one or more expert colleagues is particularly powerful in supporting the transition from the graduate to proficient career stage (AITSL, 2016a, p. 7).	Provision of a mentor	Yes
Involvement in teacher networks, including formal and informal networks within and beyond the school/education setting, to gain access to others' knowledge and skills and insights (AITSL, 2016a, p. 6).	Opportunities for collaboration	Yes
Study of teaching: This is most effective when it involves structured observations of and by the teacher to broaden the teacher's experience base and to offer feedback, evidence, and advice based on observed practice (AITSL, 2016a, p. 6).	Implementation of structured observations	Yes
Time should be made available in the initial period to enable effective conduct of the range of activities identified above (AITSL, 2016a, p. 6).	Reduced teaching and time release for the beginning teacher	Yes
Regular evaluation of induction policies and programs are essential to maximize effectiveness as well as to ensure consistency with other policies and programs (AITSL, 2016a, p. 9).	Evaluation of teaching quality	No
As part of mentoring, regular scheduled discussions and activities taking place, and sanctioned time set aside for mentor-teacher interactions (AITSL, 2016a, p. 8).	Opportunities for professional discussions and communication	No
Practice-focused mentors are the main support for early career teachers in schools and education settings, but all teachers have a role to play (AITSL, 2016a, p. 10).	Professional support and professional networking	Yes
Induction represents a more substantial and intense commitment to learning on the part of the early career teacher and those who support them than the continuing professional development available to all teachers (AITSL, 2016a, p. 2).	Continuing professional development	No

of the *Australian Guidelines* (AITSL, 2016a) with the above characteristics of effective teacher induction.

Based on Table 5.1, the initiatives of the *Guidelines* are a well-intentioned set of recommendations as they meet five of the eight characteristics for effective teacher induction as identified in the literature. However, as the literature suggests, they do not go far enough to match all the characteristics of effective teacher induction.

One of the effective teacher induction characteristics that the *Guidelines* fail to address appropriately is the structured opportunities for professional discussions beyond the mentoring relationships. Although the *Guidelines* stress the professional discussions within mentoring relationships, it does not encourage such discussions as part of professional teaching culture as suggested in the literature (Darling-Hammond et al., 2009; Fulton et al., 2005; National Commission on Teaching and America's Future, 2002; Smith & Ingersoll 2004; Wood & Stanulis, 2009).

However, if teacher induction is a form of organizational socialization in the first stage on a continuum of professional learning (Department of Education Science and Training, 2002; Kearney, 2014, 2015, 2019), it is important that the beginning teachers feel like a full member of the organization from the start (Kearney, 2015). Thus, they must have the opportunities for professional discussions with their colleagues in the school as members of a professional practice community who are interdependent in learning to teach (Little, 2012). Professional discussions and communications between beginning teachers and their colleagues also help overcome their learning limitations with mentors alone, especially when mentors could not engage beginning teachers in effectively learning to teach as expected (Cochran-Smith & Paris, 1995).

Another characteristic of effective teacher induction not mentioned in the *Guidelines* is beginning teacher evaluation. The *Guidelines* stress the program level evaluation as an essential component of teacher induction and assumed such evaluation as the responsibility of the "system, sectors, and regulatory authorities" instead of the national government (AITSL, 2016a, p. 9). They fail to emphasize the role of evaluation by beginning teachers who undertake the program to evaluate its effectiveness to complete a feedback loop for continuous improvement. The decision to relinquish the responsibility of evaluation of induction to the local level means that the quality of induction is likely to be variable and inconsistent (Kearney, 2019).

The last characteristic not met by the guidelines is teacher induction being part of continued professional development. For example, on the one hand, the *Guidelines* state that effective teacher induction "fosters the development of an early career teacher's professional identity" and "career" (AITSL, 2016a, pp. 3, 9). On the other hand, they stress, "Induction represents a more substantial and intense commitment to learning on the part of the early career teacher and those who support them, than the continuing professional development that is available to all teachers" (AITSL, 2016a, p. 2). This distinction recognizes the different learning needs of beginning teachers in the graduate stage and teachers in the Proficient stage and links the two stages to accreditation levels. However, it prevents the understanding of teacher learning as a continuum throughout teachers' careers with what they learned in the previous stage helps build what they learned in the next as suggested in the literature (Feiman-Nemser, 2001).

Broad Impacts of Australian Guidelines

Ever since implementing the guidelines, only small changes were observed in the number of beginning teachers who have received the quality support of teacher induction. For example, before the release of the guidelines, school administrators reported that 82.6% of teachers were mentored. In comparison, only 39.9% of teachers claimed that they received mentoring based on the survey data (Department of Education Science and Training, 2002). By 2019, 4 years after the release of the guidelines, school leaders indicated that 89% of beginning teachers had received formal induction, with 48% of beginning teachers reported that they had received formal induction based on the survey results from AITSL (2016b). The difference between the reports of school administrators and beginning teachers suggests different understandings about what counted as teacher induction between the two parties. Nevertheless, based on either Report, only 7%–8% more beginning teachers received teacher induction over the 20 years.

A further question can be raised regarding the nature of teacher induction programs on which teachers reported. Suppose beginning teachers' reports were more likely to reflect the reality of actual support that they received. In that case, another question can be raised on the quality of teacher induction that beginning teachers receive and whether that induction aligns with the *Guidelines*.

Summary

The *Guidelines* are primarily consistent with effective teacher induction provisions suggested in the relevant literature to a great extent. Such a consistency reflects specifically in five of the eight areas noted: Provision of a mentor, opportunities for collaboration with other teachers through mentoring, implementation of structured observations, reduced teaching time for the beginning teacher, professional support, and networking in induction programs (Kearney, 2014). The other three areas suggested in the relevant literature: Structured opportunities for professional communication beyond mentoring relationships, evaluation of teaching quality of beginning teachers, and continuing professional development (Kearney, 2014), do not feature prominently in the *Guidelines*. The three provisions are also central for beginning teachers to learn to teach effectively by benefiting from critical feedback and receiving continued support from colleagues in the school professional practice community beyond their mentors (Feiman-Nemser, 2001; Little, 2012). The critical issue is that these are only guidelines.

The *Guidelines* are a well-intentioned set of recommendations and ideas regarding good induction; however, they do not mandate such induction, which results in variation and inconsistency in implementation. As a result, there is only a small change in the number of beginning teachers who have received the quality support of teacher induction since the release of the *Guidelines*. Such weak impact demands further consideration of the process and the quality of teacher induction at the school level.

PROCESS AND QUALITY OF TEACHER INDUCTION AT SCHOOL LEVEL: CASE STUDY

One of the essential areas worth carefully examining regarding the implementation of the *Guidelines* is how well they, especially those initiatives relevant to practice-focused mentoring, were implemented and affected beginning teachers' acculturation to the Profession (AITSL, 2016a). As the *Guidelines* claim: "Of all the induction strategies available, practice-focused mentoring, by one or more expert colleagues, is particularly powerful in supporting the transition of a teacher from the Graduate to Proficient career stage" (AITSL, 2016a, p. 1). Thus, it plays the most significant role in any induction program (Matters, 2002).

Specifically, the *Guidelines* developed eight behaviors of practice-focused mentoring (AITSL, 2016a). They include: (a) beginning teachers having mentors in the same content area of teaching, (b) mentors' modeling of good practice; (c) conducting observation and encouraging reflection; (d) using data to inform practice; (e) supporting the well-being of beginning teachers; (f) having regular meetings and time working with beginning teachers; (g) supporting and challenging beginning teachers; and (h) using multiple mentors, online media, or networks.

This section examines how well the practice-focused mentoring suggested in the *Guidelines* was implemented in a primary school teacher induction program and the effects on beginning teachers. The case was part of a large study designed to examine the impact of multiple programs across various schools. It was situated in a primary school with approximately 550 students. Three beginning teachers involved in the teacher induction program at the school include one first-year teacher and the other two in their second year of teaching, who are all at the graduate stage of accreditation working towards proficiency.

My analysis of the data collected from the case led to several findings. First, only two of the eight policy initiatives regarding mentoring in the *Guidelines* were fully implemented. Table 5.2 illustrates the teachers' perceptions of their induction based on the eight behaviors of practice-focused mentoring.

The results indicate that the induction program at the school had not changed since the introduction of the *Guidelines* and that neither the teachers nor the mentor were aware of the provisions of practice-focused mentoring as indicated in the *Guidelines*. This case represents other cases where participants are either ignorant of the *Guidelines* or only partially implemented them.

Providing a mentor is arguably the most significant role in any induction program (Matters, 2002). According to the *Guidelines*, the most important strategy: "Of all the induction strategies available, practice-focused mentoring, by one or more expert colleagues, is particularly powerful in supporting the transition of a teacher from the Graduate to Proficient career stage" (AITSL, 2016a, p. 1).

TABLE 5.2 Mentoring Contexts Compared to the Guidelines' Mentoring Initiatives

Guidelines Initiatives	School Practices	Match or Not
Provision of a Mentor		
• Teacher of the same year group (primary school)	• Deputy principal who plays a non-teaching role	No
• Model good practice	• There was no modeling as the deputy principal was not teaching	No
• Observation and use of data	• Observation required data use	Partial
• Use learning outcomes to improve teaching approaches	• Student data was not considered pertinent to the program	No
• Support well-being	• The teacher reported that well-being did not come up	Yes
• Regular meetings and time allowance	• Teachers reported that meetings were irregular and rarely scheduled	No
• Coach, support, and challenge the teacher to improve practice	• Teachers did not feel challenged or supported	No
• Use multiple mentors, online media, or networks	• Only one mentor was appointed	No

First, none of the three beginning teacher participants claimed in the interviews that they had a mentor that met the *Guidelines'* recommendations. For example, the mentor assigned to each participant was the deputy principal who was in a non-teaching role and therefore not year-or content-appropriate as a mentor.

Such mentor assignments resonated with the study's overall situation of other primary school cases. For instance, about 87% of beginning teachers in teacher induction programs had mentors who were also their line managers. Over 80% of them had their deputy or assistant principals as mentors. In the high school cases of the study, all mentors were the beginning teachers' heads of the subject-specific department. As one of the deputy principals who worked as a mentor in a different case put it, "Someone has to do it and that Someone has to have the time and expertise to mentor the new teacher. We can't expect a full-time mentor."

Second, none of the teachers felt that the support they received from mentors was consistent with the intentions of a formal teacher induction program as expected by the *Guidelines*. As one of the second-year teacher participants articulated:

> We are told we are being inducted without any real sense of what that entails. [The deputy principal] is our supervisor, which we are told is the same as a mentor but is it? It doesn't seem like we are treated differently than any other staff. I mean, I don't want special treatment, but if this is what an induction program is, then I don't see any difference between me and a teacher with ten years of experience.

Another second-year teacher participant added when asked if she wanted to add anything else about the program or her experience in the program:

> I'm already looking for another job. I might just decide to do casual [substitute teaching] for a while. While I like the school and the kids, I'm just not sure it's for me. I don't get along with [the deputy principal], and it makes it hard to come to work. I know I have areas I need to improve upon, but I'm struggling, and while some of the teachers are great, they all have their classes to look after. I just feel like I don't particularly belong.

While the first-year teacher participant was more optimistic about her induction, she still didn't feel like she was being supported through an official program. She had this to say:

> I'm learning a lot. I love the school and the children, and I just feel so lucky to have this job. The support from the other teachers is amazing, especially Sarah (pseudonym). She is great and is so helpful. [The deputy/mentor] is good too. She helps when you ask, and our meetings are usually positive, but

I'm learning more from the teachers I meet and teach with than from her. She is my boss, so I don't want to bother her with my questions and problems.

My analysis of this case suggests a few things relevant to how well the mentoring practices were implemented. First, the practice-focused mentoring in the teacher induction program needs to be clearly defined with "an absolute clarity of roles, expectations, and knowledge of what constitutes the mentoring relationship" (Baker, 2002, p. 39). Unfortunately, this was not the situation in this case or the other programs of the study. For example, in this case, the clarity of the role of mentor as an expert teacher was not met. The teachers did not feel supported, and the reciprocal learning vital in mentor/mentee relationships could not be met due to the power dynamic between a deputy principal and a beginning teacher. For these reasons, the mentoring relationship was not effective.

Third, the practice-focused mentoring in the teacher induction program needs to be implemented as consistent with the expectations of the *Guidelines* reflecting the characteristics of effective teacher induction identified in the literature. In the context of the mentoring initiatives not being implemented consistently, school leaders may see these initiatives as aspirational guides. Thus, they will rely on their experience to develop teacher induction programs and acculturate new teachers to the Profession. As shown in this case, the teacher induction program was developed by ignoring the complexity of the mentoring relationship and the learning processes that underpin mentoring generally. It belies the problematic assumption that "the activity of mentoring necessarily facilitates the ability of beginning teachers to understand the central tasks of teaching and to engage in pedagogical thinking" (Feiman-Nemser et al., 1993, p. 16). Consequently, it reinforces the situation in which beginning teachers are not receiving the support they need, a problem the *Guidelines* were created to resolve in the first place.

Finally, while a manager can be a good mentor, they can reinforce a hierarchy that does not necessarily facilitate a good mentor–mentee relationship and allows for open communication, trust, and confidentiality (McCormack, 2005). As shown in the above quote by the first-year teacher, in this case, when your line manager is also your mentor, it can be difficult to see the relationship as one of mutual learning. In this situation, the mentees were challenged to know to whom to ask even if other supports were available.

Summary

It is important to note that this case was chosen for this chapter from the larger study of ten cases on the impact of beginning teacher induction in the four years since the release of the *Guidelines*. The themes and trends in this case neither reflected the worst cases (Kearney, 2016) nor those in the good ones (Kearney, 2017) that I presented elsewhere. Instead, they have been prominent in most cases, if not all, analyzed in the study. This research suggests that the *Guidelines* are not being implemented to their potential, mostly due to ignorance of what the Guidelines recommend and a false sense that their program is meeting the needs of beginning teachers despite not following the *Guidelines*. Therefore, the same practices that necessitated the creation of the *Guidelines*, namely supporting beginning teachers in the early years of their career to become proficient practitioners who stay in the Profession, are likely to continue despite the *Guidelines*. The *Guidelines* tend to be ignored because they are not embedded in policy, are not compulsory, and are poorly understood.

CONCLUSIONS AND IMPLICATIONS

The national-level policy changes in Australia over the past 15 years have been quite significant but only produced little noticeable positive effect on student achievement, if any (Organisation for Economic Co-operation and Development, 2018). One of the outcomes of these policy changes was creating and implementing the *Australian Guidelines for Teacher Induction*. Despite overwhelming evidence suggesting that teacher induction programs with mentoring at their center can improve teaching quality and student outcomes (Ingersoll & Strong, 2011), this initiative has not been embedded in policy or mandated.

As I have highlighted throughout this chapter, the *Guidelines* were an important step in recognizing the importance of an acculturation process for beginning teachers. They are designed to provide advice and recommendations for implementing beginning teacher induction nationwide to minimize the variability and inconsistencies in understanding, development, and implementing teacher induction programs in Australia (Kearney, 2019).

However, despite the continuous efforts in supporting beginning teacher induction for decades, the *Guidelines* did not mandate teacher induction nor its oversight; thus, teacher induction practices in Australia remain inconsistent.

If induction is as important as the literature and the *Guidelines* suggest, then mandating induction should have been worth consideration. However, as a national education body in a decentralized education system where school education is a state-run enterprise, it is not difficult to recognize the AITSL's limited power in policy implementation and evaluation of teacher induction programs consistently in Australia.

The question that needs to be asked is: What are the main obstacles to effective induction in schools? According to the research (Feiman-Nemser et al., 1993; Kearney, 2014, 2016, 2017, 2019; Wong et al., 2005), a lack of awareness and expertise about what good induction entails and little oversight of the process are obstacles. Thus, further action should be taken to lobby state education ministers to accept the *Guidelines* as policy so a more standardized approach can be implemented in schools in all states and territories.

The *Australian Guidelines* only provide the model for teacher induction. However, teacher induction needs school-leader buy-in and accountability procedures to ensure that the program meets its intended purpose. Until beginning teacher induction is policy-mandated, and the school leaders are held accountable for the program implementation, we may continue to see the same variation and inconsistency in beginning teacher induction reported for the past 20 years.

REFERENCES

Australian Institute for Teaching and School Leadership. (2011). *Australian professional standards for teachers.* Australian Institute for Teaching and School Leadership. https://www.aitsl.edu.au/teach/standards

Australian Institute for Teaching and School Leadership. (2015). *Australian professional standards for teachers.* AITSL. https://www.aitsl.edu.au/teach/standards

Australian Institute for Teaching and School Leadership. (2016a). *Graduate to proficient: Australian guidelines for teacher induction into the Profession.* AITSL. https://www.aitsl.edu.au/tools-resources/resource/graduate-to-proficient-australian-guidelines-for-teacher-induction-into-the-profession

Australian Institute for Teaching and School Leadership. (2016b). *Stakeholder survey results.* AITSL. https://www.aitsl.edu.au/research/measuring-our-impact/stakeholder-survey-results

Australian Institute for Teaching and School Leadership. (2018). *One teaching profession: Teacher registration in Australia.* Australian Institute for Teaching and School Leadership. https://www.aitsl.edu.au/teach/national-review-of-teacher-registration

Baker, W. (2002, July 7–10). Mentoring: Improving the quality of work life and organisational effectiveness: A case study of a formal mentoring programme implemented in a higher education organisation [Paper presentation]. *2002 Annual International Conference of the Higher Education Research and Development Society of Australasia* (HERDSA): Quality Conversations.

Bruniges, M., Lee, P., & Alegounarias, T. (2012). *Great teaching, inspired learning: A blueprint for action.* NSW Government. https://educationstandards.nsw.edu.au/wps/portal/nesa/about/initiatives/great-teaching-inspired-learning

Cochran-Smith, M., & Paris, P. (1995). Mentor and mentoring: Did Homer have it right? In J. Smith (Ed.), *Critical discourses on teacher development* (pp. 181–202). Cassell.

Darling-Hammond, L. (2000). Teacher quality and student achievement: A review of state policy evidence. *Education Policy Analysis, 8*(1), 1–44.

Darling-Hammond, L., Chung Wei, R., Andree, A., Richardson, N., & Orphanos, S. (2009). *Professional learning in the learning profession: A status report on teacher development in the United States and abroad.* National Staff Development Council.

Department of Education Science and Training. (2002). An *ethic of care: Effective programs for beginning teachers*. Australian Government Publishing Service.

Department of Education Science Training. (2003). Australia's *teachers: Australia's future—advancing innovation, science, technology, and mathematics*. Australian Government Publishing Service.

Dinham, S. (1992). Teacher induction: implications for administrators. *The Practising Administrator, 14*(4), 30–33.

Feiman-Nemser, S. (2001). From preparation to practice: Designing a continuum to strengthen and sustain teaching. *Teachers College Record, 103*(6), 1013–1055.

Feiman Nemser, S., Parker, M. B., & Zeichner, K. (1993). Are mentor teachers teacher educators? In D. McIntyre, H. Hagger, & M. Wilkin (Eds.), *Mentoring: Perspectives on school-based teacher education* (pp. 147–165). Kogan Page.

Fulton, K., Yoon, I., & Lee, C. (2005). *Induction into learning communities*. National Commission on Teaching and America's Future.

Gonski, D., Boston, K., Greiner, K., Lawrence, C., Scales, B., & Tannock, P. (2011). *Review of funding for schooling: Final Report.* Australian Government. https://www.dese.gov.au/school-funding/resources/review-funding-schooling-final-report-december-2011

Hattie, J. A. (2003). Teachers make a difference: What is the research evidence? [Keynote presentation]. *ACER Annual Conference: Building Teacher Quality*, Melbourne, Australia.

Howe, E. R. (2006). Exemplary teacher induction: An international review. *Educational Philosophy and Theory, 38*(3), 287–297.

Ingersoll, R. M., & Strong, M. (2011). The impact of induction and mentoring programs for beginning teachers: A critical review of the research. *Review of Educational Research, 81*(2), 201–233

Kearney, S. (2013). *New scheme teacher induction: Challenges and opportunities*. Scholar's Press.

Kearney, S. (2014). Understanding beginning teacher induction: A contextualised examination of best practice. *Cogent Education, 1*(1), 1–15. https://doi.org/10.1080/2331186X.2014.967477

Kearney, S. (2015). Reconceptualizing beginning teacher induction as organizational socialization: A situated learning model. *Cogent Education, 1*(2), 1–20. http://www.tandfonline.com/doi/full/10.1080/2331186X.2015.1028713#.VSxuBJOUeI

Kearney, S. (2016). What happens when induction goes wrong: Case studies from the field. *Cogent Education, 3*(1), 1–9. http://www.tandfonline.com/doi/full/10.1080/2331186X.2016.1160525

Kearney, S. (2017). Beginning teacher induction: A best practice case study. *Issues in Educational Research, 27*(4), 784–802. http://www.iier.org.au/iier27/kearney.pdf

Kearney, S. (2019). The challenges of beginning teacher induction: a collective case study. *Teaching Education, 32*(2), 1–17. https://doi.org/10.1080/10476210.2019.1679109

Khamis, M. (2000). The beginning teacher. In S. Dinham & C. Scott (Eds.), *Teaching in context* (pp. 1–17). ACER.

Lingard, B. (2000). Federalism in schooling since the Karmel Report (1973), schools in Australia: From modernist hope to postmodernist performativity. *The Australian Educational Researcher, 27*(2), 25–61.

Little, J. W. (2012). Professional community and professional development in the learning-centered school. In *Teacher learning that matters* (pp. 42–64). Routledge.

Matters, P. N. (2002, December 1–5). Mentoring: Cornerstone of teaching and learning excellence [Paper presentation]. *Conference of the Australian Association for Research in Education*, Brisbane, Australia.

Moskowitz, J., & Stephens, M. (Eds.). (1997). *From students of teaching to teachers of students: Teacher induction around the pacific rim.* Asia Pacific Economic Cooperation Secretariat.

McCormack, N. (2005, July 6–9). Mentoring the ongoing professional learning of early career teachers. In M. Cooper (Ed.), *Teacher education: Local and global.* In *Proceedings of the 33rd Annual Australian Teacher Education Association Conference* (pp. 10–17). Centre for Professional Development, Griffith University.

McCormack, A., & Thomas, K. (2003). Is survival enough? Induction experiences of beginning teachers within a New South Wales context. *Asia-Pacific Journal of Teacher Education, 31*(2), 125–138.

Ministerial Council on Education, Employment, Training and Youth Affairs. (2003). *A national framework for professional standards for teaching.* Curriculum Corporation.

National Commission on Teaching and America's Future. (2002). *Unravelling the "teacher shortage" problem: Teacher retention is the key.* https://files.eric.ed.gov/fulltext/ED475057.pdf

New South Wales Department of Education and Training. (2004). *Professional learning and leadership development: Supporting the induction of new teachers: Guidelines for schools.* NSW Government.

Organisation for Economic Co-operation and Development. (2005). *Teachers matter: Attracting, developing and retaining effective teachers.*

Organisation for Economic Co-operation and Development. (2015). *PISA 2015 results: (Volume I) Excellence and equity in education.*

Organisation for Economic Co-operation and Development. (2018). *PISA 2018 results: Combined executive summaries.*

Ramsey, G. (2000). *Quality matters: Revitalising teaching: Critical times, critical choices—Report of the review of teacher education in New South Wales.* The New South Wales Department of Education.

Rizvi, F., & Lingard, B. (2010). *Globalizing education policy.* Routledge.

Rowe, K. (2003). *The importance of teacher quality as a key determinant of students' experiences and outcomes of schooling* [Paper presentation]. The ACER annual conference: Building teacher quality, Melbourne, Australia.

Serpell, Z. (2000). *Beginning teacher induction: A review of the literature.* American Association of Colleges for Teacher Education.

Smith, T. M., & Ingersoll, R. M. (2004). What are the effects of induction and mentoring on beginning teacher attrition? *American Educational Research Journal, 41*(3), 681–714.

The Treasury. (2000). *Final budget outcome 1999–2000*. The Treasury. www.budget.gov.au/1999-00/finaloutcome/index.html

The Treasury. (2008–2011). *Final budget outcome 2007–08, 2008–09, 2009–10, 2010–11*. The Treasury. www.budget.gov.au/past_budgets.htm

Wong, H. K., Britton, T., & Ganser, T. (2005). What the world can teach us about new teacher induction. *Phi Delta Kappan, 86*(5), 379–384.

Wood, A. L., & Stanulis, R. N. (2009). Quality teacher induction: "Fourth-Wave" (1997–2006) Induction programs. *The New Educator, 5*, 1– 23.

CHAPTER 6

TEACHER INDUCTION POLICY IN CHILE

Beatrice Ávalos
University of Chile

Erika Castillo
National Accreditation Council Chile

ABSTRACT

This chapter describes how Chile's teacher induction policy was legally established in 2016 to address the difficult conditions under which teachers began to teach using research and other evidence from the early 2000s as support. The evidence pointed to young teachers abandoning the profession mainly in their second year of teaching, with around 14% of beginning teachers changing schools. Then, it discusses the complexity of the formal system of mentor preparation managed by the Ministry of Education and university-based. However, given the rigor and complexity of mentor training, it has not been possible to cover all eligible new teachers by 2022, as was expected. The chapter illustrates the impacts of the teacher induction policy using interview data with mentors and beginning teachers.

A host of reforms affecting teachers have been enacted since 1990. These include a major policy initiative to improve initial teacher education (Ávalos, 2005), efforts to widen the scope of professional development through school-based collaboration (Avalos & Bascopé, 2017; Ley 20.903, 2016), and legislation to evaluate the quality of newly graduated teachers before beginning to teach (Avalos & Reyes, 2020). Contrary to the assumption governing these policies that teacher education would adequately prepare teachers to face their early professional demands, research from the 2000s began to provide knowledge about difficulties faced by beginning to teach in Chilean classrooms (Avalos & Aylwin, 2007; Flores, 2014; León, 2016; Rufinelli, 2014). Results from this research prompted policymakers to consider a policy initiative that would support beginning teachers to address their needs, challenges, and difficulties in classrooms (Rufinelli Vargas, 2016). The outcome of such policy consideration was included in the 2016 Teacher Development Law, which established an induction system for beginning teachers (Ley 20.903, 2016).

In the first part of this chapter, we narrate the process leading to the development of the induction policy in Chile, discuss its current state, and identify its strengths and limitations. Then, we examine the effects of the second-year formal induction policy implementation from the perspective of mentors and novice teachers, drawing on interview data with those who were part of the process. Finally, we conclude the chapter by synthesizing what we learned about the Chilean teacher induction policy development, discussing its implementation challenges, and proposing research areas needed to build the knowledge base for addressing these challenges.

TEACHER INDUCTION POLICY DEVELOPMENT CONTEXT

The condition of teachers in terms of their salaries and working hours was deplorable starting in the 1980s due to policies implemented by Augusto Pinochet's Civic-Military dictatorship (1973–1990). Among other controversial measures, the dictatorship transferred responsibility for teacher preparation to tertiary-level institutions and then reversed this policy towards the end of the 1980s. These measures contributed to lessening the attractiveness of the teaching profession in the early 1990s, with the number of teacher candidates in teacher education programs oscillating from year to year during the decade.

The above conditions helped create the need for democratic governments to improve the preparation of teachers from the 1990s onwards (OECD, 2004). Specifically, between 1998 and 2002, the Chilean government provided substantial funding to reform teacher education programs in 17 public and private universities, covering around 80% of student teachers (Avalos, 2005). These efforts led to changes in the teacher education curriculum and, more importantly, future teachers' field experiences and practicum.

In the early 2000s, the inadequate working conditions of teachers in Chile began to receive research and public attention. In a review of Chile's education system, the Organisation for Economic Co-operation and Development (OECD, 2004) alerted that the teachers' workload in Chile was heavy during their first year and lacked school-based pedagogic support. Several research studies further supported this analysis. For example, Avalos and Aylwin (2007) conducted a mixed-methods study involving 242 beginning teachers in two regions of Chile. They found that participants typically taught 30 to 44 weekly periods, 45 minutes each.

Consequently, almost two-thirds of them declared being "physically exhausted" at the end of their school day. They also revealed that most new teachers were never observed nor received any feedback on their teaching that could help them improve. Thus, they had to learn to teach from experience with only occasional support from their colleagues or headteachers.

In 2006, secondary students started a major protest known as the Penguin Revolution, highlighting the poor quality of public schools. This protest led President Michelle Bachelet to set up a widely representative committee to review the conditions of the school system and submit change recommendations. Two committee recommendations directly affected beginning teachers (Avalos, 2014). The first of these called for monitoring teacher preparation using a test to assess the quality of teacher graduates' knowledge base for teaching. Chile's Ministry of Education approved this recommendation and developed 2008 the teacher beginner test in INICIAL, which was fully implemented in 2012 (Avalos, 2014). The second recommendation of the ministerial committee was to establish a support system for beginning teachers. In response, the Minister of Education convened a meeting involving teacher education authorities in 2005 (Beca & Boerr, 2020), who agreed on the need for new teacher induction and decided to commence mentor preparation (Cox, Meckes, & Bascopé, 2010). Professor Orland-Barak from the University of Haifa in Israel, with recognized mentoring experience, was invited to assist in the design of mentor preparation workshops (Orland-Barak, 2010).

The above agreements brought out the need for a future teacher induction policy. First, it became clear that being a good teacher did not necessarily make a good mentor. Teacher mentors need to understand adult learning and know how to work with beginning teachers collaboratively as professional colleagues (Beca & Boerr, 2020). Second, the Ministry of Education funded the enactment of a 200-hour formal mentor training program with a theory and practical curriculum to be delivered at three different universities in 2006 (Beca & Boerr, 2020). This preparation was later expanded in 2009 to five universities, including the three previous ones. In 2014, the Ministry of Education developed the legal framework and funding to sustain mentor preparation programs (Beca & Boerr, 2020). Finally, representatives from universities, research centers, parent associations, and teachers' unions discussed issues related to teachers, their working conditions, and the quality of their preparation programs in 2014. The outcome of these discussions was a document, The *Teachers' Plan*, that produced 141 recommendations, including the need for a beginning teacher induction policy and formal mentor preparation (Hochschield et al., 2014). These developments contributed to legislation passed during the second government of President Bachelet of the Teacher Professional Development Law (Ley 20.903, 2016), covering teacher preparation and development from initial teacher education to in-service support. Specifically, the Law establishes the right to induction for new teachers and its conditions.

In summary, the long process from 2005 to 2016 of generating professional awareness about beginning teachers' needs and working conditions, developing a knowledge assessment for those entering the teaching profession, and experimenting with mentor preparation had finally borne fruit in the new law's inclusion of beginning teacher induction. Below, we refer specifically to the resulting induction policy.

MANDATES, ASSUMPTIONS, AND IMPLEMENTATION OF THE TEACHER INDUCTION POLICY

Policy Mandates and Assumptions

The Law entrusts the Ministry of Education's professional development body, the Centro de Perfeccionamiento, Experimentación e Investigaciones Pedagógicas (CPEIP), to develop, organize, and manage the induction program. Its policy mandate reflects the assumption that an induction process with formal purposes and operation procedures is more important in supporting beginning teachers' learning to teach effectively in the school context rather than informal school-based support (https://www.cpeip.cl/mentoria-docente/).

The policy specifies the following mandates based on relevant assumptions developed in the literature. First, the Law establishes the right of all new teachers employed with contracts of at least 38-week school periods in public and subsidized private ones to receive 6-week class periods of induction during their first or second year of teaching (Ley 20.903, 2016). All newly contracted teachers are expected to apply for induction support using a specific platform developed by the Ministry of Education. Also expected is that by 2022, all eligible beginning teachers will have participated in this induction.

Second, the Law specifies that the induction processes be supported by experienced and specifically trained mentor teachers selected from those at or near the "accomplished" level of their teaching career. It requires those teachers wishing to become mentors to apply and register for university-based mentor training courses using a Ministry of Education platform. It also allows high-achieving schools, as measured by student learning results, to select competent teachers and allocate them time to mentor any beginning teacher contracted in the school.

Third, the Ministry of Education not only pays all beginning teachers and their mentors a stipend for time spent on the induction process. It also requires matching a mentor teacher with a beginning teacher based on whether they teach the same subject, at the same grade level, or in the same school. These practices for matching mentor teachers with beginning teachers are consistent with assumptions included in the legislation that they are professionally recognized as "highly competent" in the career system and have professional preparation in line with the new teachers' specialisms (https://www.cpeip.cl/mentoria-docente/).

Fourth, the government specifies two main roles for mentors working with beginning teachers in the school context (CPEIP, 2018). One is to strengthen beginning teachers' professional identities, further develop their teaching and management skills, and offer them feedback and guidance for improvement. This expected role reflects the legislation's definition of new teacher induction as "accompaniment and support" during their first teaching year to achieve those "learning, practice, and professional responsibilities" required for their professional development and integration in their school community (Ley 20.903, art.18 G, 2016). The other role is to assist new teachers in working with the school community in developing collaborative networks between the local education system, its schools, and teachers at the school level. These roles reflect those considered important in the induction literature (Malderez & Wedell, 2007).

Finally, mentors must follow mentoring procedures (Gorichon et al., 2020). Begin the process by asking beginning teachers about their learning-to-teach needs, conducting classroom visits, and engaging in co-planning with beginning teachers. These activities should include observation of beginning teachers' lessons, co-analysis of these lessons with them, as well as discussion, assessment, and other administrative tasks during mentor-novice interactions.

Through this mentoring process, new teachers are expected to understand and develop the ability to support students' ethical, social, and personal development using subject-specific and cross-sectional curricula. This requirement follows the assumption that teaching in contemporary social and cultural contexts requires teachers not just a technical but, more importantly, a social perspective (Achinstein & Athanases, 2010). More specifically, mentor teachers are asked to help beginning teachers develop the knowledge, communicative skills, and pedagogy needed to teach diverse students as required by professionals (Serpell, 2000). Finally, mentors must develop a plan and foster their and their mentee's reflective capacities by observing and assisting new teachers in lesson planning, classroom interaction, and assessment tasks, as Riveros et al. (2012) suggested. In synthesis, the mentoring process should be centered on developing beginning teachers' professional autonomy and identity, encouraging self-reflection in their teaching, and developing solutions to teaching issues.

Status of Induction Policy Implementation

Since its legislative enactment in 2016, teacher induction has been implemented in several ways. Regarding mentors, university-based preparation programs have expanded from five in three regions of the country in 2005 to nine that currently offer a diploma in mentoring. As of 2022, based on data from the CPEIP (https://impulsodocente.com)/over 2,000 mentors have received mentor training and registered officially as mentors for schools nationwide, especially in the most populated regions. Despite this number, during the 2021–2022 school year, there were only 190 beginning teachers working with mentors throughout the country (https://www.cpeip.cl/duplas-mentorias-2021-2022/), and mostly in the Metropolitan and Bio-Bío regions, which are the most populated of the 16 regions in Chile. These figures indicate that the policy expectation of mentoring for all new teachers by 2022 was not fulfilled. A couple of reasons contribute to this situation. First, despite the number of prepared mentors, they are not equally distributed throughout the country. Second, the teacher induction policy stipulates that beginning teachers must have contracts in the same school for at least 30 out of a maximum of 44 teaching periods. This requirement excludes induction for beginning teachers who do not find such jobs and must work part-time in two or more schools with fixed-term contracts (Cabezas et al., 2017). More so, the number of these teachers seems to have been increasing, as shown in a study tracking the employment history of three beginning teacher cohorts in 2000, 2005, and 2007 (Ávalos & Valenzuela, 2016). One out of ten teachers in the study changed schools, amounting to around 14% of new teachers yearly.

In short, the teacher induction policy established in 2016 (Ley 20.903, 2016) sets out the right of beginning teachers with 38-week teaching periods in schools to receive teacher induction in their first year. To this end, the Ministry of Education selects and pays experienced teachers to receive university-based mentor preparation. The induction process should match mentors with novice teachers based on content area, grade level, and school context. In substantive terms, it expects mentors to develop beginning teachers' professional identities and teaching and management skills through observation, feedback, and guidance. The system requires that mentors understand new teachers' needs and develop their capacity to teach the subject-specific and cross-sectional curriculum, including knowledge, skills, and pedagogy for diverse students, as well as foster their reflective capacities. Mentors should also encourage new teachers to participate in collaborative networks covering the local education district, its schools, and teachers. Since 2016, the policy has expanded the university-based mentor training programs and produced over 2,009 mentors to work with new teachers. However, the policy does not cover a growing number of teachers working part-time in two or more schools.

INDUCTION IMPACT ON CHILEAN BEGINNING TEACHER PROFESSIONAL LEARNING EXPERIENCES

In this section, we present the results from an interview study examining beginning teacher accounts and those of their mentors about their induction experiences. By doing so, we examine the impacts of implementing the teacher induction policy at the university level.

Contexts, Participants, and Data Sources

The study participants included three beginning teachers and their mentors from three university-based mentoring programs. It covered 8 or 9-month induction experiences during the 2019/2020 school years. All three beginning teachers interviewed worked in elementary, also known as basic schools in Chile, mostly covering preschool to eighth grade. The schools were in Valdivia, Concepción, and San Antonio. Information on all three beginning teacher participants is shown in Table 6.1.

TABLE 6.1 Basic Information of Beginning Teacher Participants

Participants	Schools	Grade Level	Content Areas	Interview
Peppa	Valdivia, Public	Elementary	Language	Zoom
Adriana	Concepción, Public	Elementary	Mathematics	Phone
Enrique	San Antonio, Private Subsidized	Elementary	History	Zoom

Peppa's school is in Valdivia, a city in the southern region of Los Ríos. In 2020, it had 340 students, 36 teachers, and a mean of 26 students per class. Adriana's school is an elementary school in Concepción in the region of Bío Bío, with 338 students, 39 teachers, and a mean of 21 students per class. In contrast, Antonio's school is in the port city of San Antonio in the region of Valparaíso, some 100 kilometers away from the capital Santiago. It had 150 students, 17 teachers, and 15 students per class. All three beginning teachers were first-year teachers who started their induction in 2019 and 2020, both complex years with disruption of normal schooling due to serious social unrest during the second part of the 2019 school year and the irruption of the COVID-19 pandemic.

Mentor interviews covered three mentors working with the beginning teachers studied and a professor at a major teacher preparation university in Santiago carrying out mentor training (see Table 6.2).

Rosa and Jimena were basic-level teachers, while Antonia taught at both basic and secondary levels. Rosa was also the principal of her school. Antonia was Adriana's mentor, Rosa mentored Pepa, and Jimena worked with Enrique. They were prepared as mentors in different university-based diploma programs sponsored by the CPEIP. Also interviewed was María, at the main pedagogic university in Santiago. At the time, she was responsible for coordinating teacher education practicum experiences and for a mentor preparation program offered by her university, though not sponsored by the CPEIP.

An interview was conducted with each beginning teacher and mentor teacher focusing on (a) their experience of the mentorship process, (b) its impact on their professional growth, (c) induction policy enactment, (d) areas for its improvement, and (e) how initial teacher preparation could support beginning teachers' learning to teach. All the participants were interviewed in 2020 after the first year of induction activities, using telephone, Zoom, and written media due to the COVID-19 pandemic and school closures through 2020. These interviews were coded and analyzed for the themes related to the interview, leading to the following results.

TABLE 6.2 Basic Information of Mentor Trainer and Mentor Teacher Participants

Participants	Training Institute	School	Roles in Program	Interview
María	Metropolitan U.	Santiago	Mentor trainer	Zoom
Rosa	San Sebastian U.	Valdivia	Mentor, principal, and teacher	Phone
Antonia	U. Concepción	Concepción	Mentor & teacher	Zoom
Jimena	Catholic U. Valparaiso	Valparaíso	Mentor & teacher	Zoom

Mentoring Focuses and Processes Under Teacher Induction Policy

The interview data analysis revealed several findings related to mentoring developments following the teacher induction policy. First, in their interactions with beginning teachers, all three mentors centered on general teaching approaches more than content-specific teaching. They made few references to the quality of the beginning teachers' subject knowledge or having to correct errors and misunderstandings in their mentees' teaching. While subject specialization was not an issue, "pedagogy," as they described it, certainly was. This situation was because their preparation as mentors was more generic than subject-specific. As explained by María, the mentor trainer, in recalling her mentor training:

> We were not prepared as subject specialist mentors...I was part of a large mentoring project in Valparaiso where I engaged in group and individual mentoring...it was a huge challenge for I had to mentor secondary teachers, including specialists in mathematics, science, and arts. Nevertheless, one must be responsible because even though mentoring does not require sharing the same subject specialization, it centers on pedagogy and how to do this or the other.

Second, despite curricular specialization differences, mentors seemed to catch on to what a beginning teacher knew or did not know. For example, as observed in other studies (Ávalos & Aylwin, 2007), beginning teachers in Chile often experience difficulties in managing day-to-day routine activities such as proper recording of student attendance in the "class book," a key requirement for school funding as it rests on a per-student-in-school voucher system. As the mentor, *Antonia*, claimed:

> I teach them how to handle the "classroom book" and to deal with parents (María, mentor trainer). The root of the problem is that universities mostly provide theoretical preparation...Thus, when teachers begin to teach, they find themselves in a new world that includes something as basic as the "classroom book."

Beginning teachers also find it difficult to set aside their former student-teacher roles and modes of interaction and catch on to the social and professional conduct required by their schools. Antonia, one of the mentor teachers interviewed, recalled how her first mentee was "immensely fearful of presenting herself to others in her new professional role and on how formal she should be when interacting with parents and colleagues." Adriana recalled her experience of beginning to teach in the same school where she had completed her preservice teacher education student practicum and the complexities of moving from one role to another. These fears reflected the regard for status and hierarchy in schools. Also, mentor interviews highlight the importance of the mentor's role in providing socio-emotional support. As Adriana, the beginning teacher, claimed, "When I began in this school, I felt very lonely. I needed strong guidance. But she trusted me."

Third, mentor–novice relationships for these mentors and beginning teachers in the study tended to be experienced more as collegial rather than hierarchical as between experienced and inexperienced teachers. For example, the beginning teacher, Adriana claimed:

> Our first meeting was fruitful, for it gave us an opportunity to learn from one another and to work in a more horizontal manner, not as between an experienced and beginning teacher.

Also valued, as noted by one of the beginning teachers interviewed, was the opportunity provided for some of them to meet as beginning teachers. As the beginning teacher, Peppa expressed.

> The best experience was when several of us from different parts of the country met to share experiences and offer suggestions about how the mentorship process could be improved, considering the contextual differences.

What Mentor Teachers Learned from the Teacher Induction Processes

Throughout interviews with the four mentors, there were many references to their professional learning and the role of reflection in this. First, as noted earlier, all three mentors learned how to understand the difficulties of beginning teachers in managing day-to-day routines that they failed to learn during their initial preparation program. They could offer mentoring support accordingly. One of the mentors, Antonia, used an interesting image of how the poor in Chile build their houses -room by room with no connecting hallways- to illustrate how mentoring had helped her in terms of professional growth:

> And this is what happens with professionals in general. They build isolated rooms...At some point in my work as a teacher, I felt the need to articulate to build hallways...and the perfect hallway turned out to be my mentoring experience...It helped to analyze my practice...mentoring made me reflect and systematize what I was doing as a teacher.

Mentors also distinguished and valued the different ways' experience' rather than "expertise" is a plus in mentoring relationships. The mentor trainer, María, shared her reflections on how personal and professional traits interlinked over time as she pursued her work:

> I think my life history has marked me as a student and person. I can prove myself to others because I can speak from experience more than from theory, although I also manage to bring theory in. But my strength is experience, and this is something on which we work together [with the mentors she prepares].

Although she completed her practicum as a preservice teacher in the same school where she was beginning to teach, Adriana still felt lonely and faced the challenge of dealing with day-to-day routine activities as she transitioned from the role of student to the role of teacher. She said, "When I began in this school, I felt very lonely. I needed strong guidance."

Her mentor teacher, Antonia, quickly learned that Adriana was "immensely fearful of presenting herself to others in her new professional role" and of "how formal she should be when interacting with parents and colleagues." Thus, Antonia offered her beginning teachers support on how to deal with day-to-day routines. As she said in the interview:

> I teach them (beginning teachers) how to handle the "classroom book" and deal with parents. The root of the problem is that universities mostly provide theoretical preparation but not on how to deal with everyday school requirements. Thus, when beginning teachers begin to teach, they often find themselves in a new world that includes something as basic as the "classroom book."

Mentor teacher Rosa also echoed that one of the important issues beginning teachers face as they start to teach is how to "deal with parents regarding their children's absences and how to communicate with them effectively" and "They often fear facing parents, as well worry about their lack of skills to handle formal teacher meetings correctly."

All mentor teachers learned how to support their beginning teachers to engage their students in active learning and to manage different kinds of students in their school contexts. For example, beginning teacher Adriana worked in a school in a poor urban area, where her students shared her socio-economic background. As she explained:

> I feel comfortable here because this is where I come from [a poor neighborhood in the city of Concepción] ... So, what if he didn't bring a lead pencil, what if he is sleepy, and what if she is hungry? Yes, I now can see what is behind every child.

Her mentor, Antonia, provided intentional and active mentoring to address student learning issues in line with the school context. As she explained:

In highly vulnerable school contexts, a beginning teacher should not be left alone to manage difficulties... As an experienced teacher, the mentor should not just lend a friendly ear to the beginning teacher's call for help: "Hey, look how those kids have behaved." The mentor should also consider the emotional components involved. If the new teacher's preparation did not include experiences with these kinds of students, it is quite possible that they will be frustrated and end up repeating what other teachers in the school do. That is, shout at the students and overpower them with rules totally unrelated to learning. I am telling you about the beginning teacher who worked hard until he got his students to take out library books and read those that meant something to them.

A well-structured and oriented mentor program needs to prepare them to assist beginning teachers in noticing the specific difficulties their students encounter in different contexts. For example, Enrique, one of the beginning teachers interviewed, faced with the reading difficulties of his second-grade students, commented on the importance of mentors assisting with relevant practical suggestions: "This could be handled this way. You might focus on these other objectives or assist with the practical meaning of some of the terms that are part of the lesson plan we have to develop."

Third, all the mentor teachers valued the central role of reflection, as stressed in the teacher induction policy, to improve their teaching and mentoring practices. Reflection, they asserted, helps them understand their role concerning the mentee's needs and their role as teachers. However, reflection can be misleading if it simply adds segmented parts of experience. To illustrate this concept, mentor teacher, Antonia, used the image of how people with low incomes in Chile build their houses room by room and without connecting hallways:

> And this (reflection) is what happens to professionals in general—they build isolated rooms... At some point in my work as a teacher, I felt the need to articulate, to build hallways... The perfect hallway turned out to be my mentoring experience... I was able to analyze my practice... Mentoring made me reflect and systematize what I was doing as a teacher.

Beginning Teachers' Learning

The beginning teacher responses to questions during the interviews mostly brought out personal and professional examples of learning rather than elaborate narratives. Here are a few of these. Responding to the question about the benefits of the induction experience, Enrique recalled help from the mentoring process and his mentor during the pandemic closed down in handling a second-grade child who lived in a home for children without a family. This child could not follow the Zoom reading lessons that others in her class could do. "I was at the other side of the camera and could not, as one does in normal circumstances, walk up to her place and assist her." Faced with this difficulty, Enrique appreciated his mentor's assistance in handling this and similar situations, for which his initial teacher training had not and probably could not prepare him. Adriana recalled the importance of the first meeting with her mentor when she began teaching in a primary school in the city of Concepción. Her mentor's collegial attitude helped to create a bond that facilitated all later interactions. Adriana's mentoring experiences also took place during the 2020 school closure. Like Enrique, she had to learn to teach at a distance." It meant assistance with the pedagogic use of the different teaching platforms available and their materials for the students she only met briefly in a face-to-face mode. Adriana learned from her mentor how to recognize her capacities and trust herself much more despite the fact that her mentor was a language teacher while Adriana had specialized in mathematics.

These perceptions about the value of the mentoring process as a stimulant for professional learning based not so much on specific advice (though including it) but on a symbiotic relationship in which advice and assistance are provided, was also found in a similar study also carried out in Chile (Salas et al., 2021). Through interviews with mentor and mentee pairs, the researchers concluded that beginning teachers more than appreciate the professional qualifications of their mentor, valued instead what the authors describe as "pedagogical capacities" to listen and assist.

ISSUES IN THE TEACHER INDUCTION POLICY AND ITS IMPLEMENTATION

The interview data brought out issues related to the teacher induction policy as currently in place. First, following the induction policy, mentors must report to the school authorities and the CPEIP regarding progress in their mentoring process and their beginning teachers' learning to teach as shaped by their mentoring actions. As commented by mentors during the interviews, the format of these reports tends to reflect more of a bureaucratic requirement rather than a base to evaluate and improve mentoring practices. Further, the systematic format in which these reports must be written produces a daunting workload of little value to the mentoring process itself. As Jimena expressed

> It is very difficult to write a systematic report on the learning of a beginning teacher, his or her development, and about all experiences that take place... there is a big gap [between what happens] and what you're able to

report on. And as far as what the Ministry of Education requires, there is lots of paperwork... We must hand in three types of paper reports: planning, enactment, and finally, a report with a reflective analysis of what we did... Besides, we are not expected to use our experiences to conduct focused research. And this is missing.

Additionally, all three beginning teachers claimed that they received little support from the school beyond that of their mentors. As Peppa commented, "Without mentoring, the first year of teaching for some beginning teachers would have been a solitary experience."

Part of the reason for the above situations might be that practicing teachers and school authorities have misconceptions regarding the beginning teachers' needs in the school context. On the one hand, they believe that after 4 to 5 years of university teacher education, beginning teachers should be fully prepared to carry out their teaching and school obligations. But also, though less recognized, is the belief that new teachers may have gained more up-to-date knowledge about the schools' curriculum from their initial preparation programs than their colleagues.

When asked what needs to be improved in the induction program, Adriana noted that schools should be more active in informing their beginning teachers of the right to induction. She stressed:

> It's all about dissemination... about what you need to know to apply for induction... It could be published on social networks. I find a lot of information about courses in such networks... Also, school principals should provide information to their new teachers on induction opportunities. Hey, Mr. Principal, you have new teachers in your school... well, we have an induction program for them. A nice, attractive brochure would also be useful.

Overall, the interview study showed that contrary to policy expectations, mentor teachers focus on general teaching pedagogies instead of content-specific teaching, possibly shaped by the mentor training they received and/or differences between the mentor and mentee's main teaching subjects. Also, relationships are more collegial without the formality expected between an experienced and beginning teacher, as the teacher induction policy assumes. On the other hand, in line with the induction policy, mentor teachers learned how to identify beginning teacher difficulties in dealing with teaching routines and in transitioning from a preservice teaching role to formal teaching roles and school responsibilities. It allowed them to offer mentor support accordingly. They also learned how to actively support their beginning teachers in complex school contexts and how reflection supports their professional growth as teachers and mentors. More than anything else, the main benefit of the mentoring process recognized by the new teachers studied was increased self-confidence and reassurance about their teaching vocation, as well as useful advice in dealing with teaching demands for which they had not been prepared. A good example was learning to teach in "zoom" form during the COVID-19 pandemic when schools were closed.

CONCLUDING THOUGHTS

The development of the teacher induction policy in Chile began with research-based and public interrogations about beginning teachers' working conditions and their preparation for teaching in the early 2000s (Ávalos & Aylwin, 2007; Flores, 2014; Rufinelli, 2014). It was built on the gradually developed university-based mentor preparation programs sponsored by the Ministry of Education starting in 2005 (Beca & Boer, 2020). It was formally established in 2016 as part of the Teacher Development Law (Ley 20.903, 2016). The policy aimed to provide induction to all eligible teachers by 2022.

As framed, the policy provides beginning teachers with mentorship support in their first or second year of teaching. Experienced teachers who are specially prepared as mentors in university diploma programs are charged with the responsibility of mentors. Mentoring is a highly structured process designed to support beginning teachers in developing professional identities, instruction, and management skills and offer them feedback and guidance for improvement. It also should assist beginning teachers to participate in collaborative networking with the local education system, its schools, and teachers based on the CPEIP at https://www.cpeip.cl/tag/induccion-y-mentoria/

In the mentoring process, mentors are expected to understand beginning teachers' learning-to-teach needs, observe their teaching, co-plan and analyze lessons with them, and discuss assessment and other issues of teaching and administration (Gorichon et al., 2020). Through this scripted mentoring process, mentor teachers are expected to develop new teacher capacity to integrate students' ethical, social, and personal development using subject-specific and cross-sectional curricula. They are also expected to develop beginning teachers' knowledge, communicative skills, and pedagogy for teaching with appropriate attention to the norms and needs of their diverse students. Finally, they must develop their and their mentee's reflective capacities in articulating lesson planning, classroom interaction, and assessment tasks.

As noted above, the teacher induction policy in Chile has well-developed intentions, specific expectations for beginning teachers, appropriate consideration of mentor selection and preparation process, and mandates informed by relevant theories and research. However, several issues emerged from our analysis in the chapter regarding the teacher induction policy development and its implementation. These issues are as follows:

First, the system has failed to cover all beginning teachers by 2022 as required by the Teacher Development Law and does not consider the growing number of beginning teachers working on a part-time basis. While over 2000 mentors have been formally trained, they still are not enough. Thus, some changes need to allow experienced teachers to take on mentoring tasks in schools where there is no prepared mentor. To meet this need, the research community should examine various teacher mentor preparation forms and identify those that can effectively prepare more mentors to work with a growing number of beginning teachers.

Second, the teacher induction legislation (Ley 20.903, 2016) expects mentors to focus on all areas of the teacher performance evaluation system, including teaching specific curriculum contents. The interview study showed that mentor teachers focus most frequently on general teaching pedagogies, day-to-day routine activities, and student management in the school context. Content-specific pedagogies were not the center of their mentoring practices in the accounts of the beginning teachers interviewed. It was the case even if the mentor and beginning teacher taught the same content in the same school. While mentor training can partially explain the situation, other influential factors and contexts shaping the focus of mentors and beginning teachers need to be identified. Thus, relevant research should identify these factors and contexts and how they shape the mentoring focuses.

Third, implicitly, the teacher induction policy expects mentors to assist beginning teachers in developing the capacity to integrate students' ethical, social, and personal development needs using subject-specific and cross-sectional curricula in line with the objectives of teaching as set out by law (Ley 20.903, 2016). The interviews in this study brought this out as a central concern of beginning teachers. In this respect, the research community must examine how such an intended policy is enacted in beginning teachers' learning to teach and how mentor teachers are being prepared accordingly in the university-led programs.

Finally, seen from the double perspective of a mentoring system carefully designed and managed as well as one that should encourage learning through reflection, collaboration, and action, it could probably be classified at the coaching level of mentoring as proposed by Kochan and Pascarelli (2012) in their continuum from tutoring to mentoring. The interview data did not show a higher mentoring involving change and innovative teaching and professional practices. Thus, in the Chilean context, as suggested by Cuellar et al. (2019), there is a need to (a) assist beginning teachers in learning about their practices through joint planning, observation, discussion, and guidance and (b) strengthen reflection-in-practice to improve teaching and the handling of other school and professional related demands. In this respect, the research community might consider innovative cases of mentoring and induction to examine what mentoring practices and contextual conditions are effective and supportive in this respect.

ACKNOWLEDGMENTS

Authors acknowledge that the funding of this chapter comes from Project FB003 from the Basal Funds for Centers of Excellence, Chile.

REFERENCES

Achinstein, B., & Athanases, S. Z. (2010). New teacher induction and mentoring for educational change. In A. Hargreaves, A. Lieberman, M. Fullan, & D. Hopkins (Eds.), *Second international handbook of educational change* (Springer International Handbooks of Education, Vol. 23). Springer. https://doi.org/10.1007/978-90-481-2660-6_33

Ávalos, B. (2005). How to affect the quality of teacher education: A four-year policy-driven project implemented at university level. In P. M. Denicolo & M. Kompf (Eds.), *Connecting policy and practice: Challenges for teaching and learning in schools and universities* (pp. 39–43). Routledge.

Ávalos, B. (2014). La formación inicial docente en Chile: Tensiones entre políticas de apoyo y control. *Estudios Pedagógicos* (Especial 1), 11–28.

Ávalos, B., & Aylwin, P. (2007). How young teachers experience their professional work in Chile. *Teaching & Teacher Education, 23*, 515–528. https://doi/10.1016/j.tate.2006.11.003

Ávalos, B., & Bascopé, M. (2017). Teacher informal collaboration for professional improvement: Beliefs, contexts, and experiences. *Education Research International. 2017*, 1–13. https://doi.org/10.1155/2017/1357180

Ávalos, B., & Reyes, L. (2020). *Historical development of teacher education in Chile. Facts, policies, and issues.* Emerald Publishing.

Ávalos, B., & Valenzuela, J. P. (2016). Education for all and attrition/retention of new teachers: A trajectory study in Chile. *International Journal of Educational Development, 49*, 279–290. https://doi.org/10.1016/j.ijedudev.2016.03.012

Beca, C. E., & Boerr, I. (2020). Políticas de inducción a profesores nóveles: Experiencia chilena y desafíos para América Latina. *Revista Electrônica de Educação, 14*, 1–23. http://doi.org/10.14244/198271994683|

Cabezas, V., Predes, R., Bogolasky, F., Rivero, R., & Zahri, M. (2017). The first job and the unequal distribution of primary school teachers: Evidence for the case of Chile. *Teaching and Teacher Education, 64*, 66–78. http://doi.org/120.1016/j.tate.20127.01.017

Cox, C., Meckes, L., & Bascopé, M. (2010). La institucionalidad formadora de profesores en Chile en la década del 2000: Velocidad del mercado y parsimonia de las políticas. *Pensamiento Educativo, 46*(1), 205–245. https://pensamiento educativo.uc.cl/index.php/pel/article/view/25567

CPEIP. (2018). *Documento de especificaciones técnicas para la formación de mentores* [Unpublished instructions for mentor preparation].

Cuéllar Becerra, C., González Vallejos, M. P., Espinosa Aguirre, M. J., & Cheung, R. (2019). 'Buen mentor' y 'buena mentoría'según actores de programas de inducción a directores novatos chilenos. *Psicoperspectivas, 18*(2), 33–46. https://doi.org/10.5027/psicoperspectivas-Vol18-Issue2-fulltext-1543

Flores, C. (2014). Inducción de profesores novatos en Chile. *Pensamiento Educativo, 51*(2) 41–55. https://doi.org10.7764/PEL.51.2.2014.4

Gorichon, S., Sálas, M., Araos, M. J., Yañez, M., Rojas-Murphy, A., & Jara, G. (2020). Prácticas de mentoría para la inducción de docentes principiantes: Análisis de cuatro casos chilenos al inicio del proceso. *Calidad en la Educación, 52*, 12–48. https://doi.org/10.1016/j.ijedudev.2016.03.012

Hochschield, H., Díaz, F., Walker, J., Schiapacasse, J., & Medeiros, M. P. (2014). El plan maestro: Diálogos para la profesion docente. *Calidad en la Educación, 41*, 131–135. https://doi.org/10.31619/caledu.n41.62

Kochan, F., & Pascarelli, J. T. (2012). Culture and mentoring in the global age. In S. Fletcher & C. A. Mullen (Eds.), *The Sage handbook of mentoring and coaching in education*. SAGE.

León, C. T. (2016). Profesores principiantes de Educación Básica: Dificultades de la enseñanza en contextos escolares básicos. *Estudios Pedagógicos, 42*(4), 31–48.

Ley 20.903. (2016). *Crea el sistema de desarrollo profesional docente y modifica otras normas*. Ministerio de Educación de Chile. https://www.docentemas.cl/download/ley-20-903-crea-el-sistema-de-desarrollo-profesional-docente-carrera-docente-y-modifica-otras-normas/

Malderez, A., & Wedell, M. (2007). Teaching teachers: Processes and practices. Continuum International Publishing Group.

OECD. (2004). *Reviews of national policies for education in Chile*. OECD.

Orland-Barak, L. (2010). *Learning to mentor-as-praxis: Foundations for a curriculum in teacher education*. Springer.

Riveros, A., Newton, P., & Burgess, D. (2012). A situated account of teacher agency and learning. Critical reflections on professional learning communities. *Canadian Journal of Education. 35*(1), 202–216.

Rufinelli, A. (2014). ¿Qué aprenden los docentes en su primer año de ejercicio profesional? Representaciones de los propios docents principiantes. *Pensamiento Educativo. 51*(2) 56–74. https://doi.org/10.7764/PEL.51.2.2014.5

Ruffinelli Vargas, A. (2016). Ley de desarrollo profesional docente en Chile: de la precarización sistemática a los logros, avances y desafíos pendientes para la profesionalización. *Estudios Pedagógicos (Valdivia), 42*(4), 261–279. http://doi.org/10.4067/S0718-07052016000500015

Salas, M., Díaz, A., & Medina, L. (2021). Mentorías en Chile: De la política diseñada a la puesta en acto. *Revista Mexicana de Investigación Educativa, 26*(89), 449–474.

Serpell, Z. (2000). *Beginning teacher induction: A review of the literature.* American Association of Colleges of Teacher Education. https://files.eric.ed.gov/full text/ED443783.pdf

Soto, F. (2013). *Historia de la educación en Chile* (2nd ed). Universidad Central.

CHAPTER 7

QUALITY TEACHER INDUCTION POLICY IN GERMANY

Development, Implementation, and Impact of the "Quality Initiative of Teacher Education"

Hans-Georg Kotthoff
University of Education Freiburg

Katharina Hellmann
University of Education Freiburg

ABSTRACT

This chapter describes the development, implementation, and impact of Germany's most important teacher induction policy. It introduces its mandates, assumptions, and intended impacts. Then, it analyses a case of policy implementation in two local universities in Southern Germany to identify the efforts to create horizontally and vertically coherent curricula and professional

---

Teacher Induction Policy in Global Contexts, pages 121–141
Copyright © 2024 by Information Age Publishing
www.infoagepub.com
All rights of reproduction in any form reserved.

orientation in their initial teacher preparation. The chapter discusses policy implementation's intended and unintended effects and challenges with the above analysis as a base. It concludes with the issues that policymakers and researchers need to tackle in the future in teacher induction.

This chapter analyzes the development, implementation, and impact of Germany's most important teacher induction policy, the "Quality Initiative of Teacher Education" (Bundesministerium für Bildung und Forschung, 2013). We begin by placing the teacher induction policy in its social and educational contexts and the historical tradition of teacher education. We then describe the teacher induction policy mandates, assumptions, implementation, funding, and evaluation. Next, we analyze the policy development, implementation, and impact in two universities through their jointly developed project funded by the policy and discuss its intended and unintended effects and the challenges in the policy implementation. Finally, we conclude with a discussion about the development and implementation of the teacher induction policy and relevant questions worth further examination in Germany.

SOCIAL AND EDUCATIONAL CONTEXTS AND HISTORICAL TRADITION OF TEACHER PREPARATION

The teacher induction policy was developed to address structural and content-related challenges in the initial teacher preparation in Germany (Bundesministerium für Bildung & Forschung, 2013). The challenges resulted from the changing social and school contexts and the historical tradition of initial teacher induction in Germany (Kotthoff & Terhart, 2013). Therefore, describing these contexts and traditions is necessary to understand the development, implementation, and impact of the teacher induction policy and its problems (Bundesministerium für Bildung & Forschung, 2013; Terhart, 2007).

The major context is that teacher induction has long been organized and administrated at the federal-state level due to the high autonomy the 16 federal German states have enjoyed in governing their school education and teacher education (Bosse, 2012). For example, the individual federal state defines the length and proportion of the initial teacher preparation curriculum, instructional approaches, and educational requirements. Universities in a particular federal state can thus translate the general federal education policy into their teacher education programs. The Federal Standing Conference of Ministers of Education and Cultural Affairs coordinates structural issues regarding teacher education contents and degrees across Germany to ensure minimum uniformity (Kultusministerkonferenz, 2004).

Under the decentralized governance of teacher education in Germany, teacher induction policy and practices reflect two characteristics. First, considerable differences exist between individual states and between single universities in teacher induction provisions (Bauer et al., 2012; Kotthoff & Symeonidis, 2021). Second, the federal government traditionally plays a limited role in shaping initial teacher preparation. It is ineffective as it is restrained or even openly rejected by the constitutionally guaranteed right of the federal state to govern their school and teacher education (Nikolai, 2020).

Another influential context is the tracking organization of the school systems in the different federal states. In Germany, all students from 6 to 10 years old must attend comprehensive primary schools, and then they are vertically tracked into four kinds of lower secondary schools. Depending on the federal state, some schools cater to students with diverse academic abilities, such as the head schools (*Hauptschule* and *Realschule*) and grammar schools (*Gymnasium*). Others, such as comprehensive schools (*Gesamtschule*), cater to those with all abilities. Finally, students are tracked to complete upper secondary education in grammar or comprehensive school, leading to the baccalaureate (Hurrelmann, 2013).

This tracking school system requires teachers to develop competencies in various subject content areas, pedagogical content areas, and educational studies. Thus, teacher preparation institutions in different federal states prepare different kinds of teachers for vertically structured secondary schools and horizontally structured primary schools. Consequently, political will has been accumulated to reduce the multi-tracked secondary school system into a more comprehensive one, eventually nurturing the need to develop coherent and integrated teacher preparation and induction.

The next context is that initial teacher preparation in Germany was traditionally a 5-year university study leading to the so-called *First State Examination* (with the *Second State Examination* following after a traineeship in schools lasting 1½ to 2 years). Now, it is organized into two different university phases in most states following the implementation of the Bologna reform (Bauer et al., 2012; Kultusministerkonferenz, 2004, 2005; Terhart, 2007; de Witte et al., 2009). The first phase is the 3-year university-based preservice teacher education geared towards acquiring academic knowledge and ending with a bachelor's degree. Depending on the federal state and university regulations, preservice teachers get awarded a Bachelor of Science, a Bachelor of Arts, or a Bachelor of Education. The first two degrees are designed in a polyvalent way and leave additional options for changing to another degree program, while the last one aims directly at the teaching profession. In any case, preservice teachers proceed with a following 2-year master's studies, awarded with a Master of Education. The Ministry of Science at the state level is typically responsible for administering the bachelor and master phases. In the bachelor phase, preservice teachers often take the following courses: (a) content knowledge courses—for example, most secondary preservice teachers take content courses in two academic subjects; (b) educational studies—including school pedagogy, educational psychology, philosophy, and/or sociology; (c) didactics courses covering pedagogical content knowledge—the educational and didactical courses are often taught separately from the relevant content knowledge and show little curricular connection; and (d) a short-period internship in school contexts. In the master courses, the focus lies more on educational studies and didactics courses and often integrates a semester-long school internship. The federal law does not explicit the amount of each course type added to students' coursework either for the bachelor or master phase, as these are estimated or specified in federal state laws and implemented by the single universities (Kultusministerkonferenz, 2004, 2008).

The following phase is the 1½ to 2-year induction phase geared towards preparing teachers for professional practice in the school context. Independent of universities, this phase is organized with special "teacher training seminars" in "training schools" administered by the Ministry for Schools and Education in each state. In this phase, teachers are placed in schools, teach regular classes, and take *teacher training seminars* weekly.

These features of initial teacher preparation in Germany pose several problems for university teacher education and the teacher induction phases. First, teacher preparation policies for preservice and induction phases are often not well aligned, featuring repetitions, gaps, and tensions in the curriculum since different ministries administer different phases (Keuffer, 2010). It is particularly the case when various political parties control the Ministry of Science and the Ministry for Schools and Education. For example, policymakers in the Ministry of Science may support comprehensive schooling, while policymakers in the Ministry for Schools and Education oppose it. Consequently, preservice teachers often experience horizontally and vertically *incoherent* curricula when moving from the preservice phase to the induction phase (Bleck & Lipowsky, 2020; Zeichner, 2010).

The second problem is the *fragmentation in knowledge delivery* within and across different institutions and phases (Hefendehl-Hebeker, 2013; Terhart, 2007). For example, professional knowledge, including content, pedagogical content, and educational studies knowledge (Baumert & Kunter, 2006; Shulman, 1987), is not well aligned within a university curriculum. Also, the central domains of professional knowledge could be delivered differently in the first phase across different universities. The knowledge and experiences are fragmented in various universities, teacher training seminars, and schools (Gröschner et al., 2015).

The third problem is the lack of *professional orientation* in initial teacher preparation in Germany (Giest, 2007; Kreutz et al., 2020). For example, the production of core courses of teacher preparation on educational studies and pedagogical content knowledge depends on the lecturers' teaching and research preferences, and again, courses are often elected based on the individual preservice teachers' preferences of instructors and lecturers. In contrast, the content knowledge courses offered in the preservice phase do not provide preservice teachers with the necessary content knowledge for school-based practice later in the induction phase (Becher & Biehler, 2016; Bosse, 2012). These fragmentations often impede teachers from acquiring elaborated and integrated professional knowledge. They result in their "inert knowledge" that cannot be used adaptively to solve complex and realistic problems in their teaching practice (Harr et al., 2015).

One of the central social contexts addressed by the policy is the ever-diversified student population in classrooms regarding linguistic, social, cultural, and performance-related heterogeneity due to the increased immigration into Germany over the past decades (Kultusministerkonferenz, 2013, 2015). Another context is the legislation regarding the inclusion of special education students into the "regular" school system due to the ratification of the United Nations convention in 2006 (United Nations, 2006). These social and school changes motivate educational policymakers to develop teacher induction policy targeting the development of new competencies amongst teachers necessary for effectively teaching students with diverse backgrounds and special education needs in their classrooms (Kultusministerkonferenz, 2013, 2015).

To sum up, several historical traditions and social and school contexts of teacher education shaped the development of Germany's teacher induction policy. These contexts include:

1. The decentralized control of initial teacher preparation at the federal state level and the separation of initial teacher preparation into preservice university and induction phases administered by different ministerial departments that further fragment teacher preparation curricula horizontally and vertically.
2. The secondary school tracking system pushes teacher preparation institutions to address the various needs of different teaching professions. It further fragments the initial teacher preparation curriculum within and across different phases and institutions.
3. The ever more diversified student population due to the increased immigration and the integration of special education students into regular classrooms. The changed classroom context demands teachers with new knowledge, expertise, and skills for effective teaching.

POLICY MANDATES, IMPLEMENTATION, AND EVALUATION

Emerging from the above contexts was the initiation of the Quality Initiative of Teacher Education (Qualitätsoffensive Lehrerbildung), Germany's most important teacher induction policy, in April 2013 (Bundesministerium für Bildung und Forschung, 2013). It was launched as a joint initiative of the federal government and the 16 federal states in Germany. It generated the funding to support various projects developed to improve various aspects of initial teacher preparation in different states of Germany associated with the problems resulting from the above mentioned teacher preparation traditions and social and school contexts.

Policy Mandates and Intended Impacts

The specific policy includes several important mandates for initial teacher preparation. These mandates aim at systematic and sustainable improvements in the following areas with different assumptions (Bundesministerium für Bildung und Forschung, 2013):

The first mandate is to develop a coherent curriculum for university-level preservice teacher education (Bundesministerium für Bildung und Forschung, 2013). This mandate assumes that the fragmentation of teacher education content is a problem that needs to be overcome (Hammerness, 2006; Hefendehl-Hebeker, 2013). In contrast, the horizontally and vertically coherent curriculum is central to the quality of teacher preparation (Blömeke et al., 2012; Canrinus et al., 2015; Hellmann, 2019) and enables a more flexible and adaptable knowledge base for effective teaching (Harr et al., 2015). Consequently, the policy is developed to fund projects that could create a coherent curriculum of initial teacher preparation by linking courses on content knowledge, pedagogical content knowledge, and educational studies and by linking courses throughout preservice teachers' studies (Bundesministerium für Bildung und Forschung, 2013).

The second mandate focuses on developing a profession-oriented curriculum at the university level to meet professional teaching needs later. This mandate suggests that the traditional teacher preparation curriculum lacks the professional orientation in both the bachelor and master phases of initial teacher preparation, which is the other problem that the teacher induction policy needs to address (Giest, 2007; Kreutz et al., 2020). Consequently, the policy funds projects that integrate extensive practical teaching internships into the initial teacher preparation university curriculum and bridge the theory–practice gap in the teacher preparation processes (Hefendehl-Hebeker, 2013). It also funds projects that connect the university-based preservice teacher preparation with teacher induction, where seminar-based practical teacher training is offered (Bundesministerium für Bildung und Forschung, 2013).

The third mandate focuses on developing support for the consultation of preservice teachers in initial teacher preparation. This mandate presumes that preservice teachers must be effectively attracted, appropriately supported, and better prepared to become qualified teachers (Bundesministerium für Bildung und Forschung, 2013).

The fourth mandate is to advance initial teacher preparation to address the teaching challenges resulting from student heterogeneity and inclusion in Germany. The teacher preparation in German is often insufficient to prepare qualified teachers who can teach diverse students effectively as it lacks a systematic and coherent curriculum in this area (Hellmann, 2019). Thus, the policy proposes to fund projects that can effectively prepare teachers with research-oriented and data-based approaches necessary for teaching diverse special education student populations. It also aims to support projects that could equip teachers with the expertise and skills to initiate reforms at the school level to address the needs of diverse and special education students (Bundesministerium für Bildung und Forschung, 2013; Kultusministerkonferenz, 2013, 2015).

The final mandate stresses the development of mutual recognition of academic credits and qualifications in initial teacher preparation across different institutions and federal states. This mandate suggests that the fragmented teacher preparation for various horizontal and vertical tracks of teaching professions in the German school systems is also a problem that the teacher induction policy needs to address (Bundesministerium für Bildung und Forschung, 2013). Therefore, the policy funds projects that build more standardized curricula and processes of initial teacher preparation within and across different states of Germany by collaborating with relevant stakeholders.

Policy Operation, Funding, Implementation, and Evaluation

The teacher induction policy is the first major joint initiative of the federal government and 16 federal states to optimize initial teacher preparation and meet the need for excellently trained teachers in Germany. It offered federal funding for innovative projects from individual universities on a competitive base to address its important mandates. It also evaluates the results of the funded projects after their implementation.

The teacher induction policy had a budget of 500 million EURO (Bundesministerium für Bildung und Forschung, 2013). According to the Federal Ministry for Education and Research guidelines (Bundesministerium für Bildung und Forschung, 2014), all universities involved in initial teacher preparation in Germany were eligible to apply. For application, they had to present how they improve the quality of their teaching practice and strengthen their teacher education profile as envisioned in the policy and how they implement their projects. The federal states and universities were also committed to recognizing the credits and qualifications that preservice teachers acquired from different programs and offering them access to teaching positions in different states once they have completed the initial teacher preparation (Bundesministerium für Bildung und Forschung, 2013).

The policy was implemented in several phases. During the first phase from 2015–2019, 49 single or joint projects were selected and funded for 59 universities in all 16 federal states. Before the first phase ended, all funded projects were subjected to an interim evaluation (Ramboll, 2018). Based on the interim evaluation results, 48 projects were granted funding for the second phase from 2019–2023, in which project products and results were to be disseminated and structurally perpetuated. In addition, some federal states have launched their teacher induction programs to provide additional funding to improve their initial teacher preparation, for example, *Strengthening Cooperative Structures in Teacher Education* in the federal state of *Baden-Württemberg*.

In March 2016, a program evaluation of the teacher induction policy was commissioned to assess its impact on the structure, process, content, and quality of teacher induction at the different project sites (Bundesministerium für Bildung und Forschung, 2019). The preliminary results of the evaluation were summarized in an interim report (Ramboll, 2018). It shows that with the financial incentives, all funded projects helped establish the link between the different knowledge domains of teacher education, between different institutions and phases, and improve the practical orientation of initial teacher preparation in the institutions whose projects were funded. Consequently, it has significantly influenced initial teacher education provisions in these teacher preparation institutions as the policy intended. As the report states, measures aimed at optimizing cross-structures within universities, creating structures for cooperation with the induction phase of teacher education, and contributing to the overall profile of the universities about teacher induction. Measures were also concerned with the practical relevance of teacher education by closing the theory-practice gap in their teaching and by enhancing existing cooperation structures with schools, seminars, and other non-university learning environments (Ramboll, 2018).

The final evaluation report published in 2020 (Ramboll, 2020) further confirmed the interim evaluation report. All the funded projects supported the successful optimization of initial teacher preparation content and structures. They provided a sound basis for improving the targeted fields of action. The strongest impacts of most measures to date can be observed in "advancement and cross-linking of subjects/disciplines, didactics, and educational studies" (Ramboll, 2020, p. 9) and "advancement of initial teacher education about the challenges of heterogeneity and inclusion" (p. 9).

In sum, the teacher education/teacher induction policy supported the efforts to create horizontal and vertical curriculum coherence and professional orientation within and across different institutions' teacher induction phases. It further endorsed the mutual recognition of the credits and qualifications across various teacher preparation institutions, allowing preservice teachers from different preparation programs to access different teaching positions in different states. It also funded projects that developed teachers' expertise for working with students with diverse backgrounds and special education needs. The policy evaluation results (Ramboll, 2018, 2020) indicate that the funded projects helped initiate the horizontal and vertical coherent curriculum reforms for preservice teacher education and professional orientation with and across different phases of initial teacher preparation associated with different institutions.

CASE OF POLICY IMPLEMENTATION IN LOCAL UNIVERSITIES

Contexts of Local Policy Implementation

This section describes the development and implementation of a joint project funded by the teacher induction policy (Bundesministerium für Bildung und Forschung, 2013) and implemented by the University of Freiburg and the University of Education Freiburg. All universities of education remained independent educational institutions in the federal state of Baden-Württemberg (Ministerium für Wissenschaft, Forschung und Kunst Baden-Württemberg, 2020), while all other universities of education throughout Germany have been converted to or integrated into universities between the 1960s and 1990s, as part of a wave of university conversion (Roessler, 2020).

In Baden-Württemberg, the University of Freiburg traditionally trains upper secondary, vocational, and grammar school teachers, focusing on content knowledge. The University of Education Freiburg is responsible for primary, lower secondary, and special education teachers. It focuses on pedagogical content and knowledge (Kurtz, 2014; Ministerium für Wissenschaft, Forschung und Kunst Baden-Württemberg, 2020).

Built on their loose collaboration in the past, both universities worked closely to apply for funding from the teacher induction policy for their joint project, which was successfully funded (Wittwer et al., 2015). The project focused mainly on developing a coherent horizontal and vertical curriculum and professional orientation through collaboration between various actors in initial teacher preparation associated with both and other institutions.

This project was initiated following the regulations of the federal state of Baden-Württemberg (Ministerium für Wissenschaft, Forschung und Kunst Baden-Württemberg, 2015) and the federal standards for teacher education (Kultusministerkonferenz, 2004, 2008).

Transformation Regarding Institution Collaboration

One of the important mandates envisioned by the teacher induction policy is to expand the collaboration among actors in initial teacher preparation from different universities, local state seminars, and local schools (Bundesministerium für Bildung und Forschung, 2013). The joint project initiated three changes to develop strong structural links between the institutions, local state seminars, and school actors in initial teacher preparation.

The first change was the establishment of the *University Partner Schools* (von Gehlen et al., 2019) and *Professional Learning Communities* (Bauer & Fabel-Lamla, 2020). The former organized and implemented preservice teachers' internships in the two institutions. The latter was responsible for addressing university actors' needs for research and evaluation relevant to teacher preparation in the school context, offering evaluation-based feedback to preservice teachers and experienced teachers. Experienced teachers could also give feedback on the research conducted regarding aspects of professional orientation.

Second, both universities co-developed and co-certified an additional professional development program for teachers in the school contexts beyond those in the certification process. This program was developed to ensure the vertical alignment of all phases of teacher preparation, including the initial university, induction, and professional phases. It was also designed to infuse research into teacher professional development.

Third, a shared institution in both universities, the *School of Education* (FACE), was developed during the second funding phase (2018/2019–2023) to consolidate the transformation and delivery of curriculum, process, and qualifications of initial teacher preparation across the two institutions. Following the concept of lateral management (Kühl, 2017), this change leaves both universities the autonomy to decide major areas of teacher preparation. At the same time, it aimed at bundling both universities' strengths and further developing these strengths in terms of curriculum content. For example, the School of Education held regular meetings between curriculum developers and administrative and scientific staff in the two institutions to adapt and modify structures and the courses on content knowledge offered at the University of Freiburg and those on pedagogical content knowledge and pedagogical knowledge provided at the University of Education Freiburg.

Transformation Regarding Curriculum Coherence Across Institutions

Another mandate of the teacher induction policy is to reduce curriculum fragmentation and make it coherent within and across different knowledge domains and phases of initial teacher preparation, and across different institutions (Bundesministerium für Bildung und Forschung, 2013). The coherent curriculum onsite was defined as the sum of all concepts and measures aiming at linking professional contents and actors of teacher preparation both *horizontally* (between the central knowledge *domains*: content knowledge, pedagogical content knowledge, and pedagogical knowledge) and *vertically* (across the *phases* of teacher preparation) to allow preservice teachers to experience their teacher preparation program as structurally and content-related interconnected and meaningful and better prepare them for professional practice (Hellmann, 2019).

Consistent with the above mentioned guidelines and literature, the project made several changes to improve the horizontal and vertical coherence of the teacher preparation curriculum in the two institutions.

First, both universities improved the courses on content knowledge, pedagogical content knowledge, and educational studies to develop a horizontally coherent curriculum (Schwichow et al., 2019). For example, courses were taught in tandem from two different teacher preparation domains, discussing topics relevant to the teaching profession (Hellmann & Kreutz, 2020). Also, courses were developed that discussed content knowledge from the perspective of subject didactics (Oettle et al., 2019). Second, they also tried to vertically connect their courses on theoretical and professional knowledge to the practical experiences of preservice teachers in their programs. For example, students enrolled in the program had to complete a course preparing them for a three-week internship in schools based on guiding questions and principles developed by both universities. Preservice teachers were expected to create a written portfolio for the courses on teachers' core practices (Forzani, 2014; McDonald et al., 2013) to reflect on their practical experiences, develop their vocational orientation, and identify future steps for their professionalization as teachers (Nückles et al., 2019). In addition, both institutions also exchanged instructors of university courses with those of the teacher training seminars to ensure that program curricula and seminars in the field were vertically coherent.

Third, both institutions also required preservice teachers to complete a *cross-study e-portfolio* to integrate their understanding of teaching developed in the horizontal and vertical curriculum as suggested (Nückles et al., 2019; Wittwer et al., 2015). In the e-portfolio, preservice teachers were expected to actively use the self-regulated learning approach to interconnect their gained knowledge in the first phase and also connect that knowledge and study experiences with their professional practice in the first and second phases of their initial teacher preparation to enhance knowledge integration (Buchmann & Floden, 1992; Hammerness, 2006).

Transformation Regarding Professional Orientation across Institutions

An important mandate of the teacher induction policy is to enhance professional orientation in initial teacher preparation. A stronger orientation towards professional practice was envisaged, resulting from a significant discrepancy between the content knowledge taught at German universities and the content knowledge needed for teaching at schools (Lorentzen et al., 2019; Neumann et al., 2017). Also, content knowledge often took much more course load than pedagogical content and pedagogical courses (Bauer et al., 2012). Several measures were taken to target this mandate, for example, an integration of aspects of school syllabi into CK lectures, the integration of language practice in foreign language courses, or the development and use of complex learning problems representing authentic opportunities to learn for students in schools (Kreutz et al., 2020; Mordellet-Roggenbuck & Zaki, 2019).

The teacher induction policy also includes the mandates for developing professional orientation in initial teacher preparation to address the needs of special education students and student heterogeneity in classrooms (Bundesministerium für Bildung und Forschung, 2013; Kultusministerkonferenz, 2013, 2015). The two institutions made several changes to their programs to address the mandates. For example, diagnostic content relevant to student diversity, that is, about student preconceptions in natural sciences, was integrated into the curriculum (Schwichow et al., 2021). Recognizing student heterogeneity concerning multilingual and cultural aspects was also added to pedagogical content and educational courses as cross-sectional competency (Wittwer et al., 2015). Therefore, the two institutions formed project teams, including faculty members from both institutions, to help integrate diversity and inclusion issues into the lectures and seminars offered in the induction phase of initial teacher preparation. Also, both institutions developed efforts to coordinate the research inquiries into the professional orientation of their teacher preparation program focusing on diversity and inclusion. For example, student composition in classrooms was researched as a relevant factor influencing academic learning and social participation of students with special education needs (Scharenberg et al., 2019). Another research strand investigated preservice teachers' beliefs about diversity and inclusion (Scharenberg & Opalinski, 2019). Results from these research projects were then mirrored back to preservice teachers or used for designing new teacher training concepts to better prepare preservice teachers for professional practice.

Challenges and Impacts of Local Policy Implementation

While institutional collaboration, curriculum coherence, and an orientation towards the teaching profession as major mandates of the policy (Bundesministerium für Bildung und Forschung, 2013) have been implemented in teaching, learning, and research at both universities, it remains unclear to date whether the mandates have been successful in terms of better preparing preservice teachers for the demands of professional practice in schools. Firstly, course evaluations and surveys with preservice teachers suggest that they did not see their teacher preparation necessarily reflect the curriculum coherence as intended by the project. Measures of students' knowledge gains, attitudes, and/or competencies have been conducted sporadically and give first indications of progress and success regarding the policy mandates (Hellmann et al., 2019; Henning-Kahmann & Hellmann, 2019; Kreutz et al., 2020). Also, descriptive data on preservice teachers' course choices, study length, or dropout rates is periodically collected by the universities' administrations and used in project teams and faculty meetings to develop initial teacher education further.

However, these results may not be conclusive since results on students' specific competencies in teaching due to the program transformations have not been conducted systematically. Moreover, interviews and surveys with university faculty members, schoolteachers, and seminar instructors demonstrate that teacher preparation actors resist the policy's innovations and activities. This indicates that the projects' expectations were not met yet and might cause detrimental effects. Furthermore, research on teacher education actors' specific perceptions about the newly developed School of Education's role in the tension between the University and University of Education in the local policy implementation is still under analysis. The overall conclusions regarding whether perceptions about the innovations in structures, cooperation, and content meet policymakers' expectations thus cannot be answered to date.

Nevertheless, implementing the teacher induction policy at the local level might have produced several unintended effects. The possibilities given by the competitive policy funding resulted in more and partly diverging federal and local university structures and contents that independently defined, shaped, and evaluated initial teacher education based on their policy mandates (Brouër et al., 2018; Glowinski et al., 2018; Hellmann et al., 2019; Meier et al., 2018). These unintended "diversification" (Arnold & Reh, 2004, p. 154) effects are, amongst others, inconsistent use of relevant terms of initial teacher education, a different focus on possible mandates of the policy, and a lack of comparability of the different measures and their effectiveness. It complicates the successful dissemination, possible adaptation, on-site implementation, and evaluation of the measures of different universities (Hellmann et al., 2021).

In short, our analysis in this section suggests that the two institutions initiated several transformations in their initial teacher preparation programs through a joint project funded by the policy. These transformations included:

1. Strengthening the collaboration across different institutions. For example, University Partner Schools and Professional Learning Communities were established to coordinate the preservice teachers' field experience and internship. A professional development program was designed for preservice and inservice teachers in the school context. A shared institution, School of Education, was established to address content, alignment, and qualification needs of initial teacher preparation across the two institutions.
2. Developing horizontal and vertical curriculum coherence in the two institutions and professional fields. For instance, the two institutions' horizontal connection of program courses on content knowledge, pedagogical content knowledge, and education studies. The vertical links of theoretical and profession-oriented courses to those practical experiences in the school contexts. The requirement of preservice teachers to complete an e-portfolio that integrates their knowledge and understanding of teaching developed in the horizontal and vertical curriculum.
3. Improving professional orientation necessary for teaching special education and heterogeneous student populations, such as integrating diagnostic and multilingual content as cross-sectional competencies into their content, pedagogical content, and educational courses. Infusing student diversity and inclusion issues into the seminars offered in initial teacher preparation. Developing research inquiries into heterogeneity and inclusion in teacher preparation to generalize the knowledge base for the future professional orientation in the program.

The evaluation of the project implementation based on the surveys with preservice teachers and teacher educators in the two institutions suggests the following. Preservice teachers partly failed to see the coherence of the horizontal and vertical curriculum transformation as intended. Their knowledge gains, attitudes, and competencies in teaching have not yet been researched systematically, so no conclusions concerning the mandates' effectiveness can be drawn. Teacher preparation actors in the two institutions also showed resistance towards the project's innovations. In addition, the implantation of the above mentioned transformation also led to several unintended effects, including competing and rather divergent structures between different funded university sites, a wealth of different measures taken regarding the federal policy, a lack of comparability of these measures and thus only limited possibilities for dissemination, adaption, and evaluation.

CONCLUSIONS

The chapter analyzed the teacher induction policy's development, implementation, and impact at the national and local level. This analysis led us to conclusions about Germany's policy development, implementation, and impact on initial teacher preparation.

First, the policy aimed to create horizontal and vertical curriculum coherence in initial teacher preparation about the different theoretical and practical fields of study within and across different phases of teacher preparation and in different institutions. Additionally, it was centrally developed to strengthen professional orientation in preservice teachers and collaboration across various institutions and phases of initial teacher preparation to ensure teachers from diverse programs can work in different teaching positions effectively in different places. The policy was also developed to address the need for increased special education and diverse student populations in the classrooms.

Second, despite the constitutionally guaranteed right for individual German states to administrate and regulate their teacher education/induction, the federal government has found a way to reform teacher induction practices through generalizing funding to support local projects aligned with the reform mandates. Evaluation of the policy implementation shows its overall success in meeting policy goals.

Third, our analysis of the policy implementation in the two institutions suggests that they developed a joint effort to coordinate the reforms on their initial teacher preparation by developing horizontally and vertically coherent curricula and professional orientation across different phases. However, preservice teachers may not sense the impact of these implemented reforms, and the reform influences on preservice teachers' competencies in teaching are yet to be investigated and established. Local actors in teacher preparation may not embrace all the initiated reforms. The unintended effects of policy implementation could occur in terms of competition and diversification of structures, a lack of comparability of measures, and limited possibilities for dissemination, adaption, and evaluation of different local reforms.

Considering the above conclusions, the following research questions about the teacher induction policy's development, implementation, and impact are worth exploring. First, how can the teacher induction policy be effectively developed to address the issues from the federal government, state-level government, and different institutions simultaneously? Secondly, how can particular teacher induction transformations shape preservice teachers' specific teaching competencies as the policy expected, and how can this increase in competencies be researched? Thirdly, how can the desired impacts of the policy implementation be maximized and the undesired policy effects be minimized in the initial teacher preparation in the local institutions? Finally, how can the positive impacts of the implemented policy be sustained, scaled up, and transferred to different institutions in different states when the funding is no longer available?

REFERENCES

Arnold, E., & Reh, S. (2004). Bachelor- und Master-Studiengänge für die Lehrerbildung. Neue Studienstrukturen als Professionalisierungschance? *Die Hochschule: Journal für Wissenschaft und Bildung, 14*(1), 143–156.

Bauer, J., Diercks, U., Roesler, L., Möller, J., & Prenzel, M. (2012). Lehramtsstudium in Deutschland: Wie groß ist die strukturelle Vielfalt? *Unterrichtswissenschaften, 40*(2), 101–120.

Bauer, P., & Fabel-Lamla, M. (2020). (Multi-)Professionelle Kooperation in der Lehrerinnen-und Lehrerbildung. In C. Cramer, J. Koenig, M. Rothland, & S. Blömeke (Eds.), *Handbuch Lehrerinnen- und Lehrerbildung* (pp. 91–97). Klinkhardt.

Baumert, J., & Kunter, M. (2006). Stichwort: Professionelle Kompetenz von Lehrkräften. *Zeitschrift für Erziehungswissenschaft, 9*(4), 469–520.

Becher, S., & Biehler, R. (2016). Beliefs on benefits from learning higher mathematics at university for future secondary school teachers. In R. Göller, R. Biehler, R. Hochmuth, & H.-G. Rück (Eds.), *Didactics of Mathematics in Higher Education as a Scientific Discipline*. Conference Proceedings (pp. 256–260). khdm.

Bleck, V., & Lipowsky, F. (2020). Dröge, nutzlos, praxisfern? Wie verändert sich die Bewertung wissenschaftlicher Studieninhalte in Praxisphasen? In I. Ulrich, & A. Gröschner (Eds.), *Praxissemester im Lehramtsstudium in Deutschland: Wirkungen auf Studierende* (pp. 97–127). Springer VS.

Blömeke, S., Suhl, U., & Döhrmann, M. (2012). Zusammenfügen was zusammengehört: Kblömekeompetenzprofile am Ende der Lehrerausbildung im internationalen Vergleich Kompetenzprofile. *Zeitschrift für Pädagogik, 4*, 422–440.

Bosse, D. (2012). Zur Situation der Lehrerbildung in Deutschland. In D. Bosse, L. Criblez, & T. Hascher (Eds.), *Reform der Lehrerbildung in Deutschland, Österreich und der Schweiz* (pp. 11–28). Prolog.

Brouër, B., Burda-Zoyke, A., Kilian, J., & Petersen, I. (2018). *Vernetzung in der Lehrerinnen- und Lehrerbildung: Ansätze, Methoden und erste Befunde aus dem LeaP-Projekt an der Christian-Albrechts-Universität zu Kiel*. Waxmann.

Buchmann, M., & Floden, R. E. (1992). Coherence, the rebel angel. *Educational Researcher, 8*, 4–9.

Bundesministerium für Bildung und Forschung. (2013). *Bund-Länder-Vereinbarung über ein gemeinsames Programm "Qualitätsoffensive Lehrerbildung" gemäß Artikel 91 b des Grundgesetzes vom 12. April 2013.* https://www.gwk-bonn.de/fileadmin/Redaktion/Dokumente/Papers/Bund-Laender-Vereinbarung-Qualitaetsoffensive-Lehrerbildung.pdf

Bundesministerium für Bildung und Forschung. (2014). *Bekanntmachung des Bundesministeriums für Bildung und Forschung von Richtlinien zur Förderung der "Qualitätsoffensive Lehrerbildung" von 10.* Juli 2014. https://www.bmbf.de/foerderungen/bekanntmachung.php?B=951

Bundesministerium für Bildung und Forschung. (2019). *Interim results of the "Qualitätsoffensive Lehrerbildung": Initial findings from research and practice.* https://www.qualitaetsoffensive-lehrerbildung.de/files/BMBF_QLB_2019_ENG_barrierefrei.pdf

Canrinus, E. T., Bergem, O. K., Klette, K., & Hammerness, K. M. (2015). Coherent teacher education programmes: Taking a student perspective. *Journal of Curriculum Studies, 39*, 1–21.

De Witte, J., Huisman, J., & Purser, L. (2009). European higher education reforms in the context of the Bologna Process. In Organisation for Economic Co-operation and Development (Ed.), *Higher education to 2030* (pp. 205–229). OECD.

Forzani, F. M. (2014). Understanding "core practices" and "practice-based" teacher education: Learning from the past. *Journal of Teacher Education, 65*(4), 357–368.

Giest, H. (2007). Lehrerbildung zwischen Berufs- und Professionsorientierung—Eine vergleichende empirische Untersuchung. *Lern-Lehr-Forschung, 22*, 27–66.

Glowinski, I., Borowski, A., Gillen, J., Schanze, S., & von Meien, J. (2018). *Kohärenz in der universitären Lehrerbildung: Vernetzung von Fachwissenschaft, Fachdidaktik und Bildungswissenschaften.* Universitätsverlag Potsdam.

Gröschner, A., Müller, K., Bauer, J., Seidel, T., Prenzel, M., Kauper, T., & Möller, J. (2015). Praxisphasen in der Lehrerausbildung–Eine Strukturanalyse am Beispiel des gymnasialen Lehramtsstudiums in Deutschland. *Zeitschrift für Erziehungswissenschaft, 18*(4), 639–665.

Hammerness, K. (2006). From coherence in theory to coherence in practice. *Teachers College Record, 108*(7), 1241–1265.

Harr, N., Eichler, A., & Renkl, A. (2015). Integrated learning: Ways of fostering the applicability of teachers' pedagogical and psychological knowledge. *Frontiers in Psychology, 6*(738), 1–16.

Hefendehl-Hebeker, L. (2013). Doppelte Diskontinuität oder die Chance der Brückenschläge. In C. Ableitinger, J. Kramer, & S. Prediger (Eds.), *Zur doppelten Diskontinuität in der Gymnasiallehrerbildung* (pp. 1–15). Springer Fachmedien.

Hellmann, K. (2019). Kohärenz in der Lehrerbildung—Theoretische Konzeptionalisierung. In K. Hellmann, J. Kreutz, M. Schwichow, & K. Zaki (Eds.), *Kohärenz in der Lehrerbildung: Theorien, Modelle und empirische Befunde* (pp. 9–30). Springer VS.

Hellmann, K., & Kreutz, J. (2020). Kooperation von Hochschuldozierenden—Professionsorientierte Lehrentwicklung in der Lehrerbildung. In J. Kreutz, T. Leuders, & K. Hellmann (Eds.), *Professionsorientierung in der Lehrerbildung—Kompetenzorientiertes Lehren nach dem 4-Component-Instructional-Design-Modell* (pp. 209–222). Springer VS.

Hellmann, K., Kreutz, J., Schwichow, M., & Zaki, K. (2019). *Kohärenz in der Lehrerbildung: Theorien, Modelle und empirische Befunde.* Springer VS.

Hellmann, K., Ziepprecht, K., Baum, M., Glowinski, I., Grospietsch, F., Heinz, T., Masanek, N., & Wehner, A. (2021). Kohärenz, Verzahnung und Vernetzung—Ein Angebots-Nutzungs-Modell für die hochschulische Lehrkräftebildung. *Lehrerbildung auf dem Prüfstand, 2,* 311–332.

Henning-Kahmann, J., & Hellmann, K. (2019). Entwicklung eines Fragebogens zur Erfassung der studentischen Kohärenzwahrnehmung im Lehramtsstudium. In K. Hellmann, J. Kreutz, M. Schwichow, & K. Zaki (Eds.), *Kohärenz in der Lehrerbildung: Theorien, Modelle und empirische Befunde* (pp. 33–50). Springer VS.

Hurrelmann, K. (2013). Das Schulsystem in Deutschland: Das "Zwei-Wege-Modell" setzt sich durch. *Zeitschrift für Pädagogik, 59*(4), 455–468.

Keuffer, J. (2010). Reform der Lehrerbildung und kein Ende? Eine Standortbestimmung. *Erziehungswissenschaft, 21,* 51–67.

Kotthoff, H.-G., & Symeonidis, V. (2021). Governing European teacher education: How great expectations are raised in Brussels and "glocalised" within Germany. *Comparative and International Education Review, 26,* 5–29.

Kotthoff, H.-G., & Terhart, E. (2013). 'New' solutions to 'old' problems? Recent reforms in teacher education in Germany. *Revista Española de Educación Comparada, 22,* 73–92.

Kreutz, J., Leuders, T., & Hellmann, K. (2020). *Professionsorientierung in der Lehrerbildung: Kompetenzorientiertes Lehren nach dem 4-Component-Instructional-Design-Modell.* Springer VS.

Kühl, S. (2017). *Laterales Führen—Eine kurze organisationstheoretisch informierte Handreichung* [Lateral leadership—A short handout informed by organizational theory]. Springer VS.

Kultusministerkonferenz. (2004). *Standards für die Lehrerbildung: Bildungswissenschaften (Beschluss der Kultusministerkonferenz vom 16.12.2004 i.d.F. vom 16.05.2019).* https://www.kmk.org/fileadmin/veroeffentlichungen_beschluesse/2004/2004_12_16-Standards-Lehrerbildung-Bildungswissenschaften.pdf

Kultusministerkonferenz. (2005). *Eckpunkte für die gegenseitige Anerkennung von Bachelor- und Masterabschlüssen in Studiengängen, mit denen die Bildungsvoraussetzungen für ein Lehramt vermittelt werden* (Beschluss der KMK vom 2.6.2005). https://www.kmk.org/fileadmin/veroeffentlichungen_beschluesse/2005/2005_06_02-Bachelor-Master-Lehramt.pdf

Kultusministerkonferenz. (2008). *Ländergemeinsame inhaltliche Anforderungen für die Fachwissenschaften und Fachdidaktiken in der Lehrerbildung* (Beschluss der Kultusministerkonferenz vom 16.10.2008 i. d. F. vom 16.05.2019). https://www.kmk.org/fileadmin/veroeffentlichungen_beschluesse/2008/2008_10_16-Fachprofile-Lehrerbildung.pdf

Kultusministerkonferenz. (2013). *Gemeinsame Erklärung der Kultusministerkonferenz und der Organisationen von Menschen mit Migrationshintergrund zur Bildungs* und *Erziehungspartnerschaft von Schule und Eltern* (Beschluss der Kultusministerkonferenz vom 10.10.2013) https://www.kmk.org/fileadmin/Dateien/ veroeffentlichungen_beschluesse/2013/2013_10_10-Bildungs-und-Erziehungs partnerschaft.pdf

Kultusministerkonferenz. (2015). *Lehrerbildung für eine Schule der Vielfalt—Gemeinsame Empfehlung von Hochschulrektorenkonferenz und Kultusministerkonferenz (Beschluss der Kultusministerkonferenz vom 12.03.2015 i.d.F. vom 18.03.2015)*. https://www .kmk.org/fileadmin/veroeffentlichungen_beschluesse/2015/2015_03_12 -Schule-der-Vielfalt.pdf

Kurtz, S. (2014). Lehrerbildung in Baden-Württemberg—Status quo und Optimierungspotenziale. In K. W. Schönherr & V. Tiberius (Eds.), *Lebenslanges Lernen: Wissen und Können als Wohlstandsfaktoren* (pp. 251–262). Springer VS.

Lorentzen, J., Friedrichs, G., Ropohl, M., & Steffensky, M. (2019). Förderung der wahrgenommenen Relevanz von fachlichen Studieninhalten: Evaluation einer Intervention im Lehramtsstudium Chemie. *Unterrichtswissenschaft, 47*(1), 29–49.

McDonald, M., Kazemi, E., & Kavanagh, S. (2013). Core practices and pedagogies of teacher education: A call for a common language and collective activity. *Journal of Teacher Education, 64*, 378–386.

Meier, M., Ziepprecht, K., & Mayer, J. (2018). *Lehrerausbildung in vernetzten Lernumgebungen*. Waxmann.

Ministerium für Wissenschaft, Forschung und Kunst Baden-Württemberg. (2015). *Rechtsverordnung des Kultusministeriums über Rahmenvorgaben für die Umstellung der allgemein bildenden Lehramtsstudiengänge an den Pädagogischen Hochschulen, den Universitäten, den Kunst- und Musikhochschulen sowie der Hochschule für Jüdische Studien Heidelberg auf die gestufte Studiengangstruktur mit Bachelor und Masterabschlüssen der Lehrkräfteausbildung in Baden-Württemberg (Rahmenvorgabenverordnung Lehramtsstudiengänge–RahmenVO-KM)*. https://www.landesrecht -bw.de/jportal/portal/page/bsbawueprod.psml/action/portlets.jw.Main Action?eventSubmit_doNavigate=searchInSubtreeTOC&showdoccase=1& doc.id=jlr-LehrRahmenVBWpAnlage6

Ministerium für Wissenschaft, Forschung und Kunst Baden-Württemberg. (2020). *Pädagogische Hochschulen*. https://mwk.baden-wuerttemberg.de/de/hochschulen -studium/hochschullandschaft/hochschularten/paedagogische-hochschulen/

Mordellet-Roggenbuck, I., & Zaki, K. (2019). Professionsorientierung im Lehramt moderner Fremdsprachen: Integrative Curriculums- und Lehrentwicklung in der Romanistik. In K. Hellmann, J. Kreutz, M. Schwichow, & K. Zaki (Eds.), *Kohärenz in der Lehrerbildung—Theorien, Modelle und empirische Befunde* (pp. 147–163). Springer VS.

Neumann, K., Härtig, H., Harms, U., & Parchmann, I. (2017). Science teacher preparation. In G. J. Pedersen, T. Isozaki, & T. Hirano (Eds.), *Science teacher education: A multi-country comparison* (pp. 29–52). Information Age Publishing.

Nikolai, R. (2020). Schulpolitik im deutschen Föderalismus. In F. Knüpling, M. Kölling, S. Kropp, & H. Scheller (Eds.), *Reformbaustelle Bundesstaat* (pp. 315–332). Springer VS.

Nückles, M., Zaki, K., Graichen, M., Liefländer, A., Burkhart, C., Klein, C., & Lösch, L. (2019). Das e-Portfolio in der Freiburger Lehrerbildung: Selbstgesteuerte

Kohärenzkonstruktion durch vernetzende Lernaufgabe. In K. Hellmann, J. Kreutz, M. Schwichow, & K. Zaki (Eds.), *Kohärenz in der Lehrerbildung: Theorien, Modelle und empirische Befunde* (pp. 217–232). Springer VS.

Oettle, M., Brandenburger, M., Mikelskis-Seifert, S., & Schwichow, M. (2019). Schaffung vertikaler und horizontaler Kohärenz in der Lehrerbildung am Beispiel der Physik. In K. Hellmann, J. Kreutz, M. Schwichow, & K. Zaki (Eds.), *Kohärenz in der Lehrerbildung: Theorien, Modelle und empirische Befunde* (pp. 167–182). Springer VS.

Ramboll. (2018). *Qualitätsoffensive Lehrerbildung. Zwischenbericht der Evaluation*. Ramboll Management Consulting GmbH.

Ramboll. (2020). *Evaluation der "Qualitätsoffensive Lehrerbildung" Abschlussbericht*. Ramboll Management Consulting GmbH.

Roessler, I. (2020). Pädagogische Hochschulen zu Übersetzungs- und Weiterbildungshochschulen weiterentwickeln—Ein unkonventionelles Gedankenspiel. In A. Tettenborn, & P. Tremp (Eds.), *Pädagogische Hochschulen in ihrer Entwicklung. Hochschulkultur im Spannungsfeld von Wissenschaftsorientierung und Berufsbezug* (pp. 144–147). Pädagogische Hochschule Luzern.

Scharenberg, K., & Opalinski, S. (2019, July 7). *Effective teacher training for inclusive education: The importance of preservice teachers' beliefs about inclusion* [Conference presentation]. 2019 Annual Meeting of the American Educational Research Association, Toronto, Canada.

Scharenberg, K., Rollett, W., & Bos, W. (2019). Do differences in classroom composition provide unequal opportunities for academic learning and social participation of SEN students in inclusive classes in primary school? *School Effectiveness and School Improvement, 30*(3), 309–327.

Schwichow, M., Hellmann, K., & Mikelskis-Seifert, S. (2021). Pre-service teachers' perception of competence, social relatedness, and autonomy in a flipped classroom: Effects on learning to notice student preconceptions. *Journal of Science Teacher Education, 33*(3), 282–302.

Schwichow, M., Zaki, K., Hellmann, K., & Kreutz, J. (2019). Quo vadis? Kohärenz in der Lehrerbildung. In K. Hellmann, J. Kreutz, M. Schwichow, & K. Zaki (Eds.), *Kohärenz in der Lehrerbildung: Theorien, Modelle und empirische Befunde* (pp. 331–350). Springer VS.

Shulman, L. (1987). Knowledge and teaching: Foundations of the new reform. *Harvard Educational Review, 57*(1), 1–23.

Terhart, E. (2007). Strukturprobleme der Lehrerausbildung in Deutschland. In A. Óhidy, E. Terhart, & J. Zsolnai (Eds.), *Lehrerbild und Lehrerbildung: Praxis und Perspektiven der Lehrerausbildung in Deutschland und Ungarn* (pp. 45–65). VS Verlag für Sozialwissenschaften.

United Nations. (2006). *Convention on the rights of persons with disabilities and optional protocol*. Retrieved from http://www.un.org/disabilities/documents/convention/convoptprot-e.pdf

von Gehlen, M., Dreher, U., Epting, B., Fesenmeier, S. J., Holzäpfel, L., & Hochbruck, W. (2019). Das Schulnetzwerk im Praxiskolleg der Albert-Ludwigs-Universität Freiburg und der Pädagogischen Hochschule Freiburg. In J. Jennek, K. Kleemann, & M. Vock (Eds.). *Kooperation von Universität und Schule fördern. Schulen stärken, Lehrerbildung verbessern* (pp. 37–56). Barbara Budrich.

Wittwer, J., Nückles, M., Mikelskis-Seifert, S., Schumacher, M., Rollett, W., & Leuders, T. (2015). Kohärenz, Kompetenz- und Forschungsorientierung–Zur Weiterentwicklung der Lehrerbildung am Standort Freiburg. In W. Benz, J. Kohler, P. Pohlenz, & U. Schmidt (Eds.), *Handbuch Qualität in Studium und Lehre* (pp. 93–115). Raabe.

Zeichner, K. (2010). Rethinking the connections between campus courses and field experiences in college- and university-based teacher education. *Journal of Teacher Education, 61*(1–2), 89–99.

PART III

PROVINCIAL AND STATE INDUCTION POLICY DEVELOPMENT IN DECENTRALIZED SYSTEM

CHAPTER 8

TEACHER INDUCTION POLICY IN CANADA

Development and Implementation of Ontario's New Teacher Induction Program

Benjamin Kutsyuruba
Queen's University

Lorraine Godden
Carleton University

Keith Walker
University of Saskatchewan

ABSTRACT

The challenges of early career teacher retention and development have garnered the attention of policymakers and educational leaders across Canada. However, due to provincial/territorial responsibility for education, pan-Canadian teacher induction efforts depend on jurisdiction-specific policies and school system organization. In this chapter, we first describe the pan-Canadian policy contexts and the factors shaping the development of Ontario's New Teacher Induction Program. Then, we describe the program's organization and mandates, identify its assumptions compared with the existing literature process, and detail its multi-level implementation process. Next, we analyze the program's impact and challenges. We conclude the chapter with the implications for further induction policy development, implementation, and practices that support early career teachers.

Teacher induction policies are intended to help early career teachers who are typically in the first five years of their teaching career to grow professionally, improve their teaching practices, and retain them in the teaching workforce. Researchers have explored the factors contributing to early-career teachers' retention and professional development (Colb, 2001; Darling-Hammond, 2003; Ingersoll & Smith, 2003; Smith & Ingersoll, 2004). However, a more focused and systematic understanding of teacher induction policy's development, implementation, effects, and challenges is necessary (Borman & Dowling, 2008). Such an understanding is important for policymakers and school leaders to make multiple and difficult policy decisions regarding supporting new teachers' retention and professional development (Ingersoll & Strong, 2011).

In Canada, high attrition among teachers with the first 5 years of teaching experience becomes a serious issue that needs to be addressed (Karsenti & Collin, 2013). Varied and multi-layered efforts have been developed to establish teacher induction and mentoring programs to increase teacher retention and enhance professional development in the pan-Canadian landscape with four categories (Kutsyuruba et al., 2016). They are (a) government-mandated and funded programs; (b) programs offered by provincial teacher associations, federations, or unions; (c) hybrid programs based upon cooperation between the provincial and territorial governments, teacher associations, universities, First Nations, and/or local communities; and (d) decentralized programs maintained by local school boards/divisions.

Although teacher induction and mentoring programs exist in all Canadian provinces and territories, only two of the fourteen jurisdictions, Ontario and Northwest Territories, have government-mandated induction programs (Kutsyuruba et al., 2016). In addition, mentoring is not always included in induction programs across Canada (Kutsyuruba et al., 2016). Various teacher induction provisions are attributed to two contexts (Kutsyuruba & Walker, 2017). The first is that the absence of a federal bureau of education in Canada makes the local provinces and territories responsible for establishing their education policies at the school district level. The second is that with great variations in school systems and policies, induction and mentoring efforts in Canada tend to be decentralized, unequal, and compartmentalized.

Ontario is the focus of this chapter as one of the two Canadian jurisdictions where comprehensive induction programs have been instituted as part of the broader government mandate for teacher induction policy. This chapter describes the context for developing and implementing Ontario's New Teacher Induction Program (NTIP). Then, we detail the program mandates, assumptions compared with the teacher induction literature, and multi-level implementation process. Next, we analyze policy outcomes and challenges. We conclude the chapter with the implications for induction policy development, implementation, and practice supporting new teachers.

TEACHER INDUCTION POLICY, ITS EVOLUTION, AND CONTEXTS

This section focuses on the development, organization, and mandates of teacher induction policy in Ontario. Teacher induction policy follows a multi-pronged approach based on the professional learning continuum for new teachers. The first step entails initial teacher education through various provincial university programs. Teacher induction is the second job-embedded stage of professional teacher learning for early career teachers (Strachan et al., 2017). In the teacher induction stage, early career teachers build on and complement what they learn in the preservice level preparation (Kustyuruba et al., 2016). The third stage entails teachers participating in the learning and leadership program designed to help them maintain their standards of excellence through continual and active engagement in learning to teach throughout their careers. Ontario's teacher induction policy and program have evolved in different processes shaped by various contexts and factors.

NTIP Development and Its Contexts

Several contexts and factors motivated its development. The NTIP program was initially developed in Ontario, Canada, by the Working Table for Teacher Development, consisting of key education partners, such as students, teachers, principals, support workers, trustees, and parents, and invited officials from representative education groups such as the Ontario College of Teachers (Wilson, 2004). Then, it was recommended to the Education Partnership Table established by the Minister of Education with its demonstration projects during 2004–2005 (Ontario Ministry of Education, 2010e). NTIP adopted effective induction practices, such as (a) orientation for all new teachers to the school and school board, (b) mentoring for new teachers by experienced teachers, and (c) professional development and training in major policies and strategies of the ministry, classroom management, communication skills, and instructional approaches, as suggested in other countries' comprehensive teacher induction literature (e.g., Glazerman et al., 2010; Huling-Austin, 1986; Ingersoll & Strong, 2011; Wong, 2004). It attempted to become more effective support for early career teachers to develop the requisite teaching skills and knowledge, increase their retention, and thus improve the levels of their student performance (Ontario Ministry of Education, 2010a).

Establishing the NTIP to increase teacher quality and improve teacher performance in Ontario can be traced to the government reforms that underscored the significance of public accountability (Cherubini, 2010; Wahlstrom & Louis, 2008). In an attempt to mandate the improvement of teacher performance, the Ontario Ministry of Education (2010a) has put into policy that all public-school boards deliver the NTIP to new teachers as "the second step in a continuum of professional development for teachers to support effective teaching, learning, and assessment practices, building on and complementing the first step: preservice education programs" (p. 5). Furthermore, NTIP was initially established to replace the Ontario Teacher Qualifying Test (OTQT) as another measure of the Ontario government's increasing demands for accountability in education (Barrett et al., 2009). This test, mandatory for all new graduates of Ontario Faculties of Education and teachers trained outside of Ontario, lasted for 4 hours and contained 50 multiple-choice and open-ended questions relating to four case studies (Portelli et al., 2010). The scope of questions spanned two domains: (a) professional knowledge (i.e., curriculum policy, planning and instruction, childhood and adolescent development, classroom management, legislation, and use of technology) and (b) teaching practice (i.e., instructional strategies, motivation, diversity and students with special needs, parents and community and reflections on teaching). Prior to being eliminated by the new Ontario government, OTQT was criticized for lack of relevance to the improvement of classroom performance and oversimplification of the knowledge needed to teach (Portelli et al., 2010)

NTIP was developed by the Working Table on Teacher Development and recommended to the Education Partnership Table established by the Minister of Education, which comprised key education partners. Demonstration projects were undertaken during 2004–2005, and the effective practices and lessons learned were synthesized into the NTIP model (Ministry of Education, 2010e). Based on a comprehensive literature review examining induction in other countries and a pilot project, the final shape and form of the NTIP came into legislation through the passing of the *Student Performance Bill* in June 2006 (Kane, 2010).

In its original format, NTIP was a mandatory 1-year program for all first-year teachers certified by the Ontario College of Teachers and hired into permanent teaching positions (Ontario Ministry of Education, 2010a) as a step in a continuum of professional learning for teachers to support effective teaching, learning, and assessment practices. All Ontario publicly funded district school boards were required to offer a full year of professional support facilitating the new teachers' continuous development of the requisite skills and knowledge; thus, the program aimed to support teachers' increased success in Ontario and help them achieve high levels of student performance. In 2010, because of the program evaluation initiated by the Ministry of Education and based on the ongoing research and feedback from consultation with educational partners, the program underwent significant revisions in terms of scope and participant eligibility (Kane, 2010). Long-term occasional (LTO) teachers in their first long-term assignment as substitute teachers (97 or more consecutive school days) were included in the Induction elements of NTIP. Furthermore, the program was amended in 2010 to allow district school boards to allocate their NTIP funding to support second-year teachers in either category (permanent or LTO). It was the direct outcome of program evaluation recommendations (Kane, 2010) that teachers in their second year can more readily identify and implement strategies to improve proficiency more quickly. Ongoing program evaluations and feedback from partners resulted in further revision of the program in 2019, further expanding the program scope to teachers in their first five years who fall outside the NTIP required definition. Thus, the development of NTIP is a complex, messy, and iterative learning journey, as Strachan et al. (2017) called it, with NTIP continuing to evolve by seeking to meet the diverse needs of new teachers in Ontario and being responsive to the changing educational landscape.

Induction Policy Goals and Mandates

Several goals were designed in the NTIP policy to espouse what early career teachers need to learn during induction from the perspective of their expected learning outcomes (Ontario Ministry of Education, 2019a). These outcomes include:

- Confidence: I can do it... I have the support to be a successful teacher.
- Efficacy: My teaching makes a difference in the lives and learning of every single student.
- Instructional Practice: I can respond to the diverse learning needs of my students with an array of effective instructional strategies.
- Commitment to Continuous Learning: I want to continue learning and growing as a professional in collaboration with my students,

colleagues, administration, parents/guardians, and school community (Ontario Ministry of Education, 2019a, p. 3).

The espoused goals of NTIP include the development of new teachers' confidence, efficacy, instructional practice to improve their student's well-being and learning, and commitment to continuous professional development (Ontario Ministry of Education, 2010a). Additionally, such professional development is not only embedded into the program for early career teachers but also specified for policymakers and program coordinators.

The present NTIP has evolved to meet the diverse needs of early career teachers in Ontario and respond to the changing educational landscape with consistent programmatic goals (Ontario Ministry of Education, 2019a). For example, its initial focus on the core content topics and a checklist of prescribed early career teachers' learning to teach has been changed to the focus on the voice, choice, and agency of authentic learning responsive to their contexts, experiences, assignments, and learning goals (Ontario Ministry of Education, 2010a). Its initial focus on the program structure, such as mentoring match, training, and principal engagement, has also evolved to focus on relationships within the mentoring web, foundational skills, trust, and principal encouragement. Additionally, NTIP has moved away from the initial "*NTIP for some*" to include as many new teachers as possible in their first 5 years of teaching. This change addresses the Calls to Action of the Truth and Reconciliation Commission (TRC) to ensure early career teachers receive training on integrating indigenous knowledge and teaching methods into their classrooms (Ontario Ministry of Education, 2019a). Finally, the change has been made from providing "professional development appropriate to the individual needs of new teachers" in the initial NTIP (Strachan et al., 2017, p. 247) to "professional learning relevant to the individual needs of new teachers" in the present one (Ontario Ministry of Education, 2019a, p. 4).

NTIP defines the role of mentors as providing ongoing support for early career teachers to improve confidence and skills of teaching through an effective, professional, and confidential mentoring relationship (Ontario Ministry of Education, 2010a). It envisions the mentoring relationship to be supportive, with mentors acting as role models, coaches, and advisors to early career teachers, sharing their experience and knowledge about teaching on an ongoing basis. It also stresses that mentoring needs to appropriately meet the needs of early career teachers through observing their teaching, co-planning lessons, developing face-to-face and online professional dialogue with them, and participating in inservice sessions and professional development with them. Additionally, NTIP asks mentors and early career teachers to work together to determine the early career teachers' individual needs by completing the Individual NTIP Strategy Form, which is revised throughout the year. Finally, it expects school principals to ensure opportunities for early career teachers to improve their teaching confidence and skills through an effective professional mentoring relationship with mentors and adequate release time.

The NTIP policy further required the school district boards and schools to implement three induction mandates from its inception (Ontario Ministry of Education, 2010a). It asked the school districts and schools to (a) offer an orientation for all new teachers to their schools; (b) select experienced teachers to mentor early career teachers; and (c) provide them professional development and training on curriculum, classroom management, communication skills, and instructional approaches expected by the provincial ministry (Ontario Ministry of Education, 2010b). The present NTIP also expects the induction support to be a web personalized in nature, including (a) mentoring web, (b) differentiated learning, (c) principal encouragement, and (d) school culture specifically to make the three induction mandates work effectively for early career teachers (Strachan et al., 2017).

It also mandates all early career teachers to participate in the induction program, including its orientation, mentoring, and professional development support in publicly funded schools in Ontario (Ontario Ministry of Education, 2010a). These teachers include those certified by the Ontario College of Teachers or trained out of province who have been hired into full-time or part-time permanent teaching positions for the first time in Ontario (Ontario Ministry of Education, 2019a). All early career teachers in the induction program are evaluated by their school principal two times during their first 12 months of employment through the teacher performance appraisal (TPA) process. Appraisals focus on eight competency statements related to three domains: commitment to pupils and pupil learning, professional knowledge, and teaching practice (Ontario Ministry of Education, 2010b). TPA outcomes include *satisfactory, development needed,* or *unsatisfactory*. Rating options include *satisfactory* or *development needed* in the first appraisal; *satisfactory, development needed,* or *unsatisfactory* in the second appraisal; and *satisfactory* or *unsatisfactory* in the third appraisal (if needed). Completing two evaluations with a *satisfactory* rating indicates successful completion of NTIP, a note of which appears on the teacher's certificate of qualification and registration (Ontario Ministry of Education, 2010a). Additional appraisals are required to be conducted by the principal in instances where a teacher's performance appraisal results in a *development needed* or *unsatisfactory* rating. If a new teacher's performance is rated as *unsatisfactory* and has not improved to a *satisfactory* rating, and after steps have been taken to provide support (e.g., an improvement plan that identifies very specific areas in which the teacher must improve to move forward successfully), the result will be a recommendation by the principal for termination of the teacher's employment (Ontario Ministry of Education,

2010b). It is also worth noting that while the NTIP includes teacher performance appraisal by the principal, the mentoring process is designed to be non-evaluative, separate from the teacher performance appraisal.

Assumptions of Teacher Induction Policy

Several underlying assumptions guided Ontario's NTIP program development, which is consistent with the relevant research literature. First, NTIP assumes that effective professional support for early career teachers should focus on transitioning from the teacher preparation stage to actual classroom instruction and developing the requisite skills and knowledge necessary for effective teaching teachers in the first two years of their teaching career (Ontario Ministry of Education, 2019a). This assumption reflects the research that effective teacher induction programs often focus on early career teachers' transition into the teaching profession, developing skills and knowledge central to preventing or reducing their difficulties encountered in instruction and classroom management and retaining them in the profession (Anhorn, 2008; Glazerman et al., 2010; Kang & Berliner, 2012; Kearney, 2014; Strong, 2005; Wynn et al., 2007). It also resonates with the research evidence that longer induction supports, 2 and even 3 years, are more effective than the typical one-year induction programs (Goldrick et al., 2012; Kearney, 2014; Kutsyuruba et al., 2016).

Second, NTIP assumes that systematic support for early career teachers using induction, mentoring, and professional development is more likely to move them toward becoming effective classroom teachers (Kane & Francis, 2013). This assumption is firmly rooted in the research literature that the most effective approach helps new teachers improve instructional effectiveness and student learning often combines induction, mentoring, and professional development (Glazerman et al., 2010; Guarino et al., 2006; Ingersoll & Strong, 2011).

Third, NTIP assumes that ongoing, teaching skill-focused, and non-evaluative mentoring support is an integral support for early career teachers in learning to teach effectively, while older, more experienced, and wiser teachers could provide such support (Ontario Ministry of Education, 2019a). This assumption echoes the research evidence that the more effective mentors were often older, more experienced, and wiser in teaching and thinking about teaching (Cumming-Potvin & MacCallum, 2010) and could offer guidance, instruction, and encouragement to less experienced mentees/protégé along with other components of the induction process (Smith & Ingersoll, 2004).

Finally, NTIP assumes that while preservice teacher education is the initial process of becoming a teacher, their continued professional learning through induction and inservice professional development was deemed critical for them to become effective teachers (Ontario Ministry of Education, 2019a). This assumption reflects the notion of teacher learning as a continuum starting from the preservice level, moving through the induction level, and continuing at the inservice level with different supports at each level in the literature (Feiman-Nemser, 2001b). Such a continuum has been effectively used to guide the development of support for second-year and long-term substitute teachers, respectively (Kane, 2010; Kane & Francis, 2013).

MULTI-LEVEL NTIP IMPLEMENTATION

Although the NTIP is designed primarily as a school-based program by the provincial government, its implementation occurred at the provincial, district school board, and individual school levels (Ministry of Education, 2010a). Such a multi-level implementation strategy was developed based on the assumption that the contexts and circumstances of different local school boards were unique and required individual interpretation and application during implementation (Ministry of Education, 2010a).

Provincial Level Implementation

The Ontario Ministry of Education led the development of the NTIP mandates and financially supported its implementation in several ways (Ontario Ministry of Education, 2010a). Initially, approximately $15 million was allocated annually to support the induction of the province's 10,000 new teachers, and subsequently, about 13.7 million has been allocated annually for the NTIP implementation. These funds are provided to 72 school district boards in the province with a base amount of $50,000 for each and an additional $1,200–$1,500 per early career teacher in each school district board, which fluctuates each year based on the number of new hires. These funds are used for salaries for board staff to oversee and coordinate the NTIP implementation, release time for NTIP-eligible teachers, mentors, and resources for professional learning.

In addition to the funding, the Ministry supports capacity building for the NTIP program implementations (Ontario Ministry of Education, 2019a). These supports include (a) facilitating professional development for mentors and board teams, (b) creating and disseminating mentoring resources, (c) monitoring the program implementation by making monitoring visits to school district boards and schools, (d) measuring impacts and evaluating program outcomes to inform program redesign (Strachan et al., 2017). More recently, the ministry has expanded NTIP funds to include more beginning teachers in the NTIP (Ontario Ministry of Education, 2019a).

As Cherubini (2010) noted over a decade ago, the ministry's mandates and capacity building for the NTIP program and its financial investment have significantly backed the NTIP implementation. These provincial-level implementation efforts are important for the effectiveness and success of induction programs (Kearney, 2014). For example, dedicated funding from government agencies to school district boards, quality standards, protected time, and mentor training is key to effective induction and mentoring support for new teachers in the United States (Goldrick, 2016). As demonstrated in the Canadian context, when lacking government funding, the beginning teacher induction program in New Brunswick, a model program for Ontario's NTIP, quickly dissolved (Kutsyuruba et al., 2016).

School Board Level Implementation

School district boards are accountable for using the received funds to implement the NTIP in the following ways (Ontario Ministry of Education, 2019a). A superintendent responsible for program oversight selects an NTIP coordinator from current or retired board employees and allocates up to $50,000 as salary to support this role. Besides, the school board was required to establish an NTIP steering committee to help schools implement the NTIP and build capacity by coordinating board-wide supports, policies, procedures, and program reviews (Ontario Ministry of Education, 2019a). The steering committee is also responsible for developing a process for mentor selection, matching, exit strategy, and offering training to principals to deliver school orientation programs and to key stakeholders of the program, including local federation affiliates, new teachers, mentors, principals, faculty of education representatives, and other staff and community partners, such as partners in the Indigenous communities. In addition, it will identify early career teachers to participate in the program as NTIP required, for example, first-year permanent hires and any teachers in their first 5 years of teaching who fall outside of the NTIP required definition (Ontario Ministry of Education, 2019a).

The leadership at the board level is considered instrumental in the successful NTIP implementation in schools (Ontario Ministry of Education, 2019a). The NTIP policy implementations offered some district-level support to address the profound challenges presented to early career teachers (Cherubini, 2010). They offered some district and predominantly school-based support, including mentors, to assist new teachers' transition and negotiation of their professional roles and responsibilities. District school boards (with the assistance of principals) are responsible for providing all new teachers with a process that orientates them to working in education in Ontario, their district school board, their school, and the classroom where they predominantly work. Reporting of the completion of the program is also a joint venture; the principal signs the NTIP Strategy Form once new teachers receive two satisfactory performance ratings, which is then forwarded to the designated NTIP superintendent. The designated NTIP superintendent submits the names of all new teachers who have completed NTIP to the Ontario College of Teachers within 60 calendar days of the new teachers' second satisfactory performance rating.

School Level Implementation

School principals exercise a critical role in the NTIP implementation in the following ways (Ontario Ministry of Education, 2010d). They are responsible for orientating early career teachers to school boards, schools, and classrooms where they predominantly teach. They also assign teaching duties for early career teachers based on their qualifications and strengths and how these assignments might support them in improving student learning. They also need to foster a school culture where new teachers feel supported and not isolated, ensuring they access essential resources and student assessment (Ontario Ministry of Education, 2010d). Additionally, they will work closely with new teachers and their mentors to complete the Individual NTIP Strategy Form, which serves as a vehicle for focusing early career teachers' learning on teaching, recording their participation, and completing induction elements. Then, principals are expected to select and develop other teacher leaders and experienced teachers to serve as mentors in a non-evaluative manner that benefits both mentors and mentees. Finally, they will complete teacher performance appraisals (TPA) for early career teachers using classroom observations, appraisal meetings, summative ratings, and reports and provide additional support depending on the appraisal outcome (Ontario Ministry of Education, 2010d).

The NTIP policy implementation was designed to offer predominantly school-based support for early career teachers' retention and professional development (Ontario Ministry of Education, 2010d). School principals shoulder the ten duties for most NTIP implementation, which are significantly more than any other stakeholders (Cherubini, 2010). Research (Kutsyuruba & Walker, 2020) suggests that the principals exerted direct and indirect impacts on the effective outcomes of teacher induction and mentoring programs, including early career teacher retention, development, and actions and beliefs related to district and government policies (Coburn, 2005). Studies (Cherian & Daniel, 2008; Wood, 2005; Wynn et al., 2007) also indicate that the early career teachers' morale improves, and their self-concept is strengthened when principals build up the school culture, exhibit supportive and shared leadership, create the opportunity for shared values and vision, and promote professional relationships among early career and experienced teachers, then. These research findings are consistent with the assumption that principal engagement is critical for the effectiveness of induction and mentoring programs as these programs depend on a school's context and are aligned with the vision, instructional focus, and priorities that school administrators set (Moir et al., 2009).

IMPACTS AND CHALLENGES OF TEACHER INDUCTION PROGRAM

Impacts on Teachers' Professional Development Opportunities

Since the NTIP's inception, it offered professional support to approximately 8,000 newly hired teachers annually (Strachan et al., 2017). The total number of teachers, including second-year participants and mentors in NTIP, has exceeded 18,000. The program has expanded since 2019 to address teacher shortages in some content areas, increasing demand for substitute teaching. It is needed for early career teachers' professional development resulting from the emerging accountability assessments in the education system (Ontario Ministry of Education, 2019a). It is now accessible for teachers in their first 5-year teaching career, many of whom traditionally fall outside the NTIP required definition, such as various categories of substitute teachers, such as daily, short- and long-term, and permanent hires. The program has also allowed school district boards to respond flexibly to local teacher hiring needs and support early career teachers for a longer time (Ontario Ministry of Education, 2019a). For example, the local school district boards can now decide to include an entire category of eligible teachers for NTIP and offer support on a case-by-case basis.

Impact on Expected Outcomes for Early Career Teachers

We reviewed two longitudinal studies (Frank et al., 2020; Kane, 2010) to understand the NTIP impact on the expected program outcomes and other aspects of the program implementation. This review led to the following results.

First, two longitudinal studies showed the NTIP implementations' positive impacts on the program's expected outcomes (Frank et al., 2020; Kane,

2010). These expected policy outcomes include (a) *confidence*, feeling that they have the support they need to be a successful teacher; (b) *efficacy*, believing that they can help all students learn; (c) *commitment to continuous learning*, having a desire and willingness to improve their teaching; and (d) *instructional practice*, having a strong repertoire of teaching skills (Barrett et al., 2009).

For example, Kane (2010) analyzed multiple data sources from early career teachers, mentors, principals, and school board contacts over the three NTIP annual cycles. The researcher found that the participants perceived the NTIP as a necessary and worthwhile initiative supporting early career teachers progressing toward the HTIP program's goals. For example, it increased their confidence in teaching, enriched their job satisfaction central to retention, enhanced their sense of belonging and value, and contributed to their professional growth.

In a 5-year longitudinal study, Frank et al. (2020) analyzed learning journeys from early career teachers collected in the past month and when they started teaching using a retrospective baseline approach. The researchers found that the participants made meaningful and sustained improvements in all four program goal areas. For example, all participants except occasional long-term teachers significantly improved their teaching confidence. Participants with permanent and substitute teaching assignments also significantly improved their efficacy scores in helping all students learn. Additionally, those participants, often observed by mentors and colleagues followed by observation-based discussions, became slightly stronger in instructional practice and commitment to ongoing learning. Finally, participants who had a mentoring relationship with colleagues and whose teaching was often observed by mentors, followed by observation-based discussions, had slightly stronger growth in their commitment to lifelong learning.

The above research findings in Canada relevant to the NTIP impact on the quality of early career teachers' teaching and learning to teach resonate with international research (e.g., Cochran-Smith, 2003; Darling-Hammond, 2003). While many factors influence student learning, what teachers know and can do in the classroom is the most important contributor (Timperly et al., 2007). Recognition of the limitations of initial teacher education programs to fully prepare new teachers for the reality of 21st-century classrooms has given rise to many Ministries of Education, professional bodies, and district school boards implementing mentoring and induction programs to support new teachers through a prolonged period of further learning and development (Anthony et al., 2011; Ingersoll & Kralik, 2004).

Second, the two longitude studies also demonstrated that mentoring was one of the most influential components of the NTIP program on the expected professional development of early career teachers (Frank et al., 2020; Kane, 2010). Kane (2010) found that early career teachers perceived mentoring as integral to their NTIP support. It is especially the case when they ask mentors for help with questions and challenges they encounter in daily teaching and when mentoring becomes an integral component of the combined support as the NTIP program intended (Ontario Ministry of Education, 2019a). Frank et al. (2020) also revealed that the early career participants perceived the most helpful support they received in the NTIP program was their mentor and colleagues, who provided them with helpful information, advice, resources, and relevant information learning opportunities.

The above finding resonates with the research from international contexts (Hobson et al. 2009) that mentoring produces a range of benefits for early career teachers, mentors, and schools, especially when mentors receive release time to play their mentor roles. The finding also supports the scholarship assumption that mentoring in a properly funded and permanent teacher induction program will offer a great promise in supporting new teachers to develop effective teaching and, thus, high-level student achievement (Glassford & Salinitri, 2007), especially when mentoring is an integral part of the web of personalized supports aligned with NTIP goals (Strachan et al., 2017). Additionally, it is consistent with the research literature on the role of peer support (Kutsyuruba et al., 2016) in improving new teachers' instruction, classroom management, and teaching techniques (Anhorn, 2008; Wynn et al., 2007) and their teacher efficacy (Haggarty et al., 2011).

Challenges Facing NTIP Implementation

Our analysis led to several challenges in developing and implementing the NTIP teacher induction policy and program. One of the challenges was balancing the original goals and the emerging needs of teacher induction over time, as Ontario's education system had multiple changes ever since the NTIP was initially developed (Glassford & Salinitri, 2007). These policy changes included a blended, jagged, and protracted path to permanent teaching, the newly developed regulation limiting early career teachers' entry into the profession, and the repelled regulation guarding the hiring process of substitute teaching in terms of seniority and time (Broad & Muling, 2017). As a result, the NTIP program has been modified to respond to changes while maintaining its goals consistently over time, which created the constant situation that Strachan et al. (2017) described as "stones in our shoes" (p. 263). Such a situation produced significant opportunity gaps among early career teachers in formal mentorship and access to relevant professional learning, especially for those daily substitute teachers and LTO teachers who have not met the previous NTIP support criteria (Ontario Ministry of Education, 2019a).

Another challenge is that school principals often face several tensions in supporting new teacher development, measuring performance, sustaining funding, and developing new teachers' skills (Glassford & Salinitri, 2007). These tensions created issues for the school principals in maintaining long-term program viability for early career teachers. In examining the hidden curriculum within the NTIP, Barrett et al. (2009) identified that school principals often faced tensions in offering orientation, developing effective mentoring, and creating professional development and training for early career teachers in the NTIP program. For example, the tensions among different philosophical and pedagogical assumptions and goals underlying the instructional and classroom management practices that school principals are expected to support early career teachers to develop (Barrett et al., 2009). The tensions among school principals' roles in supporting these early career teachers and assessing their job performance (Cherian & Daniel, 2008). Although both support and evaluation of their teachers are essential to the program (Kearney, 2014), their dual roles in supporting and evaluating new teachers could lead them to "judgementoring" and, thus, prevent early career teachers from flourishing professionally (Hobson & Malderez, 2013). In this situation, it is difficult for the school principals to maintain the trust between them and early career teachers (Frank et al., 2020) "since the principal has the authority to recommend termination of the new teacher's employment" (Cherubini, 2010, p. 25).

Finally, the school board also faces the challenge of scheduling times for mentors to meet with, offer meaningful feedback, and find ways to support occasional teachers daily. The role of effective feedback was important for new teachers' continued development, but this feedback was not without risk due to overlaps with an evaluation of performance (Cameron, 2007). highlighted how the process by which new teachers are evaluated can be contentious due to teachers being seen as autonomous professionals operating in a "culture of individualism" (Fullan & Hargreaves, 2000, p. 51). Teaching has been seen as an isolating profession where teachers work alone in their classrooms (Feiman-Nemser, 2006). It remains an ongoing challenge for the NTIP program.

CONCLUSIONS AND IMPLICATIONS

Conclusions

Our analysis of the development, implementation, impact, and challenges of Ontario's NTIP program leads us to the following conclusions. First, Ontario's NTIP teacher induction policy and program have been developed in an evolving nature with modifications to address emerging needs and contexts (Ontario Ministry of Education, 2010c). These needs and contexts are based on the view of professional learning for new teachers that were relationally rich and characterized by balanced incentives, resources, defined parameters, accountability, and flexibility. NTIP was built in a fashion designed to complement teacher education efforts and the requisite skills and knowledge associated with teacher effectiveness beyond preservice education. The program evolved due to continuous evaluations, partner feedback, and government incentives. While well incentivized and supported by the central authority, the NTIP has been at the grassroots in its implementation with numerous local initiatives and improvisations to match the particularities of challenges the local needs.

Second, despite the evolving nature, the NTIP teacher induction policy and program maintain consistent mandates following the assumptions in the relevant literature (Ontario Ministry of Education, 2010c). It is designed to develop early career teachers' confidence, efficacy, instructional practice to improve their student's well-being and learning, and commitment to continuous professional learning. The NTIP policy and program stresses the role of mentors in providing ongoing support for early career teachers by acting as role models, coaches, and advisors and sharing their experience and knowledge about teaching. It expects school principals to support early career teachers in improving their teaching skills and confidence through developing an effective mentor-novice relationship with adequate release time and assessing what early career teachers learn directly. Additionally, it requires the school district boards to offer an orientation and training to all new teachers on curriculum, classroom management, communication skills, and instructional approaches.

Third, the NTIP adopted a multi-level strategy to implement its program with various roles that the providential ministry, school district boards, and schools can play (Ontario Ministry of Education, 2010a, 2019a). For example, the Ministry led the NTIP mandate development and generated financial support for its implementation. School district boards are responsible for distributing the funds to the schools, coordinating board-wide supports, policies, procedures, and program reviews, and overseeing its implementation. In contrast, school principals are charged to orientate early career teachers, assign them teaching duties, select mentor teachers, foster a school culture, ensure resources to support new teachers, and assess what they learned.

Fourth, the NTIP policy expanded and improved early career teachers' opportunities to access induction support from mentors, principals, and professional development (Ontario Ministry of Education 2019a). With self-report as a base (Frank et al., 2020; Kane, 2010), it impacted its four expected learning outcomes. For example, it has supported early career teachers to be more confident in teaching, believe that they can help all students learn, develop a strong repertoire of teaching skills, and improve their teaching continuously (Barrett et al., 2009).

Finally, despite the positive impacts, the NTIP program also faces several challenges in its implementation. These challenges include how to balance the consistent goals and the changed needs for teacher induction overtime at the program implementation level (Ontario Ministry of Education, 2019a), how to address the tensions that school principals encounter among different assumptions underlying the instructional practices that early career teachers to develop and between their dual roles in supporting and evaluating new teachers (Ontario Ministry of Education, 2019a), and how to resolve the issue in scheduling times for mentors to meet with, offer meaningful feedback to, and find ways to support occasional daily teachers (Ontario Ministry of Education, 2019a).

Implications

Based on our review of NTIP, we offer several implications for further policy development and implementation and practice of supporting early career teachers. First, the NTIP program should maintain multi-level implementation to address the changed needs and its original goals (Ontario Ministry of Education, 2019a). Such an NTIP implementation approach will actively involve different stakeholders and generate various resources in program implementation (Strachan et al., 2017) while addressing the needs of the changing nature of the education system (Broad & Muling, 2017). However, it also needs to find ways to balance the two to ensure effective support for early career teachers in their professional development. Consequently, the research community in teacher induction needs to examine various ways of balancing the two in different contexts. Such an examination will offer the knowledge base and exemplary approaches useful in guiding policymakers and practitioners in teacher induction to appropriately balance the needs to address the emerging changes and long-term goals of teacher induction.

Second, the NTIP programs should nurture and develop the supporting web of mentoring, differentiated learning, principal encouragement, and school culture to make the three induction mandates work effectively for early career teachers (Strachan et al., 2017). Such a web of supporting early career teachers is the modified vision of the NTIP program consistent with the idea of a professional learning community central to effective teacher induction in the literature (Clandinin et al., 1993). Thus, the research community should examine various ways to nurture and develop a web of supporting early career teachers in various school contexts. Hopefully, this examination will help ensure the knowledge base and exemplary approaches central to developing an effective supporting web for early career teachers' professional development in different school contexts.

Third, the NTIP program needs to actualize its vision of teacher learning as the continuum of professional learning development from the preservice level, through the induction level to the inservice level (Ontario Ministry of Education, 2019a). Such a continuum has effectively guided the professional development of second-year and long-term substitute teachers, respectively (Kane, 2010; Kane & Francis, 2013). It is seen as especially useful to support teacher learning continuously when different yet related supports at each level (Feiman-Nemser, 2001b). Thus, the research community needs to examine what teachers need to learn, what support is necessary for teachers to learn at different levels, and how their learning to teach at different levels can be integrated. This examination could build the knowledge base and develop examples of teacher development paths central for policymakers and practitioners to support long-term teacher development and lifelong learning to teach.

Finally, while school principals are identified as central to the NTIP's successful operationalization (Kearney, 2014), it is necessary to note that their role in implementing the teacher induction program is an increased demand for their time and efforts on the top of their existing work responsibilities, which could cause stress and tensions that they must resolve (Cherubini, 2010, p. 25). Thus, it is important to equip them with the appropriate resources, knowledge, and strategies to effectively address their work priorities, stress, and tensions as they offer professional support for teacher induction. Such support is especially necessary for less experienced school principals. Therefore, the research community needs to examine the specific tensions and pressures that school principals may experience and find effective ways to address their tensions and stress in offering induction support to early career teachers in their school contexts. Hopefully, this examination will help develop the knowledge base and exemplary approaches central to developing the necessary support for school principals to effectively enact their roles of supporting teacher induction in their school contexts.

REFERENCES

Anhorn, R. (2008). The profession that eats its young. *The Delta Kappa Gamma Bulletin, 74*(3), 15–26.

Anthony, G. J., Haig, M., & Kane, R. G. (2011). The power of 'object' to influence teacher induction outcomes. *Teaching and Teacher Education, 27*(5), 861–870.

Barrett, S. E., Solomon, R. P., Singer, J., Portelli, J. P., & Mujuwamariya, D. (2009). The hidden curriculum of a teacher induction program: Ontario teacher educators' perspectives. *Canadian Journal of Education, 32*(4), 677–702.

Borman, G. D., & Dowling, N. M. (2008). Teacher attrition and retention: A meta-analytic and narrative review of the research. *Review of Educational Research, 78*(3), 367–409.

Broad, K., & Muhling, S. (2017). Voices of hope: Sustaining learning and optimism through a protracted and jagged entry to the teaching profession in Ontario. In B. Kutsyuruba & K. D. Walker (Eds.), *The bliss and blisters of early career teaching: A pan-Canadian perspective* (pp. 139–153). Word & Deed.

Cameron, M. (2007). *Induction of teachers: Literature review.* New Zealand Council for Educational Research. http://www.teacherscouncil.govt.nz/communication/publications/research0009.stm#h10

Cherian, F., & Daniel, Y. (2008). Principal leadership in new teacher induction: Becoming agents of change. *International Journal of Education Policy and Leadership, 3*(2), 1–11.

Cherubini, L. (2010). An analysis of the implications between the theoretical framework and the policy context of provincial education policy in Ontario. *Journal of Contemporary Issues in Education, 5*(1), 20–33.

Clandinin, D. J., Davies, A., Hogan, P., & Kennard, B. (Eds.). (1993). *Learning to teach, teaching to learn: Stories of collaboration in teacher education.* Teachers College Press.

Coburn, C. E. (2005). Shaping teacher sense-making: School leaders and the enactment of reading policy. *Educational Policy, 19,* 476–509.

Cochran-Smith, M. (2003). Teaching quality matters. *Journal of Teacher Education, 54*(2), 95–99.

Colb, N. M. (2001). A survival guide for the teacher shortage. *Independent School, 61*(1), 72–77.

Cumming-Potvin, W. M., & MacCallum, J. A. (2010). Intergenerational practice: Mentoring and social capital for twenty-first century communities of practice. *McGill Journal of Education, 45*(2), 305–323.

Darling-Hammond, L. (2003). Keeping good teachers: Why it matters, what leaders can do. *Educational Leadership, 60*(8), 6–13.

Feiman-Nemser, S. (2001b). From preparation to practice: Designing a continuum to strengthen and sustain teaching. *Teachers College Record, 103,* 1013–1055.

Feiman-Nemser, S. (2006). Foreword. In J. H. Shulman & M. Sato (Eds.), *Mentoring teachers toward excellence: Supporting and developing highly qualified teachers.* Jossey-Bass.

Frank, C., Zorzi, R., McGinnis-Dunphy, M., Dourado, L., Dare, L. Van den Daele, G., Brooker, A.-S. (2020). *Beginning teachers' learning journeys: Longitudinal study year 4 report.* CFA.

Fullan, M., & Hargreaves, A. (2000). Mentoring in the new millennium. *Theory into Practice, 39*(1), 50–56.

Glassford, L. A., & Salinitri, G. (2007). Designing a successful new teacher induction program: An assessment of the Ontario experience, 2003–2006. *Canadian Journal of Educational Administration and Policy, 60*(March 11), 1–34.

Glazerman, S., Isenberg, E., Dolfin, S., Bleeker, M., Johnson, A., Grider, M., & Jacobus, M. (2010). *Impacts of comprehensive teacher induction: Final results from a randomized controlled study* (NCEE 2010-4027). Institute of Education Sciences.

Goldrick, L. (2016). *Support from the start: A 50-state review of policies on new educator induction and mentoring.* New Teacher Center.

Goldrick, L., Osta, D., Barlin, D., & Burn, J. (2012). *Review of state policies on teacher induction.* New Teacher Center.

Guarino, C. M., Santibañez, L., & Daley, G. A. (2006). Teacher recruitment and retention: A review of the recent empirical literature. *Review of Educational Research, 76*(2), 173–208. https://doi.org/10.3102/00346543076002173

Haggarty, L., Postlethwaite, K., Diment, K., & Ellins, J. (2011). Improving the learning of newly qualified teachers in the induction year. *British Educational Research Journal, 37*(6), 935–954.

Hobson, A. J., Ashby, P., Malderez, A., & Tomlinson, P. D. (2009). Mentoring beginning teachers: What we know and what we don't. *Teaching and Teacher Education, 25*(1), 207–216. https://doi.org/10.1016/j.tate.2008.09.001

Hobson, A. J., & Malderez, A. (2013). Judgementoring and other threats to realizing the potential of school-based mentoring in teacher education. *International Journal of Mentoring and Coaching in Education, 2*(2), 89–108. https://doi.org/10.1108/IJMCE-03-2013-0019

Huling-Austin, L. (1986). What can and cannot reasonably be expected from teacher induction programs. *Journal of Teacher Education, 37*(1), 2–5. https://doi.org/10.1177/002248718603700101

Ingersoll, R. M., & Kralik, J. M. (2004). *The impact of mentoring on teacher retention: What the research says.* Education Commission of the States.

Ingersoll, R. M., & Smith, T. M. (2003). The wrong solution to the teacher shortage, *Educational Leadership, 60*(8), 30–33.

Ingersoll, R. M., & Strong, M. (2011). The impact of induction and mentoring programs for beginning teachers: A critical review of the research. *Review of Education Research, 81*(2), 201–233.

Kane, R. G. (2010). *NTIP Evaluation Final Report—Executive summary (Cycle III).* Ministry of Education of Ontario. Retrieved from http://cal2.edu.gov.on.ca/may2010/NTIP_Evaluation_Report_2010.pdf

Kane, R. G., & Francis, A. (2013). Preparing teachers for professional learning: Is there a future for teacher education in new teacher induction? *Teacher Development, 17*(3), 362–379. https://doi.org/10.1080/13664530.2013.813763

Kang, S., & Berliner, D. C. (2012). Characteristics of teacher induction programs and turnover rates of beginning teachers. *The Teacher Educator, 47*(4), 268–282. https://doi.org/10.1080/08878730.2012.707758

Karsenti, T., & Collin, S. (2013). Why are new teachers leaving the profession? Results of a Canada-wide survey. *Education, 3*(3), 141–149. https://doi.org/10.5923/j.edu.20130303.01

Kearney, S. (2014). Understanding beginning teacher induction: A contextualized examination of best practice. *Cogent Education, 1*(967477), 1–15. https://doi.org/10.1080/2331186X.2014.967477

Kutsyuruba, B., Godden, L., Matheson, I., & Walker, K. D. (2016). *Pan-Canadian document analysis study: Understanding the role of teacher induction and mentoring programs in teacher attrition and retention.* Queen's University.

Kutsyuruba, B., & Walker, K. D. (Eds.). (2017). *The bliss and blisters of early career teaching: A pan-Canadian perspective.* Word & Deed.

Kutsyuruba, B., & Walker, K. D. (2020, April 30). The role of school principal in induction and mentoring of early career teachers. *Oxford Research Encyclopedia of Education,* 1–27. https://doi.org/10.1093/acrefore/9780190264093.013.659

Moir, E., Barlin, D., Gless, J., & Miles, J. (2009). *New teacher mentoring: Hopes and promise for improving teacher effectiveness.* Harvard Education Press.

Ontario Ministry of Education. (2010a). *New teacher induction program: Induction elements manual.* Queen's Printer for Ontario. Retrieved from http://www.edu.gov.on.ca/eng/teacher/pdfs/NTIP-English_Elements-september2010.pdf

Ontario Ministry of Education. (2010b). *Teacher performance appraisal: Technical requirements manual.* http://www.edu.gov.on.ca/eng/teacher/NTIPPrincipal.pdf

Ontario Ministry of Education. (2010c). *Complication of professional development core content to support the new teacher induction program (NTIP): A resource for board NTIP teams.* http://www.edu.gov.on.ca/eng/teacher/NTIPCore.pdf

Ontario Ministry of Education. (2010d). *Teacher performance appraisal: Technical requirements manual.* http://www.edu.gov.on.ca/eng/teacher/pdfs/TPA_Manual_English_september2010l.pdf

Ontario Ministry of Education. (2010e). *Partnering for success, getting the most from Ontario's new teacher induction program: A resource book for principals.* Queen's Printer for Ontario.

Ontario Ministry of Education. (2019a). *New teacher induction program: Induction elements manual.* http://www.edu.gov.on.ca/eng/teacher/pdfs/NTIPInductionElements2019.pdf

Portelli, J. P., Solomon, P., Barrett, S., Mujawamariya, D., Pinto, L. E., & Singer, J. (2010). *Stakeholders' perspectives on induction for new teachers: Critical analysis of teacher testing and mentorship.* Ontario Institute for Studies in Education.

Salinitri, G., Howitt, C., & Donohoo, J. (2007, July). *The new teacher induction program: A case study on its effect on new teachers and their mentors* [Paper presentation]. International Study Association on Teachers and Teaching, St. Catharines, Ontario, Canada.

Smith, T. M., & Ingersoll, R. M. (2004). What are the effects of induction and mentoring on beginning teacher turnover? *American Educational Research Journal, 41*(3), 681–714.

Strachan, J., Creery, K., & Nemes, A. (2017). Ontario's new teacher induction program: Our continuing learning journey. In B. Kutsyuruba & K. D. Walker (Eds.), *The bliss and blisters of early career teaching: A pan-Canadian perspective* (pp. 247–266). Word & Deed.

Strong, M. (2005). Teacher induction, mentoring, and retention: A summary of the research. *The New Educator, 1*(3), 181–198. https://doi.org/10.1080/154768.80590966295

Timperly, H., Wilson, A., Barrar, H., & Fung, I. (2007). *Teacher professional learning and development: Best evidence synthesis iteration (BES).* New Zealand Ministry of Education.

Wahlstrom, K. L., & Louis, K. S. (2008). How teachers experience principal leadership: The roles of professional community, trust, efficacy, and shared responsibility. *Educational Administration Quarterly, 44*(4), 458–495.

Wilson, D. (2004). *Minister launches partnership forum.* Professionally Speaking. Ontario College of Teachers. https://professionallyspeaking.oct.ca/june_2004/registrar.asp

Wong, H. K. (2004). Induction programs that keep new teachers teaching and improving. *NASSP Bulletin, 88*(638), 41–58.

Wood, A. (2005). The importance of principals: Site administrators' roles in novice teacher induction. *American Secondary Education, 33*(2), 39–62.

Wynn, S. R., Carboni, L. W., & Patall, E. A. (2007). Beginning teachers' perceptions of mentoring, climate, and leadership: Promoting retention through a learning communities perspective. *Leadership and Policy in Schools, 6*(3), 209–229. https://doi.org/10.1080/15700760701263790

CHAPTER 9

POLICY RELATED TO TEACHER INDUCTION AND INSTRUCTIONAL COACHING IN THE UNITED STATES

Peter Youngs
University of Virginia

Jacob Elmore
University of Virginia

Rachel van Aswegen
University of Virginia

ABSTRACT

Beginning teacher induction and instructional coaching have been two policy foci in the United States during the past 20 years. Induction programs serving beginning teachers typically feature formally assigned mentors, orientation activities, professional development, and formative teacher assessment. Instructional coaches usually work with teachers at all experience levels by observing their instruction, modeling lessons, meeting with teacher teams, and coordinating their professional development. This chapter first describes contexts in which traditional mentoring-focused teacher induction and instructional coaching emerged over the past two decades, offers examples of beginning teacher induction and instructional coaching policies and programs, and describes theoretical assumptions underlying them. Then, it reviews research on both types of initiatives and identifies strengths and limitations of each. Next, we consider theoretical assumptions underlying integrated approaches to induction and describe research findings on these approaches. Finally, we identify implications for practice and research about integrated approaches to teacher induction.

Research indicates that teachers have a stronger influence on student achievement than any other school-based variable, and they vary considerably regarding their teaching effectiveness (Chetty et al., 2014; Rivkin et al., 2005). These findings have led United States policymakers and researchers to focus extensively during the past 20 years on two areas of educational policy: beginning teacher induction and instructional coaching (Kraft et al., 2018; Youngs et al., 2019). Induction programs serving beginning teachers typically feature formally assigned mentors, orientation activities, professional development, and formative teacher assessment to promote teacher retention and effectiveness (Youngs et al., 2019). In contrast, instructional coaches typically work with teachers of all experience levels, including beginning teachers. They usually observe instruction, model lessons, meet with grade-level or subject-area teams and provide or connect teachers with professional development to support teachers' instructional improvement and effectiveness and promote school or school district priorities (Kraft et al., 2018).

Several studies indicate that having access to formal mentors helps beginning teachers remain in the teaching profession (Ingersoll & Strong, 2011; Kapadia et al., 2007; Ronfeldt & McQueen, 2017; Smith & Ingersoll, 2004; Youngs et al., 2019). In addition, there is strong evidence that instructional coaching is associated with changes in teachers' instructional practices and student learning (Biancarosa et al., 2010; Campbell & Malkus, 2011; Kraft et al., 2018; Matsumura et al., 2013). Further, some teacher induction approaches that integrate aspects of both traditional induction and instructional coaching, such as the New Teacher Center's induction model, improve early career teachers' effects on student achievement (Glazerman et al., 2010; Schmidt et al., 2017). At the same time, there is less evidence that integrated approaches have a stronger impact on novices' retention decisions or instructional quality than traditional induction programs.

In this chapter, we first describe (a) contexts in which traditional approaches to induction and instructional coaching emerged over the past two decades, (b) examples of a state's beginning teacher induction policy and a school district's instructional coaching initiative, and (c) theoretical assumptions underlying them. Second, we review findings from research on both types of initiatives to identify the strengths and limitations of each. Third, we consider theoretical assumptions underlying integrated approaches to induction and how they are similar to and different from those undergirding traditional teacher induction and instructional coaching. We review research findings on the effects of integrated approaches and identify implications for practice and research regarding integrated approaches to teacher induction.

TRADITIONAL INDUCTION AND INSTRUCTIONAL COACHING

Teacher Induction Policy Development, Enactment, and Underlying Assumptions

Policies related to beginning teacher induction and instructional coaching became prevalent in the United States during different periods in response to various factors. Between 1990–1991 and 1999–2000, the percentage of U.S. first-year teachers who reported participating in a formal induction program increased dramatically from about 40% to approximately 80% (Smith & Ingersoll, 2004). During this time, many states and school districts required novice teachers to be assigned to formal mentors and compensated for their mentoring work and/or participate in induction programs, such as completing formative or summative teacher assessments (Porter et al., 2001).

This growth in induction programs can be attributed to two main factors that created the need for beginning teachers. First, the teaching profession changed considerably over time. In the 1960s, limited professional opportunities were available to women (Corcoran et al., 2004). In the 1970s and 1980s, many women worked as K–12 teachers for 25 or 30 years, which led to little need for new teachers; starting in the 1970s, women had increasing professional opportunities in fields outside of teaching, including medicine, law, and academia (Corcoran et al., 2004). In addition, baby boomers began to retire from K–12 teaching, and it became more common for adults to change careers frequently, including moving into or out of teaching (Lankford et al., 2014). Second, the K–12 student population increased significantly in the 1990s due to immigration and more children of the baby boom generation approaching school age.

These factors contributed to greater demand for new teachers. Consequently, states started to develop beginning teacher induction policies and programs in the 1980s in response to increases in novice teachers, which grew further throughout the 1990s and 2000s (Youngs et al., 2010). The underlying belief was that these induction initiatives could help beginning teachers transition to full-time teaching (Smith & Ingersoll, 2004), reduce turnover rates among them (Ingersoll & Strong, 2011), and improve their instruction through the use of teacher assessments (Porter et al., 2001).

One example of a comprehensive state induction policy is Connecticut's Teacher Education and Mentoring (TEAM) program (Connecticut State Department of Education, 2020). The program is designed to help beginning teachers transition to full-time teaching and continue developing instruction, assessment, classroom management, and student engagement skills during their first two years. It is also intended to help novice teachers understand moral and ethical behavior expectations and connect with students' families and the broader school communities (Connecticut State Department of Education, 2020).

As part of the TEAM Program, beginning teachers were required to work with assigned mentors in their school districts over two years using five modules focusing on lesson planning, instruction, assessment, classroom environment and student engagement, and professional responsibilities, respectively. For each module, beginning teachers were expected to develop a professional growth action plan and share it with their mentor and principal. The districts then required beginning teachers to work on reflection papers or projects as formative assessments to show that they had completed a given module. Only those who completed all five modules during their first 2 years could renew their teaching certificates based on summative evaluation of their work on the modules (Connecticut State Department of Education, 2020).

The program also selected accomplished teachers as mentors for beginning teachers in core content areas who were from the same school and taught the same grade level or content area. These individuals were expected to participate in 3 days of initial support teacher training through the TEAM program and then provide at least 50 hours of mentoring support to each mentee over 2 years, including approximately 10 hours per module (Connecticut State Department of Education, 2020). For each module, mentors supported novice teachers in establishing professional goals and action plans, identifying sources and opportunities for professional learning, applying their learning in classrooms, and documenting, analyzing, and reflecting on their instruction and students' learning outcomes. These mentors received at least $500 per year from their district as long as they documented their mentoring work in the mentor/beginning teacher log.

In addition, beginning teachers in the TEAM program were required to work with their mentors to complete a series of modules by analyzing data related to their instruction and student learning. These modules constitute an unstructured formative assessment process that guides novices to identify goals and activities for professional development, create lesson plans, apply what they learn in instruction, and analyze the effects of their instruction on their students. The state also required the reviewers of beginning teachers' reflection papers and projects to complete reviewer training and provide a degree of accountability to this process (Connecticut State Department of Education, 2020).

Several theoretical assumptions undergird these teacher induction policies and programs. These assumptions differ from the underlying instructional coaching policies and programs described below. One of the assumptions is that a novice teacher should have a designated support person who is not an administrator even though they may seek assistance from other teachers and administrators. For example, the districts involved in the TEAM program were required to assign mentors to all first- and second-year teachers in most core content areas.

Another assumption is that it can help beginning teachers access mentors who are knowledgeable about their school context and their teaching assignment. As shown in the TEAM Program, districts were also expected to match those beginning teachers teaching core content with mentors from the same school, grade level, and content area.

Finally, it is assumed that novices will benefit from mentoring even if their interactions with mentors are not based on formative teacher assessments or other structured support. For instance, in the TEAM program, mentoring was the major component of the program; this was consistent with the general nature of teacher induction programs documented in the literature (Feiman-Nemser, 2001; Wang et al., 2008)

INSTRUCTIONAL COACHING POLICY DEVELOPMENT, ENACTMENT, AND UNDERLYING

Assumptions

Instructional coaching initiatives emerged and grew tremendously in the 2000s and 2010s in response to concerns about the limited impact of traditional approaches to professional development on teaching effectiveness. In the 1980s and 1990s, states and districts allocated significant amounts of funding for professional development activities, often in short-term workshops offered by external providers (Desimone et al., 2002; Little, 1993). These workshops introduced teachers to new instructional technology, management strategies, or approaches to student assessment by placing teachers in passive learning roles, offering them little follow-up support, if any, and taking little account of their teaching contexts (Desimone et al., 2002; Little, 1993). Consequently, scholars called for ongoing professional development to address subject matter, involve teachers in active learning with colleagues, and consider their work contexts (Cohen & Hill, 2001; Desimone et al., 2002; Little, 1993; Wilson & Berne, 1999).

Instructional coaching involves a coach observing teachers, modeling lessons for them, meeting with teams of teachers as they plan for and analyze instruction, and connecting them with other learning opportunities (Biancarosa et al., 2010; Campbell & Malkus, 2011; Kraft et al., 2018; Matsumura et al., 2013). Therefore, it became an alternative to traditional professional development activities by addressing its limitations.

Instructional coaching became more widespread as a result of the 1999 Reading Excellence Act, the 2002 No Child Left Behind Act, and the reauthorization of the 2004 Individuals with Disabilities Act. These federal laws supported the enactment of literacy coaching programs at the early childhood and elementary levels and led to a notable amount of research on literacy coaching initiatives over the past two decades (Kraft et al., 2018). In addition, they also created a policy context that led many districts to implement instructional coaching programs focused on mathematics, English learners, equity and diversity, effective teacher–child interactions, and classroom management (Allen et al., 2015; Campbell & Malkus, 2011; Olson et al., 2017; Teemant, 2014).

An example of a comprehensive approach to instructional coaching is the systemic reform in Indiana's Bengtsson (a pseudonym) School District. As of 2015–2016, Bengtsson had closely aligned its district standards and assessments with the state's content and performance standards in literacy and mathematics and aligned instructional coaching, coherent and centralized curricula in literacy and mathematics, and data-driven improvement with each other continually over time.

For example, elementary coaches in Bengtsson developed expertise in and closely monitored teachers' implementation of the district's curricula: Everyday Mathematics, Reading Street, and 6 + 1 Traits of Writing to help improve teachers' instructional practices in several ways (Galey, 2017). They regularly interacted with grade-team leaders, principals, and individual teachers to identify needs for teacher improvement. They also interpreted state standards, aligned curriculum, and designed professional development based on teachers' needs to address the gap between district expectations and teachers' instructional practices. They coordinated resources across multiple schools for teacher instructional improvement and supported their data-based decision-making through learning labs focusing on interventions for low-performing students. In this process, beginning teachers participated in regular professional development activities based on their professional needs and data on their teaching and student learning as they enacted district reading, mathematics, and writing curricula (Galey, 2017).

Unlike traditional induction programs, instructional coaching initiatives were developed based on different theoretical assumptions. First, instead of focusing only on beginning teachers as induction programs do, instructional coaching assumes that teachers of all experience levels need opportunities to learn to teach continuously over a sustained period (Pianta et al., 2014). For example, the instructional coaching program in Bengtsson engaged all teachers in continuously developing and enacting effective teaching practices by working with coaches and teacher colleagues.

In addition, while induction programs generally focus on supporting beginning teachers to increase their retention levels, instructional coaching assumes that teacher induction should improve the quality of their instructional knowledge and practice and, thus, student learning outcomes (Pianta et al., 2014). For example, as Galey (2017) documented, coaches in the Bengtsson program regularly interacted with grade-team leaders, principals, and individual teachers to identify needs for teacher instructional improvement. They supported teachers' efforts to align curriculum standards with instruction based on their needs to address the gap between district expectations and teachers' instructional practices. And they coordinated resources for teacher instructional improvement and supported teachers' efforts to engage in data-based decision-making to improve students' performance.

Finally, coaching programs presume that to improve instructional quality and student learning, teachers need to play active learning roles and acquire deep knowledge of subject matter, and support should account for their work contexts as suggested in the teacher learning literature (Desimone, 2009; Little, 1993; Wilson & Berne, 1999). As shown in Bengtsson, the coaching initiative was designed to ensure that elementary teachers enacted district mathematics, reading, and writing curricula with fidelity while providing some autonomy to teachers concerning choosing instructional strategies and approaches (Galey, 2017).

In summary, beginning teacher mentoring and induction policies were developed as state-level responses to the increased need for beginning teachers and their higher attrition rates in the 1980s and 1990s. They mainly focused on mentors' support for novice teachers as they transitioned to full-time teaching so that they would continue working in their schools and remain in the profession. They also assume that an important characteristic of an effective mentor is to be a full-time teacher who works in the same school, grade level, and/or content area as their mentee.

In contrast, instructional coaching policy was developed primarily as a district-level response to the limitations of traditional teacher professional development and to several federal laws established to improve teacher quality and student learning in the 2000s and 2010s. It mainly focuses on coaches supporting teachers of all experience levels to implement curriculum standards, develop high-quality instruction, and improve student learning. It also assumes that coaching is central in helping teachers acquire deep knowledge of subject matter and a repertoire of teaching practices and improve instructional quality and student learning.

EFFECTS OF INDUCTION AND INSTRUCTIONAL COACHING

In this section, we review research examining the effects of teacher induction and instructional coaching. This review first considered experimental or quasi-experimental studies in the U.S. context. In addition, we also focused on qualitative and mixed-methods studies in both the United States and international contexts.

Research on Effects of Teacher Induction

Several quantitative studies on the effects of teacher induction policy have been conducted in the U.S. context; here, we focus on three of these studies. Smith and Ingersoll (2004) examined associations between mentoring and other supports and first-year teacher retention drawing on the 1999–2000 Schools and Staffing Survey (SASS) and the 2000–2001 Teacher Follow-Up Survey (TFS); their sample included 3,235 beginning teachers. They found that having a mentor in one's field reduced the risk of leaving at the end of the first year by 30%, and having opportunities to meet frequently with colleagues about instruction reduced the risk of quitting by 43%.

Kapadia et al. (2007) collected survey data in 2004–2005 from first- and second-year teachers in grades Kindergarten through 8 (K–8) in Chicago Public Schools (CPS) and found that novice teachers "were much more likely (than other novices) to report a good experience, intend to continue teaching, and plan to remain in the same school" when receiving strong mentoring (p. 28). The authors defined strong mentoring as mentors who observed and discussed teaching with beginning teachers and supported them in using effective instructional, assessment, and classroom management strategies; communicating with parents; and enacting CPS induction policies and procedures. In contrast, novice teachers receiving average levels of mentoring experienced most types of assistance and found them somewhat or very helpful. Teachers receiving weak mentoring either received no mentoring assistance or participated in some mentoring activities but found them somewhat helpful at best.

Ronfeldt and McQueen (2017) drew on data from the 2003–2004, 2007–2008, and 2011–2012 SASS and TFS and the Beginning Teacher Longitudinal Survey (BTLS). They reported that having a mentor reduced the odds of first-year teachers leaving their schools by 36% to 45% and leaving the profession by 35% to 50%. They also found that participating in regular workshops with other novices, experiencing supportive communication with school administrators, and having shared time to collaborate with colleagues had similar effects on reducing first-year teacher migration and attrition.

In the international context, Hobson and Maxwell (2020) conducted a mixed-methods study of teachers and mentors drawing on (a) interview data from a sample of beginning teachers, experienced teachers, and mentors in England; and (b) policy documents. The authors found that how mentors and mentees were paired and how schools structured support for mentoring, including the institutional commitment to training and supporting mentors and the degree of clarity and specificity in defining mentors' roles and mentorship, affected the quality of mentoring support.

In a qualitative study in Ireland, O'Sullivan and Conway (2016) conducted three rounds of interviews to examine nine novice teachers' experiences with mentoring. They reported that teachers found that mentoring was poorly structured and consisted of passive interactions with mentors based on completing checklists and few substantive interactions. O'Sullivan and Conway found that the mentorship embedded in the probationary period for teachers in Ireland reinforced the procedural nature of traditional teaching in the Irish school system, rather than encouraging more dynamic instruction. The context in which the probationary mentorship policy was enacted—with direct oversight from a national board and specific criteria to meet—ultimately worked against the stated mentorship goals to empower teachers to guide their profession.

Research on Effects of Instructional Coaching

In contrast to research on induction, several studies on the effects of instructional coaching have been conducted over the past 20 years. Here, we focus on three experimental or quasi-experimental studies in the U.S. context. Biancarosa et al. (2010) conducted a quasi-experimental study on the effects of literacy collaborative (LC), a schoolwide reform approach featuring one-on-one literacy coaching for K–2 teachers in 17 elementary schools. In the study, coaches participated in one year of training on literacy learning theory and content and how to use LC's instructional framework to teach children through site-based professional development and coaching and continued to teach half-time after participating in training. The authors reported significant gains in students' literacy achievement during the first year of LC implementation, and the effect magnitude increased during next two years.

Campbell and Malkus (2011) carried out an experimental study on the effects of a mathematics instructional coaching initiative focusing on teachers in Grades 3–5 from 36 elementary schools with teachers in 12 schools exposed to the coaching treatment for 3 years, teachers in 12 schools exposed to the treatment for one year, and teachers in 12 receiving no treatment. In both treatment conditions, teachers worked with coaches who completed five mathematics content courses and one leadership-coaching course. The authors found no difference in students' mathematics achievement among the two treatment and control groups in the first year. However, students' mathematics achievement in the schools exposed to the treatment for three years was consistently better than in the control groups during the second and third years. The 12 schools in the 1-year treatment group were exposed to the treatment in the final year of data collection; thus, it was impossible to compare the mathematics achievement of students in this group two years after the treatment with that of students in the other groups.

Matsumura et al. (2013) conducted an experimental study on the effects of content-focused coaching (CFC), an elementary literacy coaching initiative, on teachers' reading instruction and, thus, student reading comprehension, involving 15 treatment and 14 control schools. In the treatment schools, coaches participated in training on the QtA approach to reading comprehension, emphasizing discussion and its theoretical base. They were also engaged in co-planning QtA lessons and observed coach trainers as they modeled QtA lessons, met with individual teachers, and led grade-level team meetings as part of the training. The study revealed that this approach to coaching positively affected the quality of text discussion in treatment teachers' classrooms, which was significantly associated with student achievement by the end of the second year of the policy implementation.

The other two studies in the United States also investigated the effects of coaching programs on helping teachers teach culturally diverse learners effectively, including those from racial/ethnic minority backgrounds, those from low-income families, and English language learners in urban school contexts. In a longitudinal quantitative study, Teemant et al. (2011) collected classroom observation data on 21 elementary teachers working in diverse settings. After attending an initial intensive 5-day and 30-hour workshop, the teachers worked with three coaches during one school year to complete seven coaching cycles, each featuring a 45-minute observation of their instruction and a 30-minute post-observation meeting. Teemant and colleagues reported statistically significant growth in teacher observation ratings from cycles one to seven in the areas of attention to students' language and literacy development and cognitive demand of language arts lessons.

In a follow-up quasi-experimental study, Teemant (2014) further investigated the effects of instructional coaching on 36 urban elementary teachers' instructional practices with 21 teachers exposed to the intervention (the same teachers who participated in the intervention in Teemant et al., 2011) and 15 teachers who did not receive instructional coaching until after the intervention and the data collection were completed. The author reported statistically significant differences between the two groups in the ratings of their instruction on language and literacy development, cognitive demand, and contextualization based on observations conducted toward the end of the intervention year and 1 year later. In the focus group interviews, Teemant found that the teachers exposed to the intervention viewed the coaching as valuable, personalized, and practical, and they also shifted their beliefs regarding working with diverse students.

In summary, existing research offered some large-scale evidence that implementing mentoring-based teacher induction policy was positively associated with beginning teacher retention in U.S. contexts (Kapadia et al., 2007; Ronfeldt & McQueen, 2017; Smith & Ingersoll, 2004). In addition, research from England and Ireland also indicated that several factors associated with induction policy implementation could affect beginning teachers' learning to teach, including mentor training, role clarification, institutional commitment, and program oversight. However, none of these studies examined whether or the extent to which mentoring-based induction contributes to novices' instructional quality.

Research provided some large-scale evidence that instructional coaching was associated with teachers' instructional effectiveness (i.e., student achievement) in literacy and mathematics (Biancarosa et al., 2010; Campbell & Malkus, 2011; Matsumura et al., 2013). Further, research from urban U.S. districts also documented ways instructional coaching could help teachers teach culturally diverse learners more effectively (Teemant, 2014; Teemant et al., 2011). However, few of these studies focused on how instructional coaching was associated with beginning teachers' instructional quality.

INTEGRATED APPROACHES TO INDUCTION, THEIR ASSUMPTIONS, AND EFFECTS

In this section, we describe two integrated approaches to beginning teacher induction. These approaches explicitly combine the strengths of traditional mentoring-based induction programs and instructional coaching programs to support improvements in beginning teachers' instruction quality. We analyzed the theoretical assumptions underlying these approaches and reviewed research on their effectiveness.

Integrated Induction Models

It is not sufficient for induction policy to only focus on retaining beginning teachers; it also needs to address their instructional quality and their effects on student learning. Otherwise, induction policy may succeed in keeping high percentages of novice teachers in the profession without supporting their development of rigorous, high-quality instructional practices or promoting student achievement. In this section, we describe two integrated approaches to induction that combine aspects of traditional induction and instructional coaching.

The first approach is the New Teacher Center (NTC) induction model, which has been implemented in many U.S. school districts, including two large urban districts, Broward County (Florida) Public Schools and Chicago Public Schools, as documented in the literature (Schmidt et al. 2017). Developed and implemented over 20 years, the NTC model features the assignment of a full-time, trained mentor, who is typically an accomplished teacher, to work with novice teachers whose teaching assignment may differ from the mentor's former teaching assignment in terms of the content area and grade level (Schmidt et al., 2017). These mentors are required to participate in 100 hours of professional development each year provided by NTC staff and supported by the districts and schools as well as leading coaches in the field. Beginning teachers are expected to meet with their mentors 3 to 4 times for at least 180 minutes per month for one or more school years. The mentors use formative assessments to observe and provide feedback on novice teachers' instruction and help them plan lessons, enact equitable instructional practices, and analyze student work.

The second model was developed based on the Framework for Teaching (Danielson, 2013) and implemented in one large Midwestern U.S. urban district to improve beginning special education teachers' instructional quality through mentoring (Israel et al., 2014). In this model, special education teachers designated as lead teachers, the highest professional teaching rank by the district, were selected as mentors for novice special education teachers. These mentors were required to participate in 10 days of professional development on using the teacher evaluation system, a modified version of the Framework for Teaching, to summatively assess beginning special educators' instruction and how to provide mentoring support to mentees. One of the major foci of the training "included thorough work in scoring new teachers based on the evaluation system, including a great deal of interrater reliability with the evaluation instrument" (Israel et al., 2014, pp. 49–50). Mentors were required to demonstrate the ability to observe and provide feedback on instruction with fidelity. In particular, if beginning teachers were having difficulty or performing poorly for one or more aspects of the Framework for Teaching, mentors were expected to provide detailed, specific recommendations directly related to those aspects.

Assumptions Underlying Integrated Approaches

Several theoretical assumptions underlie integrated approaches to beginning teacher induction. Similar to those underlying instructional coaching policy initiatives, integrated induction policy initiatives focus on instructional improvement and assume that beginning teachers need support over long periods to develop teaching skills, attain knowledge, and implement effective instructional practices. Such integrated initiatives assume that induction should engage novices in active learning, take account of their school contexts, and be sustained over time (Desimone, 2009; Little, 1993; Wilson & Berne, 1999). Similar to traditional mentoring programs, integrated induction assumes that it is valuable for a beginning teacher to have access to designated mentors who are accomplished teachers and can help them learn to teach effectively (Feiman-Nemser, 2001; Wang et al., 2008).

At the same time, several theoretical assumptions underlying integrated induction programs differ from those undergirding traditional mentoring programs. First, integrated induction programs assume that it is essential for mentors to participate in comprehensive professional development. For example, both integrated teacher induction models featured extensive training for mentors with 100 hours of mentor training for the NTC model and 10 days per year for the special education induction program. In contrast, mentor training in traditional mentoring-based programs, such as the TEAM program, is typically much shorter. Second, integrated induction programs assume that beginning teachers will benefit from working with structured teacher assessments. For example, the NTC model features formative assessments while the special education induction program used a summative assessment based on the Framework for Teaching.

In contrast, many traditional mentoring programs, including the TEAM program, do not rely on structured teacher assessments. Third, integrated induction programs assume that mentors can work productively with mentees as full-time mentors across different schools, contents, and grade levels, as in the NTC model. In contrast, traditional mentoring programs often concentrate on helping novices acclimate to their schools and function productively in particular teaching assignments, grade levels, and school contexts.

Effects of Integrated Approaches

Several studies examined the effects of integrated approaches to induction on both beginning teachers' instructional quality and students' mathematics and reading achievement. In an experimental study, Schmidt and colleagues (2017) assigned 342 first- and second-year elementary and secondary mathematics and English teachers in 108 schools from Broward County and Chicago districts to the NTC induction model (i.e., the treatment) for 2 years. They then assigned 287 beginning teachers in 119 schools to a control group in which they worked with mentors who were not working full-time as mentors and did not receive mentor training, observe their mentees regularly, or use a formative teacher assessment to evaluate their instruction. The researchers found no significant differences between the two groups in their ability to communicate with students, engage and facilitate students in discussion, assess students' learning, establish a productive learning environment, or manage student behavior. However, the study revealed that students in the classrooms of beginning teachers who received two years of induction support using the NTC model performed 0.15 standard deviation ($p < .01$) higher in mathematics and 0.09 standard deviation ($p < .05$) higher in English than students in the classrooms of teachers in the control group at the end of their teachers' second year teaching.

In another experimental study, Glazerman and colleagues (2010) examined the effects of integrated teacher induction programs on beginning teachers' instruction and their students' mathematics and reading performance. Their study included 1,009 beginning teachers in 418 elementary schools in 17 urban school districts. Teachers were randomly assigned at the school level to one of two treatment conditions (i.e., the NTC or Educational Testing Service's Pathwise model) or the control condition. Pathwise is similar to the NTC model in that mentors participated in extensive training and were released from teaching to work full-time as mentors; they used classroom observations and formative assessments to support novices. Ten of the seventeen districts participated in the treatments for one year and seven participated for 2 years. Beginning teachers in the control condition were assigned to mentors at their schools who were not working full-time as mentors and did not receive mentor training, observe their mentees regularly, or use a formative teacher assessment to evaluate their instruction.

Glazerman et al. (2010) found no statistically significant differences between the treatment and control groups in (a) reading language arts instructional practices during the first year of teaching or (b) retention levels after any of the first 3 years of teaching. At the same time, they reported that beginning teachers in the seven districts that provided 2 years of integrated induction support had significantly more positive effects on student achievement in mathematics and reading than teachers in the control group in those districts.

Israel et al. (2014) included 5 mentors and 16 beginning special educators in their qualitative study of one large urban district's integrated induction program. The authors drew on document analysis and interviews with the novices. Israel and colleagues reported that the five mentors mostly provided feedback to their mentees about practices evaluated by the district's summative assessment, the Framework for Teaching. In particular, the mentors made recommendations regarding classroom organization, rules and routines, lesson plans, and instructional practices for students with disabilities. Israel et al. also found that mentors identified professional development activities for their mentees, observed them teach, modeled lessons for them, and helped them complete required paperwork. In addition, the authors reported that mentors advised the beginning special educators to improve their ratings on the Framework for Teaching assessment. Finally, they found that mentors helped novices identify resources and responded to their requests for assistance with instructional strategies, setting up routines, and addressing student behavior (Israel et al., 2014).

In summary, the growth of instructional coaching in the United States in the 2000s and 2010s created pressure on induction programs to go beyond their traditional focus on promoting beginning teacher retention and addressing instructional quality and improvement. In response, integrated approaches to induction became more prevalent during this time. Such approaches are based on several assumptions that differ from traditional mentoring programs.

First, integrated approaches to induction assume that mentors should participate in comprehensive professional development. Second, they assume that structured teacher assessments can support novice teacher development. Third, integrated induction programs assume that mentors who are released from teaching and who work full-time as mentors can work productively with beginning teachers across different schools, grades, and subject areas.

However, existing research on the effects of the integrated approach to teacher induction reveals mixed results. On the other hand, it suggests that students in the classrooms of beginning teachers exposed to integrated approaches to teacher induction for 2 full years demonstrated more significant achievement gains in mathematics and reading than those of beginning teachers in the control group. On the other hand, it showed no significant differences in instructional quality or retention between beginning teachers in the two groups (Glazerman et al., 2010; Schmidt et al., 2017).

IMPLEMENTING INTEGRATED INDUCTION PROGRAMS

Compared to traditional mentoring programs that mainly focus on beginning teacher retention, integrated induction programs focus on helping beginning teachers improve the quality of their instructional practices. The change in focus of teacher induction is important because it can potentially promote student learning. However, existing research on the effects of integrated approaches to teacher induction is limited in sustaining the assumptions underlying such approaches (Glazerman et al., 2010; Schmidt et al., 2017). Consequently, school districts that seek to implement integrated induction programs face some challenges. Therefore, the research community in teacher induction needs to understand challenges associated with integrated approaches to teacher induction.

First, school districts need to identify the qualities of mentor teachers who can work effectively with beginning teachers and offer mentor training that can help them learn to mentor effectively to help improve beginning teachers' teaching quality (Youngs et al., 2010). For example, for existing integrated programs, such as the NTC model (Schmidt et al., 2017) and the model for supporting beginning special education teachers (Israel et al., 2014), whether training helps mentors learn to mentor effectively is still an unsettled question. Future research could examine how mentor selection and mentor training are associated with beginning teachers' instructional quality to develop a knowledge base for school districts in making these policy decisions.

Second, school districts must decide whether to have mentors use a formative teacher assessment or a summative teacher assessment or both in their work with beginning teachers and when and how often to use them (Youngs et al., 2010). Formative assessment is crucial to the NTC model (Schmidt et al., 2017). It is presumably helpful in mentors' efforts to form trusting relationships in which novices are willing to be open about their challenges and vulnerabilities. In contrast, summative assessment can give mentors structure and accountability in their work with beginning teachers when used reliably (Israel et al., 2014). Therefore, whether and how formative and/or summative assessments are used in integrated induction to improve beginning teachers' instructional practices is worth investigating.

Finally, districts need to determine whether mentors will continue to teach part- or full-time while mentoring small numbers of novice teachers in the same content areas, grade levels, and schools or working as a full-time mentor with a dozen of novices across different content areas, grade levels, and/or schools. One advantage of releasing mentors from teaching is that they will be more likely to develop mentoring skills necessary for supporting beginning teachers in teaching multiple content areas and different grade levels in various school contexts (Glazerman et al., 2010; Schmidt et al., 2017). These mentors may not know the school contexts that beginning teachers need to navigate, understand the students they are teaching, or know content-specific pedagogies necessary to support beginning teachers in enacting curriculum in their classrooms (Youngs et al., 2019). Future research could explore the relative benefits of school-, grade level- and content-based mentoring compared to mentoring provided by full-time mentors who may be less familiar with novice teachers' school contexts, grade levels, and content.

REFERENCES

Allen, J. P., Hafen, C. A., Gregory, A. C., Mikami, A. Y., & Pianta, R. (2015). Enhancing secondary school instruction and student achievement: Replication and extension of the my teaching partner-secondary intervention. *Journal of Research on Educational Effectiveness, 8*(4), 475–489.

Biancarosa, G., Bryk, A. S., & Dexter, E. R. (2010). Assessing the value-added effects of literacy collaborative professional development on student learning. *Elementary School Journal, 111*(1), 7–34.

Campbell, P. F., & Malkus, N. N. (2011). The impact of elementary mathematics coaches on student achievement. *Elementary School Journal, 111*(3), 430–454.

Chetty, R., Friedman, J. N., & Rockoff, J. E. (2014). Measuring the impacts of teachers II: Teacher value-added and student outcomes in adulthood. *American Economic Review, 104*(9), 2633–2679.

Cohen, D. K., & Hill, H. C. (2001). *Learning policy: When state education reform works*. Yale University Press.

Connecticut State Department of Education. (2020). *TEAM: Teacher education and mentoring program. Program manual 2020–21*.

Corcoran, S. P., Evans, W. N., & Schwab, R. M. (2004). Women, the labor market, and the declining relative quality of teachers. *Journal of Policy Analysis and Management, 23*(3), 449–470.

Danielson, C. (2013). *The framework for teaching evaluation instrument*. The Danielson Group.

Desimone, L. M. (2009). Improving impact studies of teachers' professional development: Toward better conceptualizations and measures. *Educational Researcher, 38*(3), 181–199.

Desimone, L. M., Porter, A. C., Garet, M., Yoon, K. S., & Birman, B. (2002). Does professional development change teachers' instruction? Results from a three-year study. *Educational Evaluation and Policy Analysis, 24*(2), 81–112.

Feiman-Nemser, S. (2001). From preparation to practice: Designing a continuum to strengthen and sustain teaching. *Teachers College Record, 103*(6), 1013–1055.

Galey, S. (2017). *Organized ideas: How idea-based policy change shapes conflict and collaboration in district-level instructional coach teams* [Unpublished doctoral dissertation]. Michigan State University.

Glazerman, S., Isenberg, E., Dolfin, S., Bleeker, M., Johnson, A., Grider, M., Jacobus, M., & Ali, M. (2010). *Impacts of comprehensive teacher induction: Final results from a randomized controlled study*. U.S. Department of Education, Institute of Education Sciences.

Hobson A. J., & Maxwell, B. (2020). Mentoring substructures and superstructures: An extension and reconceptualisation of the architecture for teacher mentoring. *Journal of Education for Teaching, 46*(2), 184–206.

Ingersoll, R. M., & Strong, M. (2011). The impact of induction and mentoring programs for beginning teachers: A critical review of the research. *Review of Educational Research, 81*(2), 201–233.

Israel, M., Kamman, M. L., McCray, E. D., & Sindelar, P. T. (2014). Mentoring in action: The interplay among professional assistance, emotional support, and evaluation. *Exceptional Children, 81*(1), 45–63.

Kapadia, K., Coca, V., & Easton, J. Q. (2007). *Keeping new teachers: A first look at induction influences in the Chicago public schools.* Consortium on Chicago School Research, University of Chicago.

Kraft, M. A., Blazar, D., & Hogan, D. (2018). The effect of teacher coaching on instruction and achievement: A meta-analysis of the causal evidence. *Review of Educational Research, 88*(4), 547–588.

Lankford, H., Loeb, S., McEachin, A., Miller, L. C., & Wyckoff, J. (2014). Who enters teaching? Encouraging evidence that the status of teaching is improving. *Educational Researcher, 43,* 444–453.

Little, J. W. (1993). Teachers' professional development in a climate of educational reform. *Educational Evaluation and Policy Analysis, 15*(2), 129–151.

Matsumura, L. C., Garnier, H. E., & Spybrook, J. (2013). Literacy coaching to improve student reading achievement: A multi-level mediation model. *Learning and Instruction, 25,* 35–48.

Olson, C. B., Matuchniak, T., Chung, H. Q., Stumpf, R., & Farkas, G. (2017). Reducing achievement gaps in academic writing for Latinos and English learners in Grades 7–12. *Journal of Educational Psychology, 109*(1), 1–21.

O'Sullivan, D., & Conway, P. F. (2016). Underwhelmed and playing it safe: Newly qualified primary teachers' mentoring and probationary-related experiences during induction. *Irish Educational Studies, 35*(4), 403–420.

Pianta, R. C., Burchinal, M., Jamil, F. M., Sabol, T., Grimm, K., Hamre, B. K., Downer, J., LoCasale-Crouch, J., & Howes, C. (2014). A cross-lag analysis of longitudinal associations between preschool teachers' instructional support identification skills and observed behavior. *Early Childhood Research Quarterly, 29*(2), 144–154.

Porter, A. C., Youngs, P., & Odden, A. (2001). Advances in teacher assessment and their uses. In V. Richardson (Ed.), *Handbook of research on teaching* (4th ed., pp. 259–297). Macmillan.

Rivkin, S. G., Hanushek, E. A., & Kain, J. F. (2005). Teachers, schools, and academic achievement. *Econometrica, 73*(2), 471.

Ronfeldt, M., & McQueen, K. (2017). Does new teacher induction really improve retention? *Journal of Teacher Education, 68*(4), 394–410.

Schmidt, R., Young, V., Cassidy, L., Wang, H., & Laguarda, K. (2017). *Impact of the New Teacher Center's new teacher induction model on teachers and students.* SRI International.

Smith, T. M., & Ingersoll, R. M. (2004). What are the effects of induction and mentoring on beginning teacher turnover? *American Educational Research Journal, 41*(3), 681–714.

Teemant, A. (2014). A mixed-methods investigation of instructional coaching for teachers of diverse learners. *Urban Education, 49*(5), 574–604.

Teemant, A., Wink, J., & Tyra, S. (2011). Effects of coaching on teacher use of sociocultural instructional practices. *Teaching and Teacher Education, 27,* 683–693.

Wang, J., Odell, S. J., & Schwille, S. A. (2008). Effects of teacher induction on beginning teachers' teaching: A critical review of the literature. *Journal of Teacher Education, 59*(2), 132–152.

Wilson, S. M., & Berne, J. (1999). Teacher learning and the acquisition of professional knowledge: An examination of research on contemporary professional development. *Review of Research in Education, 24,* 173–209.

Youngs, P., Bieda, K., & Kim, J. (2019). *Teacher induction programs that lead to retention in the STEM teaching workforce.* American Association for the Advancement of Science.

Youngs, P., Pogodzinski, B., & Low, M. (2010). The role of formative assessments in new teacher induction. In M. Kennedy (Ed.), *Teacher assessment and teacher quality: A handbook* (pp. 165–199). Jossey-Bass.

PART IV

LOCAL INDUCTION POLICY DEVELOPMENT IN DECENTRALIZED SYSTEM

CHAPTER 10

TEACHER INDUCTION POLICIES AND PROGRAMS IN BRAZIL

Aline Maria de Medeiros Rodrigues Reali
Federal University of São Carlos, Brazil

Ana Paula Gestoso de Souza
Federal University of São Carlos, Brazil

Rosa Maria Moraes Anunciato
Federal University of São Carlos, Brazil

ABSTRACT

This chapter outlines and analyzes the development of beginning teacher induction policies in Brazil and discusses the issues and future actions regarding teacher induction policies. It begins with a panoramic description of contexts and factors shaping the situation in which specific teacher induction policies at the national level are absent in Brazil. Then, it describes educational and teacher education policies enacted in the last 35 years associated with teacher induction. Next, it presents teacher induction and mentoring policy initiatives developed at municipal government levels. It introduces three mentoring programs for beginning teachers and analyzes their program characteristics, conception, methodology, data, and results. The chapter concludes with a summary and a discussion about Brazil's beginning teacher induction contributions and challenges from a policy perspective. It proposes relevant research to advance its beginning teacher induction policy and practices.

Brazil, the largest country in South America with a population of 212,000,000 people, is a federal republic that includes 27 states, a federal district, and different municipalities. It is also a country with a younger generation. For example, people from 0 to 17 years old comprise 24.2% of the population. Children and adolescents between the ages of 4 to 17 receive mandatory basic education composed of daycares, pre-schools, elementary schools, and high schools, and offers regular education, special education, and youth and adult education. By 2019, the school enrollment rates for children aged 0 to 3 years was 35.6%, 4 to 5 years old was 92.9%, 6 to 14 years old was 99.7%, and 15 to 17 years old 89.2%, including 12.5% and 28.6% of 11 to 14 and 15 to 17 of year-old adolescents, respectively, who were delayed or dropped out of school (Instituto Nacional de Estudos E Pesquisas Educacionais Anísio Teixeira, n.d.). In Brazil, teacher professional development and induction policies are developed in the above school contexts and are affected by complex and controversial factors.

CONTEXTS SHAPING TEACHER INDUCTION NEEDS

Several political contexts, education policies, and manners of how professional educators react to the political contexts and policies at the local levels shape teacher professional development, especially those at the beginning of their teaching career in Brazil (Mainardes, 2006).

First, the economic and social inequalities across different regions of Brazil have generated an immense educational disparity. According to Indicador de Permanência (2020), Brazil had already had difficulty keeping children born in 2003 in school even before the pandemic, especially to keep the most vulnerable students in schools. There is a strong correlation between the school permanence indicator and the socioeconomic level of students in the network. The worst permanence rates were always associated with the lowest results in the socioeconomic indicator, especially in the country's northeast region. However, such a situation gets better in the southeast and southern regions. This context calls for more teachers with adequate training, especially for schools with higher school failure rates and faculty turnover.

Historically, social groups, such as landowners, received the land from Portuguese colonizers and educated their children in European universities in the 18th and 19th centuries. They generated wealth by benefiting from Afro-descendant slave labor. The descendants of these slave laborers mostly remain struggling to overcome the limitations and impediments of social and economic resources until today. Their children could only receive an undignified education, which strongly marks Brazilian society. The same happened with other minorities, such as native peoples and poor populations of different ethnic groups. As Cury (2013) claimed, these educational inequalities have resulted from the converged factors of "the elitist, oligarchic, and slavery past and the exclusionary inclusion" (p. 3).

Gatti et al. (2019) highlight that the above circumstances strongly affect the teachers' profession due to the strength of the social and cultural markers in determining the students' school trajectories and the low general level of schooling of the families of those who choose to become a teacher.

Second, Brazil established a decentralized system and maintained the compulsory school system in 1988 (*Constituição da República Federativa do Brasil*, 1997). Under the influences of specific historical, political, economic, and social contexts (Mainardes, 2016), the federal government's role is limited to organizing and regulating the different educational systems and acting as an agent for distributing and complementing resources. The states and the Federal District are responsible for elementary and secondary education, while the municipalities are responsible for elementary and early childhood education. As Roggero and Zanini da Silva (2021) stated, in this decentralized system, resources for school education and teaching forces are not uniformly distributed among schools and teachers, which is reflected in teachers' salaries and continuing. Notably, the financing of Brazilian education is permeated by disputes of different interests and still needs to guarantee equality of educational opportunities. Although with advances, technical, operational, and managerial procedures have been predominant, typical of collective processes of autonomy, decision-making, and improvement of the quality of education, even though the mechanisms for such are present in the legislation, with the political dimension remaining in the background. It has assumed a character of *deconcentration*, as it adds little money to schools while maintaining centralized decision-making power in central bodies; moreover, it does not relate to the inputs necessary for quality assurance.

One of the consequences of this decentralized school system is that teachers from less favored families often received their basic education in public schools and teacher preparation in private universities since there are few vacancies in free public universities, and are considered the best, are generally occupied by the children of wealthy families, in contrast to what happens in basic education, where private schools are generally seen as of higher quality. Private teacher education institutions often have inadequate laboratories, libraries, and insufficient curricula on disciplinary and pedagogical knowledge central to maintaining quality teacher education and training (André, 2015). Consequently, the egress teachers could develop a reductionist view of teaching as a technocratic school management approach consistent with school administrative power (Papi & Martins, 2014). As a result, it is essential to offer beginning teachers additional training on pedagogical and disciplinary knowledge and effective instruction (Gatti et al., 2019).

Third, the Education Guidelines and Bases Law were established in 1996 to offer several specific requirements for initial teacher training courses for teacher certification at any school level (Lei 9.394, 1996). For example, it requires a university degree for basic education teaching. Consequently, based on Gatti et al. (2019), this legislation expanded teacher training courses, such as pedagogy courses, in teacher preparation programs, especially those preparing early childhood and elementary teachers, and preservice teachers enrolled in the pedagogy courses increased by 300%. Much of the enrollment increase occurred in private teacher preparation institutions; the increase was only 13% in public institutions.

It also led to the increased enrollment of preservice teachers who are working on weekdays and only available for study at night and weekends in teacher preparation programs and, thus, the development of distance learning courses on pedagogy (55.9%), especially in the private institutions (Almeida et al., 2020). Additionally, it led to teacher preparation programs' challenges in offering school-based instruction support to all the preservice teachers and supervising their teaching practices (Gatti et al., 2019).

The above development of teacher preparation programs influenced teacher professional development and beginning teachers' induction in several ways. Expanding pedagogical courses, especially online ones, challenged teacher preparation programs to offer their pedagogy courses of adequate quality. Many of these initiatives appear to be hastened, requiring little dedication from students and rigor from their teachers, resulting in a deficient formation that strengthens the need for induction policies (André, 2015).

Considering the above circumstances, the increased need for teacher preparation programs to offer school-based instruction activities and supervised teaching practices could be more satisfying during preservice teacher preparations (Gallavan, 2015). Thus, it is necessary to offer beginning teachers contextualized support for professional development while teaching, as in many Latin American countries (Beca & Boerr, 2020).

POLICY INITIATIVES OF INITIAL AND CONTINUED TEACHER DEVELOPMENT

The above contextual factors in Brazil and its school system demanded and motivated proposition policies by the federal government to address the issues of initial and continued teacher training that states and municipalities should implement. The 2001 National Education Plan (PNE) approved for 2001–2010 was a policy initiative (Lei n.º 10.172, 2001). It introduced the National Basic Education Training Plan regarding teacher professional development and stressed continued teacher development as part of the movement to improve the teaching profession. Thus, it was essential to ensure adequate working conditions, study time, course preparation, salary scale, and career plans to support their professional development. However, beginning teachers were not the plan's focus (Mira & Romanowski, 2016).

2014, the National Education Plan was updated for 2014–2024 with propositional policies for states and municipalities to implement (Lei n.º 13.005, 2014). It contemplated the guidelines, goals, strategies, and provisions for teachers' initial and continued professional development (Mira & Romanowski, 2016). This plan tied teachers' career plans and salaries to their professional development. It stressed the role of mentoring in supporting beginning teachers' professional development in public basic and higher education. It emphasized the role of experienced teachers' professional team substantiating support and implementing documented evaluation for teachers starting in their probationary stage as beginning teachers. During this period, the teacher's professional development content should focus on teaching methodologies specific to different subjects (PNE-Strategy 18.2). However, this plan did not consider the complexity of initial and continued teacher professional development, for example, mentor teachers' training, monitoring of their mentoring practices, organizational resources, and working conditions guaranteeing the adequate development of induction or mentoring programs (Mira & Romanowski, 2016).

More recently, other policy actions were developed regarding increasing the quality of teacher training in the country, including those explicitly targeting teachers at the beginning of their careers. Aligned with the Common National Curricular Base (Ministério da Educação, 2018), the National Curricular Guidelines were developed in 2017 to leverage initial and continued teacher preparation and development, including undergraduate courses, pedagogical educational courses for graduates, and second-degree courses (Ministério da Educação, 2019). The National Curriculum Guidelines and the Common National Base also offered essential guidelines for initial and continued teacher professional development at the same time (Ministério da Educação, 2019).

These guidelines expected the continued teacher professional development to focus on the pedagogical content knowledge and active learning methodologies that would exert a coherent and positive impact on teachers' social and quality practices. Such professional development would engage teachers in learning to teach with their peers collaboratively through sharing their lesson plans and implementations with the support of an experienced mentor or tutor. Long-term training with flexible and modular program courses should allow complementation, updating, or improvement of teacher professional development processes.

The above policies were developed to empower local governments to develop programs according to their demands. Although the federal government offers financial support for professional development programs focusing on diverse themes, teacher induction was still necessary and not contemplated in any federal initiative.

In sum, beginning teacher induction policies must be developed more closely with continued teacher professional development policies. They were embedded in developing the National Education Plan since 2001 and in the Common National Curricular Base and the National Curricular Guidelines. These initiatives were criticized as top–down policies with little collaboration with teachers' unions, educational research associations, and universities (Aguiar & Dourado, 2019).

LOCAL LEVEL TEACHER INDUCTION PROGRAMS

In Brazil, "training institutions—the school itself, the university, the Secretariats and the Ministry of Education—have been seeking ways, still timid and punctual, to support teachers who start their career" (Azevedo et al., 2014, p. 342). However, relatively few programs or provisions have been developed to support beginning teacher induction, specifically at the local school, despite the initiation of the national-level propositional teacher induction policies. In a nationwide survey by Gatti et al. (2011), three were found to have been developed to offer beginning teacher induction in their probationary stage.

The Sobral municipal education department has developed two local teacher induction programs to offer compulsory support for beginning teacher elementary teachers in the area during their probationary period since 2005 (Calil & André, 2016). In the first program, beginning teacher elementary teachers received 25% of the 4-hour base salary to attend 200-hour professional development over 2 years to become newly qualified teachers. In the second program, the requirements included specific induction training on content-based pedagogies to address beginning teachers' weaknesses in the area on top of the required hours.

The Campo Grande municipal education department developed a teacher induction program with several provisions (Ferreira et al., 2017). First, beginning teachers were required to brief what they learned about teaching and how they taught when entering the probational stage to help diagnose their needs for on-site induction training in the school. Then, mentor teachers offered them contextualized pedagogical support, and school administrators evaluated their training process and students' learning outcomes. Following the Campo Grande Quality Education Policy, they were guided to understand how various sectors of their school system and policies are central to their professional work in the schools.

The Manaus Municipal Secretariat of Education also offered an induction program in its school system to assist beginning teachers during their probationary internship (Fernandes et al., 2021). In the program, more experienced teachers were assigned to offer induction training based on their knowledge and experience in professional teaching practices, focusing on improving beginning teachers' teaching practices in the school context for 1 year. The mentoring support involved observing the beginning teachers' teaching and offering feedback, familiarizing them with the school context, norms, and policy for pedagogical purposes, and role-play using active listening, questioning, and communication in teaching. The mentor–beginning teacher relationship and the responsibility for each were clearly defined, weekly mentor–beginning teacher meetings were required, and a flexible yet established plan was developed to assess the processes, outcomes, and challenges of beginning teachers' learning to teach with mentors. At the end of the program, mentor and beginning teachers were also encouraged to write a research paper documenting their experience during the program.

However, these locally initiated teacher induction programs shared the following characteristics. First, any broader educational policy involving teacher training, especially those developed for beginning teachers, often lacks the solid theoretical and methodological bases to support the training processes and disseminate their results. Second, as Nascimento et al. (2019) claimed, their implementation was easily affected by the local educational system's periodic changes in leadership and priorities. Consequently, they were often unstable since they were financed with municipal funds.

However, Almeida et al. (2020) point out that after 2014, there was a significant increase in publications on the topic. In recent years, interest appeared in continuing education actions proposed by state and municipal educational departments and secretariats. Studies have also been increasingly focusing on training actions to support and monitor teachers who enter the profession, highlighting contributions made by using training devices and collaborative groups proposed by state and municipal departments and some universities.

UNIVERSITY-LEVEL TEACHER INDUCTION PROGRAMS

Another line of teacher induction program development is those university-based teacher mentoring programs with the support of federal and state scientific funding agencies, grants, and scholarships (Tancredi & Reali,

2003). These programs were developed to train experienced teachers to mentor and work with earlier career teachers. Relevant teacher induction literature and a research agenda to develop a knowledge base for teacher induction policies in Brazilian contexts were also considered in such programs (Mizukami et al, 2015).

For example, the three programs developed at the Federal University of São Carlos are such (Reali, 2012, 2016; Tancredi & Reali, 2003). They used constructive-collaborative research interventions and the Internet to help train experienced teachers to be mentors and to work with early career teachers for 3–4 years. They developed a research agenda to understand the impacts of virtual, hybrid, and face-to-face mentoring training on mentoring activities (Vaughan, 2010) and promote partnerships between the university and school (Zeichner, 2010). In the following, we analyze these programs and their impacts using.

Program Characteristics and Mandates

The first program was an online mentoring program sponsored by grant #401506/2004-5 from the National Council for Scientific and Technological Development (CNPQ; Reali, 2004) and grant #04/00160-9 from the São Paulo Research Foundation (FAPESP; Tancredi & Reali, 2003). Developed and implemented from 2004 to 2007, the program involved 10 experienced teachers with more than 20 years of teaching experience, half retired teachers, and 52 elementary teachers in their first five years of teaching.

The program aimed to help mentor teachers understand beginning teachers' teaching difficulties and professional socialization in the school culture. Then, they used what they learned to support elementary school beginning teachers through online communications via emails and virtual letters in mentor-beginning teacher dyads. Then, it engaged them in designing a mentoring program collaboratively and using what they learned to mentor beginning teachers in their elementary school years.

The mentors were awarded a FAPESP scholarship to work at least eight hours weekly to develop mentoring activities and participate in weekly meetings with the researchers. Beginning teachers were expected to work with their mentors four hours per week and 120 to 180 hours in total, leading to certification by the university.

Within the program, a research project was also structured to evaluate the program's contributions to the learning of mentors and beginning teachers. It interviewed mentors and beginning teachers, recorded weekly face-to-face meetings between mentors and trainers, and collected documents and narratives developed in the virtual environment regarding mentoring activities.

The second program was a mentor online training program from 2013 to 2016, sponsored by grant #474921/2012-3 from the National Council of Research (Reali, 2012). It offered 5- or 6-month Moodle-based training to 68 mentor teachers, principals, and pedagogical coordinators from two municipal school systems in the interior of São Paulo based on an agreement with the university and municipalities to be mentors. These participants all had more than 10 years of teaching experience. The training focused on face-to-face mentoring with beginning teachers and developing participants' identity as professional mentors.

Then, 28 mentors participating in the training were assigned to work with 52 beginning teachers from their school systems and schools at least 8 hours a week for 4 to 8 months. In contrast, beginning teachers were expected to work with their mentors four hours a week to receive the university certificate, which could impact their promotion in the school associated with their financial package.

The structured program research project collected audio recordings of mentors' virtual interactions with the researcher-trainers and written narratives documented in Moodle dealing with beginning teachers' difficulties in teaching, learning, and professional development. It also collected written forums and daily entries from mentors on their work with beginning teachers, audio recordings of biweekly face-to-face interactions between mentors and beginning teachers in dyads or triads, and recordings of mentors' interactions with trainers regarding their mentoring work.

The third program was the hybrid mentoring program from 2017 to 2021, sponsored by grant #2016-/25412-8 from the São Paulo Research Foundation (Reali, 2016). Due to the COVID-19 pandemic in 2020, the program was transformed to online delivery only. The beginning teachers and mentors started to teach their classes remotely in April 2020 until the end of the year.

It offered face-to-face and online training for 14 experienced teachers with ten or more years of teaching practice to be mentors. The training supported the mentors in conducting face-to-face and virtual mentoring involving Moodle, Skype, Google Meet, and other applications such as WhatsApp. It developed their understanding of the curriculum and activities related to the program and different levels of education contemplated in the program, such as early childhood education, elementary education, youth, and adult education. Then, these mentors were assigned to work with 72 beginning teachers in early childhood education, early years, and youth and adult education with less than five years of professional experience. In this case, mentors were awarded FAPESP grants to conduct the program's activities for at least 8 hours a week. In contrast, beginning teachers worked with their mentors at least 4 hours a week for 6 to 18 months and then received the UFSCar certification.

The program collected the recordings of weekly face-to-face or virtual meetings between mentors and the trainer and face-to-face and virtual interactions between mentor and beginning teacher. The video- and audiotaped conversations, journal entries, reports, and written narratives documented in Moodle and WhatsApp were also collected. Table 10.1 offers the detailed information about all three programs.

TABLE 10.1 Background Information of Teacher Induction and Mentor Training Programs

Research-Interventions	Mentoring programs for primary school teachers (Tancredi & Reali, 2003).	Online training program for mentors mentoring (Reali, 2012).	Professional development program for experienced and beginning teachers (Reali, 2017).
Focuses	How to implement a continuum of teacher learning.	Develop a knowledge base for mentoring and professional identity.	Develop hybrid mentoring practices.
Characteristics	Online Mentoring Program (2004–2007).	Online Mentor Education Program (2012–2016).	Hybrid Mentoring Program (2017–2021).
Data Sources	Interviews with mentors and beginning teachers, records of follow-up meetings with mentors, weekly face-to-face mentoring data, and systematic register of mentoring activities in the virtual environment.	Discussion forums, journals, and reports on Moodle from mentors. Audio recordings of their interactions with researcher-trainers in groups of two or three.	Recordings of face-to-face or virtual meetings between mentors and trainers, mentor-beginning teacher interactions, journals, reports, and written narratives in Moodle and WhatsApp.
Mentor Profile	Elementary experienced teachers with more than twenty years of teaching practices and other educational roles.	Early childhood and first-year elementary principals, pedagogical coordinators, and supervisors with more than ten years of teaching practice.	Early childhood, elementary, youth, and adult education experienced teachers with more than ten years of teaching practice.
Beginning Teacher Profile	Elementary beginning teachers with no more than 5 years of teaching practice.	Early Childhood elementary teachers with no more than 5-year teaching practices considering teaching level.	Early childhood, elementary, youth, and adult education teachers with no more than 5-year teaching practices, considering teaching level.

(continued)

TABLE 10.1 Background Information of Teacher Induction and Mentor Training Programs (continued)

Program Delivery	Weekly face-to-face meetings between mentor teachers and researchers.	Moodle training involving mentor teachers and researchers.	Hybrid training and online training during the pandemic involving mentor teachers and researchers
Mentoring Activities	Online mentoring activities between mentors and beginning teachers.	Face-to-face mentoring between mentors and beginning teachers.	Hybrid and online mentoring between mentors and beginning teachers.
Mentor and Beginning Teacher Grouping	One mentor with one beginning teacher.	One mentor with one or two beginning teachers.	One mentor with one, two, or three beginning teachers. Two mentors and two or more beginning teachers at the same level.
Mentoring Curricula	Open.	Open with pre-established activities.	Open with pre-established activities.
Mentoring Practice	Inquiry, suggestion, reflection, support, offer beginning teachers readings and written feedback.	Observe beginning teacher teaching, orientation, rehearsal, inquiry, face-to-face conversations, and oral feedback.	Inquiry, suggestion, reflection, support, audio and written feedback, illustrating videos, synchronous conversations, virtual observation, orientation, and written feedback.
Mentoring Focuses	Beginning teachers' formative demands and negotiating mentoring plans with beginning teachers.	Beginning teachers' formative demands and negotiating mentoring plans with beginning teachers.	Beginning teachers' formative demands and negotiating mentoring plans with beginning teachers.
Effects on Beginning Teachers	Develop relations with the school community, and perceive the classroom as a place for dialogue, sharing, and socialization. Manage class, improve pedagogical practices and reflection, generate questions, overcome difficulties, understand others, and develop professional identity	Address immediate beginning teacher demands, improve their school socialization process, teaching experiences, exchanges with mentors and other mentees, receive specialist support from mentors, and learn how to use hierarchies and different attentions.	Broaden beginning teachers' views on teaching practices, improve their interactions with other mentees about teaching knowledge and practices, receive mentors' online observation-based feedback, offer space to express anxieties, and receive support in the COVID-19 pandemic.

(continued)

TABLE 10.1 Background Information of Teacher Induction and Mentor Training Programs (continued)

Effects on Mentor Teachers	Expand their professional knowledge, develop their identity as teacher educators, and improve their computer, internet use, and writing skills	Broaden their knowledge about early career and learning processes. Improve their professional development through Moodle	Expand knowledge of beginning teachers, teacher learning, and development, develop teaching knowledge base and identity as teacher educators, understand characteristics of other levels, and improve Moodle and virtual activity design skills
Mentoring Duration	9–22 months	4–6 months	6–18 months
Beginning Teachers' Weekly Dedication	4 hours	4 hours	4 hours
Mentors' Weekly Dedication	8 hours	8 hours	8 hours
Mentors' Financial Support	Yes[a]	No	Yes[b]

[a] Each mentor received a FAPESP scholarship during their participation in the research.
[b] Each mentor received a FAPESP scholarship during their participation in the research.

Shared Program Practices and Literature Bases

Despite some specific content and characteristics in training, all three mentoring shared several characteristics. These similarities are reflected in the program focuses, literature-based mentoring approaches, and contextualized research agenda developed to address the limitations of locally initiated teacher induction specified in the earlier section.

First, each program demonstrated that mentors played an essential role in supporting beginning teachers to overcome their challenges and limitations in mastering content-specific pedagogies and reducing their feelings of isolation in the classroom. Such a focus on teacher mentoring considers the following characteristics of Brazilian beginning teachers. They often needed more content-specific pedagogies to address challenges and difficulties encountered in teaching while struggling to be socialized into the school norms and cultures (Horn et al., 2017).

This mentoring focus reflects that beginning teachers initially develop pedagogical content knowledge (Shulman, 1987) and construct specific knowledge in content, students, school, and public policies (Cole &

Knowles, 1993) as central to developing effective teaching. It is consistent with the idea that beginning teachers' personal, socio-cultural, and professional profile presumably functions as lenses to filter what they learn and shape how they learn to teach (Fairbanks et al., 2010). Additionally, it reflects the assumption that beginning teachers' professional development is a complex endeavor shaped by the school curriculum and teaching policies, culture, teaching organization, and their students' characteristics in the context of their teaching and learning to teach.

Second, each program stressed face-to-face and virtual approaches to develop effective communication between mentors and beginning teachers and support beginning teachers to teach effectively. This program focus suggests that face-to-face or virtual mentor–beginning teacher conversations can reveal school curriculum and teaching issues, bridge the gap between practice and theory, and create significant sources for teacher professional development (Timperley, 2001). Considering Vaughan (2010), using face-to-face and virtual mentoring practices could enrich the choices of mentoring practices central to supporting beginning teachers to learn to teach when traditional mentoring or teaching alternatives are not available and helpful, such as in the context of the COVID-19 pandemic.

Third, all three programs were developed with particular attention to building partnerships between researchers in universities and administrators and teachers in school contexts and connecting the national and municipal educational policies to specific mentoring program contexts. For example, the experienced teachers in the second and third programs understood mentoring characteristics, organization, and operation based on critical analyses of their training and personal experiences. As the literature suggests, partnerships and connections could promote closer relations between theory and practice and policy initiative and implementation relating to teaching, teacher learning, and professional growth (Cole & Knowles, 1993).

Fourth, each program understood that it takes time and training for mentors to establish mutual trust with their beginning teachers, understand their formative needs in learning to teach, and develop mentoring practices to address these formative needs. Such needs of mentor teachers reflect the idea that while valuable in helping beginning teachers learn to teach, mentor teachers' teaching experiences alone are insufficient for them to develop effective mentoring practices. Effective mentoring practices rely on mentors' broader and deeper knowledge for effective teaching and how beginning teachers learn from each, including how they "see" classroom events, their teaching knowledge "stock," and how they act, especially in dilemmatic and their challenging situations (Gallavan, 2015). Like beginning teachers, mentor teachers also faced dilemmas and difficulties in acting in their new role as mentors. They must adapt their knowledge and experiences to the new context of their mentoring work (Murray & Male, 2005).

Consequently, all three programs were designed with mentor training as an important part of their programs. In the mentor training, the researchers–teacher educators engaged mentor teachers in learning to identify beginning teachers' tensions in teaching and use them to trigger opportunities for beginning teachers to experiment with alternative teaching practices and develop effective solutions. They also support mentor teachers in developing reflective processes to address unique difficulties and challenges in their mentoring practices. Additionally, they offered opportunities for mentor teachers to learn how to monitor their mentoring practices to inform their further mentoring work through feedback. Lastly, they all sustained mentor teachers to learn how to work collaboratively with fellow mentor teachers, university researchers, school administrators, and fellow teachers to develop a supportive environment to improve their mentoring practices and for beginning teachers to learn how to teach effectively.

All three programs were designed and implemented with similar research goals that would lead to a theory–practice connection regarding teaching, teacher training, and teacher professional development (Cole & Knowles, 1993). The mentor teachers were conceived to generate knowledge about beginning teachers' professional development processes and to understand the mentoring processes by mentors directed to support beginning teachers from different fields and levels, considering diverse delivery methods (virtual, face-to-face, and hybrid). They have implemented data collection and analysis to examine how mentors, beginning teachers, and university researchers interact with each other using various Internet platforms.

Programs Impacts

As shown in Table 10.1, the following data were collected from each program to understand the impacts of the three mentoring programs on beginning teachers' professional development, mentoring practices, and partnerships between beginning teachers, mentors, and university researchers.

The data analysis led us to the following overall results regarding the program's impacts on beginning teachers. First, the programs expanded beginning teachers' knowledge base for teaching specific content and general pedagogical knowledge by training mentors to understand the beginning teachers' needs for learning to teach. They also allowed mentors to develop mentoring practices based on their beginning teachers' demands. These program influences were documented in a series of studies on the programs (Barros, 2022; Borges, 2017; Bueno, 2008; Cesário, 2021; Gobato, 2020; Malheiro, 2017; Massetto, 2014; Massetto, 2018; Pieri, 2010; Pinheiro, 2020). Also shown in the literature above, beginning teachers developed the need to understand literacy instructions for students at different levels of elementary schools, adapt learning rhythms, pedagogical models, and learning strategies to meet the special needs of students in early childhood, youth, and adult education levels, and learn how to teach Libras and the Braille writing system to special education students.

Second, the beginning teachers in all three programs also reported that their professional conversations with mentors promoted their learning to teach relevant to their content and content of teaching, especially when these conversations often focused on the following cycle (Souza & Reali, 2022). The cycle included analyzing their teaching situations, weighing and selecting alternative actions, planning practices, projecting, and analyzing results.

Third, the programs helped beginning teachers develop specific resources for specific teaching practices as their mentors shared the suggested curriculum and instruction materials related to the content and pedagogical practices (Souza & Reali, 2022). Their mentor teachers developed and acquired these materials in their mentor training and continued consultations with their trainers after their program training (Borges, 2017; Reali et al., 2020).

The programs also impacted mentor teachers based on a series of research reports. First, mentor teachers in the programs reported that they were able to conduct their mentoring practices with their beginning teachers safely and reflectively due to the relevant training and continued support afterward that they received in the programs (Mizukami & Reali, 2019; Reali & Souza, 2022; Reali et al., 2008, 2010; Souza et al., 2019). They especially benefited from their continued and systematic dialogue with their trainers built in all three programs after training (Malheiro, 2017; Reali et al., 2008; Souza et al., 2019).

Second, mentor teachers also reported that they were able to develop their understanding of how to teach and develop a stronger professional identity as teacher educators (Tancredi & Reali, 2003). They attributed their development in the above area to their mentoring work and program training (Gobato & Reali, 2017; Reali et al., 2017; Souza & Reali, 2022).

Third, mentor teachers further reported that they could improve their trust relationship with their beginning teachers and develop a safe environment for beginning teachers to pose difficulties in their mentoring practices (Cesário, 2021; Massetto, 2018; Migliorança, 2010). They claimed that their detailed documentation about their mentoring practices and their chances to know local policies and the school's culture, as required by the online and hybrid programs, helped them develop these relationships and environments (Borges, 2017).

Finally, mentor teachers felt they could stimulate and engage beginning teachers to reflect and analyze their teaching practices (Borges, 2017; Carvalho & Reali, 2022; Malheiro, 2017; Migliorança, 2010). They learned how to do the above as the results of their training programs focusing on how to observe and analyze beginning teachers' teaching and provide formative feedback to them using appropriate explanations, suggestions, praise, and evaluations (Borges, 2017; Carvalho & Reali, 2022; Malheiro, 2017; Migliorança, 2010).

The three programs further impacted the development of the online professional community among the program trainer, mentor teacher, and beginning teachers by positively analyzing data generated on various Internet platforms based on a series of reports. By interviewing participants in the online mentoring program in a follow-up study over 7 years, Massetto (2014) showed that trainers, mentors, and beginning teachers were able to use the internet platform to develop dialogue, share, and socialize in terms of mentoring, teaching, and learning to teach after their program training. Such impacts were also reported by the trainers in the programs because of the specific design of initial training actions (Borges, 2013) and experienced by the trainers, beginning teachers, and mentor teachers experienced teachers based on dialogue among them (Batista, 2018; Cardoso, 2016; Cruz, 2019).

Those Brazilian university-based teacher induction programs were often developed to address issues the initial teacher education courses failed to address with the support of various federal or local foundation grants. These issues included mentoring training, literature-based mentoring practices, newly emerged mentoring forms, such as virtual mentoring and mentor training, the partnership between beginning teachers, mentor teachers, university researchers, and faculty members, and research agenda to build knowledge bases for further development of teacher induction policies, programs, and practices. The obtained results have shown the impacts of mentoring support on beginning teachers' learning to teach, the relevance of considering the needs of their learning to teach as a guide to mentors' actions, and the research knowledge of mentoring from universities.

CONCLUSIONS AND IMPLICATIONS

Our analysis of teacher induction policies and programs in Brazil suggests that teacher induction policies and programs are emerging. They are situated in the contexts of traditional social and educational inequality, decentralized schooling systems, and newly developed needs for teaching.

At the Federal level, the teacher induction policy initiatives are positionally embedded in and derived from the overall policies on newly developed beginning teacher qualifications (Marcelo & Vaillant, 2017), reformed basic curriculum standards demanding teachers to support students to develop the higher-order and effective communications, and affective capacities (Pérez Gómez. 2019), and the relevant teacher professional developments

(Conselho Nacional de Educação, 2015). The mentoring programs are mainly developed to address specific local needs of beginning teachers learning to teach and documents that reveal their theoretical-methodological bases were not localized. The federal-level policy influences on these programs are only suggestive and disparate, and their impacts are not carefully documented. The university-based teacher induction programs are developed by competing with the national and local foundations, focusing on mentor training, literature-based mentor training, mentoring practice, emerging needs of mentoring practices focus, and research agenda. These programs impacted beginning teachers' professional development, mentoring practices, and patroonships between beginning teachers, mentors, and university researchers.

Our analysis of the status and development of teacher induction policies and programs in Brazil also led us to several challenges faced in future teacher induction policy and program development. These challenges are specified below.

First, since mentor teachers are central to induction programs, the programs in Brazil need to develop the necessary profile for mentor teachers who effectively support beginning teachers' learning to teach (Wang, 2019). Such a profile is an essential basis for teacher mentor selection and training. Our analysis of the university-based mentoring programs showed some crucial aspects of this profile, such as influential mentors who are knowledgeable about effective teaching pedagogies, can articulate practice, and are committed to developing effective mentoring practices to support beginning teachers' professional development and their teaching.

However, whether these aspects of mentor teacher profile are sufficient in mentor selection, ensuring the necessary profile of mentor teachers in the mentor training program, and developing mentoring practices are still questions. Thus, the research community in teacher induction needs to inquire into essential aspects of such a mentor profile. It needs to examine how it can be effectively used to select effective mentor teachers, train them for their mentoring role, and guide mentoring practices with beginning teachers.

Second, understanding the needs and characteristics of beginning teachers in learning to teach is essential for mentors to develop their mentoring practices accordingly (Hobson et al., 2009). Our analysis of the three university-based mentoring programs shows that mentor teachers often developed mentoring practices based on beginning teachers' needs and characteristics during specific times of the academic year. Thus, an appropriate conception of various beginning teachers' needs and characteristics is central to providing a critical conceptual base for mentor teachers to effectively identify their beginning teachers' needs and characteristics in learning to teach formatively and develop mentoring practices accordingly. Thus, the research community in teacher induction needs to inquire into important profiles of beginning teachers' needs and characteristics in learning to teach. It must also examine how to support mentor teachers using such profiles in mentoring training and mentoring practices. Additionally, it needs to explore how it can be used to select effective mentor teachers, train them for their mentoring role, and guide their mentoring practices with beginning teachers.

Third, when mentor and beginning teachers are appropriately matched, productive professional relationships can be developed, which can help build effective mentoring practices and beginning teachers' learning to teach during their programs (Kardos & Johnson, 2010). Thus, it becomes an avoidable part of program needs for almost any program. Research literature suggests that mentor and beginning teacher matchings have been identified as necessary for an effective mentor–beginning teacher relationship, such as content areas, grade levels, and teaching contexts. However, our understanding needs to be developed regarding what engages in matching mentors and beginning teachers to develop their supporting mentoring practices and their learning to teach in the field, related to certain skills, open-mind, sensibility, care, and so on (Kochan, 2017). Our second teacher induction program analysis suggests that when principals, supervisors, and retired teachers become mentors, their relationship with their beginning teachers can be significantly affected. Consequently, the research community needs to inquire into what participates in mentor and beginning teacher matching for what purpose, how to use this understanding in matching and nurturing their relationships to support mentoring practices, and the necessary contexts, training, and support in nurturing effective mentor–beginning teacher relationships.

Finally, an appropriate partnership between beginning teachers, mentors, and university faculty members or researchers is central to building necessary knowledge bases for developing and improving research-based mentoring policies, practices, and training programs (Zeichner, 2010) and, thus building and sustaining such a relationship into the professional learning community through mentor training and mentoring programs (Grossman et al., 2000). At the same time, it is also helpful for the research community to identify important and emerging issues of mentoring practice and develop the necessary understanding of them in time (Wang, 2019). Our analysis of the three teacher induction programs indicates the benefits of developing an appropriate relationship between beginning teachers, mentors, and university researchers. However, our understanding of how participants developed their relationships and addressed the issues of sustaining them in different contexts is limited (Mizukami & Reali, 2019). Thus, the research community must inquire into what engages in an effective partnership between beginning teachers, mentors, and researchers and examine how to use this understanding to develop and sustain such relationships to support mentoring practices.

REFERENCES

Aguiar, M. A. S., & Dourado, L. F. (2019). BNCC e formação de professores: concepções, tensões, atores e estratégias. *Retratos Da Escola, 13*(25), 33–37. https://doi.org/10.22420/rde.v13i25.990

Almeida, P. C. A. de, Reis, A. T., Gomboeff, A. L. M., & André, M. E. D. A. de. (2020). As pesquisas sobre professores iniciantes: uma revisão integrativa. *Revista Eletrônica De Educação, 14*, e4152113. https://doi.org/10.14244/198271994152

André, M. E. A. D. (2015). Políticas de valorização do trabalho docente no Brasil: algumas questões. *Ensaio: Avaliação e Políticas Públicas em Educação 23*(86). 213–230. https://doi.org/10.1590/S0104-40362015000100008

Azevedo, A. A., Fernandes, C. M., & Bonifácio, R. M. (2014). Professores em início de carreira: Políticas públicas no contexto da América Latina. *Formação Docente—Revista Brasileira de Pesquisa sobre Formação de Professores, 6*(10), 31–44. https://doi.org/10.31639/rbpfp.v13i25.426

Barros, B. C. (2022). *Mentoras de professoras iniciantes da educação infantil: enfrentando e superando tensões no processo de ensinar a ensinar.* Universidade Federal de São Carlos. https://repositorio.ufscar.br/handle/ufscar/17216

Batista, M. L. M. (2018). *Aprendendo a ser professor: contribuições da rede de aprendizagem da docência.* Universidade Federal de São Carlos. https://repositorio.ufscar.br/handle/ufscar/10030

Beca, C. E., & Boerr, I. (2020). Políticas de inducción a profesores nóveles: Experiencia Chilena y desafíos para América Latina. *Revista Eletrônica de Educação, 14*, 4683111. https://doi.org/10.14244/198271994683

Borges, F. V. A. (2013). *Professor-tutor-regente: Base de conhecimento e aprendizagens.* Universidade Federal de São Carlos. https://repositorio.ufscar.br/handle/ufscar/2655

Borges, F. V. A. (2017). *Os especialistas escolares no trabalho de mentoria: Desafios e possibilidades.* Universidade Federal de São Carlos. https://repositorio.ufscar.br/handle/ufscar/9374

Bueno, A. H. (2008). *Contribuições do programa de mentoria do portal dos professores-UFSCar: Autoestudo de uma professora iniciante.* Universidade Federal de São Carlos. https://repositorio.ufscar.br/handle/ufscar/2473

Calil, A. M. G. C., & André, M. E. D. A. (2016). Uma política de formação voltada aos professores iniciantes de Sobral—CE. *Revista Diálogo Educacional, 16*(50), 891–909. https://doi.org/10.7213/1981-416X.16.050.DS05

Cardoso, L. C. (2016). *Aprendizagem e desenvolvimento profissional da docência em um espaço híbrido de formação: O terceiro espaço.* Universidade Federal de São Carlos. https://repositorio.ufscar.br/handle/ufscar/7787

Carvalho, B. K. R. de, & Reali, A. M. M. R. (2022). TUTOR EM AÇÃO. *Imagens Da Educação, 12*(3), 80–100. https://doi.org/10.4025/imagenseduc.v12i3.58478

Cesário, P. M. (2021). *Programa híbrido de mentoria: Contribuições para a aprendizagem da docência de professoras iniciantes.* Universidade Federal de São Carlos. https://repositorio.ufscar.br/handle/ufscar/14989

Cole, A. L., & Knowles, J. G. (1993). Teacher development partnership research: A focus on methods and issues. *American Educational Research Journal, 30*(3), 473–495. https://doi.org/10.3102/00028312030003473

Conselho Nacional de Educação. (2015). *Resolução que define as diretrizes curriculares nacionais para a formação inicial em nível superior (cursos de licenciatura, cursos de formação pedagógica para graduados e cursos de segunda licenciatura) e para a formação continuada*. Diário Oficial da União.

Constituição da República Federativa do Brasil de 1988. (1997). Saraiva.

Cruz, E. M. R. (2019). *Professoras experientes e a base de conhecimento para o ensino: Pontas de icebergs*. Universidade Federal de São Carlos. https://repositorio.ufscar.br/handle/ufscar/11234

Cury, C. R. J. (2013). Plano nacional de educação: Questões emblemáticas. In I. R. Pino, D. D. P. e Zan, & A. N. de Souza (Eds.), *Plano nacional da educação (PNE): Questões desafiadoras e embates emblemáticos* (pp. 35–45). INEP.

Fairbanks, C. M., Duffy, G. G., Faircloth, B. S., Ye He, Levin, B., Rohr, J., & Stein, C. (2010). Beyond knowledge: Exploring why some teachers are more thoughtfully adaptive than others. *Journal of Teacher Education, 61*(1–2), 161–171. https://doi.org/10.1177/0022487109347874

Fernandes, F. S., Gimenes, N., Pimenta, C. O., Silva, V. G., & Pereira, R. (2021) Implementação de uma metodologia de formação docente em serviço: O programa de tutoria em Manaus. *Revista Educação e Humanidade, 2*(1), 187–211. https://www.periodicos.ufam.edu.br/index.php/reh/article/view/8505

Ferreira, A. D. P., Calil, A. M. G., Pinto, J. A., & Souza, M. A. (2017). A inserção profissional sob o olhar dos professores iniciantes: Possibilidades de implantação de políticas públicas, *Educação, 40*(3), 431–439. https://doi.org/10.15448/1981-2582.2017.3.26148

Gallavan, N. P. (2015). Mediating the sources and benefits of teacher self-efficacy for systematic transformative meaning-making. In T. Petty, A. Good, & M. Putman (Eds.), *Handbook of research on professional development for quality teaching and learning* (1st ed.; pp. 321–341). IGI Global. https://doi.org/10.4018/978-1-5225-0204-3.ch016

Gatti, B. A., Barreto, E. S. S., & André, M. E. D. A. (2011). *Políticas docentes no Brasil: Um estado da arte*. UNESCO. https://unesdoc.unesco.org/ark:/48223/pf0000212183

Gatti, B. A., Barreto, E. S. S. B, André, M. E. D. A., & Almeida, P. C. A. (2019). *Professores do Brasil: Novos cenários de formação*. UNESCO. https://unesdoc.unesco.org/ark:/48223/pf0000367919

Gobato, P. G. (2020). *Programa de formação online de mentores da UFSCar: Contribuições para o desenvolvimento profissional de professores iniciantes participantes*. Universidade Federal de São Carlos. https://repositorio.ufscar.br/handle/ufscar/13298

Gobato, P. G., & Reali, A. M. de M. R. (2017). A base de conhecimentos e a identidade de mentores participantes do programa de formação online de mentores da UFSCar-Brasil. *Revista Portuguesa De Educação, 30*(2), 133–157. https://doi.org/10.21814/rpe.10844

Grossman P., Wineburg, S., & Woolworth, S. (2000) *What makes teacher community different from a gathering of teachers* [Occasional paper]. Center for the Study of Teaching and Policy. https://www.education.uw.edu/ctp/sites/default/files/ctpmail/PDFs/Community-GWW-01-2001.pdf

Hobson, A. J., Ashby, P., Malderez, A., & Tomlinson, P. D. (2009). Mentoring beginning teachers: What we know and what we don't. *Teaching and Teacher Education, 25*, 207–216.

Horn, I. S., Garner, B., Kane, B. D., & Brasel, J. (2017). A taxonomy of instructional learning opportunities in teachers' workgroup conversations. *Journal of Teacher Education, 68*(1), 41–54. https://doi.org/10.1177/0022487116676315

Indicador de Permanência. (2020). *Em interdisciplinaridade e evidências no debate educacional.* https://www.portaliede.com.br/Wp-Content/Uploads/2021/07/Indicador-De-Permanencia-Escolar_Julho2021.pdf

Instituto Nacional de Estudos E Pesquisas Educacionais Anísio Teixeira. (n.d). *Adequação da formação docente.* Instituto Nacional de Estudos E Pesquisas Educacionais Anísio Teixeira. Retrieved January 25, 2023, from https://www.gov.br/inep/pt-br/acesso-a-informacao/dados-abertos/indicadores-educacionais/adequacao-da-formacao-docente

Kardos, S. M., & Johnson, S. M. (2010). New teachers' experiences of mentoring: The good, the bad, and the inequity. *Journal of Educational Change, 11*, 23–44. https://doi.org/10.1007/s10833-008-9096-4

Kochan, F. (2017). Part 1 The landscape of mentoring: Past, present, and future. In D. A. Clutterbuck, F. Kochan, L. G. Lunsford, J. Haddock-Millar (Eds.), *The Sage handbook of mentoring* (pp. 11–13). SAGE.

Lei 9.394. (1996, December 20). *Estabelece as diretrizes e bases da educação nacional.* Brasil. https://www2.camara.leg.br/legin/fed/lei/1996/lei-9394-20-dezembro-1996-362578-publicacaooriginal-1-pl.html

Lei n.º 10.172. (2001, January 9). *Aprova o plano nacional de educação e dá outras providências.* Brasil. https://www2.camara.leg.br/legin/fed/lei/2001/lei-10172-9-janeiro-2001-359024-publicacaooriginal-1-pl.html

Lei n. °13.005. (2014, June 25). *Aprova o plano nacional de educação—PNE e dá outras providências.* Brasil. https://www2.camara.leg.br/legin/fed/lei/2014/lei-13005-25-junho-2014-778970-publicacaooriginal-144468-pl.html

Mainardes, J. (2006). Abordagem do ciclo de políticas: Uma contribuição para a análise de políticas educacionais. *Educação & Sociedade, 27*(94), 47–69. https://doi.org/10.1590/s0101-73302006000100003

Mainardes, J. (2016). Políticas educacionais contemporâneas e algumas consequências para o trabalho docente. In M. F. Cóssio (Ed.), *Políticas públicas de educação* (pp. 65–80). UFPEL.

Malheiro, C. A. L. (2017). *Mapeamento das necessidades formativas do formador de professores atuante no programa de formação online de mentores.* Universidade Federal de São Carlos. https://repositorio.ufscar.br/handle/ufscar/8957

Marcelo, C., & Vaillant, D. (2017). Políticas e programas de indução na docência na América Latina. *Cadernos De Pesquisa, 47*(166), 1224–1249. https://publicacoes.fcc.org.br/cp/article/view/4322

Massetto, D. C. (2014). *Formação de professores iniciantes: O programa de mentoria online da UFSCar em foco.* Universidade Federal de São Carlos. https://repositorio.ufscar.br/handle/ufscar/2708

Massetto, D. C. (2018). *Experiências emocionais e aprendizagens de mentoras no programa de formação online de mentores.* Universidade Federal de São Carlos. https://repositorio.ufscar.br/handle/ufscar/10143

Migliorança, F. (2010). *Programa de mentoria da UFSCar e desenvolvimento profissional de três professoras iniciantes*. Universidade Federal de São Carlos. https://repositorio.ufscar.br/handle/ufscar/2236

Ministério da Educação. (2018). *Base nacional comum curricular*. http://basenacionalcomum.mec.gov.br/images/BNCC_EI_EF_110518_versaofinal_site.pdf

Ministério da Educação. (2019). *Resolução que define as diretrizes curriculares nacionais para a formação inicial de professores para a educação básica e institui a base nacional comum para a cormação inicial de professores da educação básica*. Ministério da Educação.

Mira, M., & Romanowski, J. P. (2016). Processos de inserção profissional docente nas políticas de formação: O que documentos legais revelam. *Acta Scientiarium, 38*(3), 283–292. https://doi.org/10.4025/actascieduc.v38i3.2764

Mizukami, M. G. N., & Reali, A. M. M. R. (2019). Aprender a ser mentora: um estudo sobre reflexões de professoras experientes e seu desenvolvimento profissional. *Currículo sem Fronteiras, 19*(1), 113–133. https://www.curriculosemfronteiras.org/vol19iss1articles/mizukami-reali.pdf

Mizukami, M. G. N., Tancredi, R. M. S., & Reali, A. M. M. R. (2015). Construction of professional teaching knowledge: Collaboration between experienced primary school teachers and university teachers through an online mentoring program. *Journal of Education for Teaching, 5*, 1–21. https://doi.org/10.1080/02607476.2015.1108626

Murray, J., & Male, T. (2005). Becoming a teacher educator: Evidence from the field. *Teaching and Teacher Education, 21*(2), 125–142. https://doi.org/10.1016/j.tate.2004.12.006

Nascimento, M. G., Flores, M. J. B. P., & Xavier, D. B. (2019). Indução profissional docente: Desafios e tensões no contexto de uma política pública. *Currículo sem Fronteiras, 19*(1), 151–166. https://www.curriculosemfronteiras.org/vol19iss1articles/nascimento-flores-xavier.pdf

Papi, S. O. G., & Martins, P. L. O. (2014). Políticas de descentralização impactam negativamente a aprendizagem de professoras iniciantes. *Linhas Críticas, 20*(42), 421–441. http://educa.fcc.org.br/scielo.php?script=sci_arttext&pid=S1981-04312014000200011&lng=pt&tlng=pt.

Pérez Gómez, Á. I. (2019). Ser docente en tiempos de incertidumbre y perplejidad. *Márgenes Revista de Educación de la Universidad de Málaga, (0)*(0), 3–17. http://doi.org/10.24310/mgnmar.v0i0.6497

Pieri, G. S. (2010). *Experiências de ensino e aprendizagem: Estratégia para a formação online de professores iniciantes no programa de mentoria da UFSCar*. Universidade Federal de São Carlos. https://repositorio.ufscar.br/handle/ufscar/2523

Pinheiro, T. S. (2020). *Elementos da constituição da identidade docente de professoras iniciantes da educação infantil e do ensino fundamental—Anos iniciais*. Universidade Federal de São Carlos. https://repositorio.ufscar.br/handle/ufscar/12387

Reali, A. M. M. R. (2004). *A participação em um grupo de pesquisa como ferramenta de aprendizagem profissional da docência para professores experientes: O caso do programa de mentoria da UFSCar*. Projeto de pesquisa.

Reali, A. M. M. R. (2012). *Formação online de mentoras: Base de conhecimentos—Identidade profissional—Práticas*. Projeto de Pesquisa.

Reali, A. M. M. R. (2016). *Desenvolvimento profissional docente de professores experientes e iniciantes: Programa híbrido de mentoria*. Projeto de Pesquisa.
Reali, A. M. de M. R., Massetto, D. C, Gobato, P. G., Borges, F. V. A. (2017). A construção da identidade de uma mentora: o Programa de Formação Online de Mentores em foco. *Práxis Educativa, 13*(2), 330–347. https://doi.org/10.5212/PraxEduc.v.13i2.0005
Reali, A. M. M. R., Souza, A. P. P. G., & Barros, B. B. C. (2020). O WhatsApp na formação de professores iniciantes no programa híbrido de mentoria da UFSCar. *Revista da FAEEBA–Educação e Contemporaneidade, 29(58)*, 344–257. https://doi.org/10.21879/faeeba2358-0194.2020.v29.n58.p344-3
Reali, A. M. M. R., Tancredi, R. M. S. P., & Mizukami, M. G. N. (2008). Programa de mentoria online: Espaço para o desenvolvimento profissional de professoras iniciantes e experientes. *Educação e Pesquisa, 34*(1), 77–95. https://doi.org/10.1590/s1517-97022008000100006
Reali, A. M. M. R., Tancredi, R. M. S. P., & Mizukami, M. G. N. (2010). Programa de mentoria online para professores iniciantes: Cases de um processo. *Cadernos de Pesquisa, 40*, 479–506. https://doi.org/10.1590/S0100-15742010000200009
Roggero, R., & Zanini da Silva, A. (2021). A disputa dos recursos públicos da educação básica, os arranjos do estado com o mercado e seus impactos na gestão democrática e participativa da educação no âmbito dos municípios. *EccoS—Revista Científica, 0*(58), e20847. https://doi.org/10.5585/eccos.n58.20847
Shulman, L. (1987). Knowledge and teaching: Foundations of the new reform. *Harvard Educational Review, 57*(1), 1–23. https://doi.org/10.17763/haer.57.1.j463w79r56455411
Souza, A. P. G., & Reali, A. M. M. R. (2022). Construção de práticas pedagógicas na educação básica em tempos de pandemia. *Práxis Educacional, 18*(49). e9099. https://doi.org/10.22481/praxisedu.v18i49.9099
Souza, A. P. G., Reali, A. M. de M. R., Barros, B. C. de, & Anunciato, R. M. M. (2019). Formação e aprendizagens de mentoras iniciantes em um programa de indução à docência. *Imagens da Educação, 9*(2), 141–156. https://doi.org/10.4025/imagenseduc.v9i2.46711
Tancredi, R. M. S. P., & Reali, A. M. M. R. (2003). *Programa de mentoria para professores das séries iniciais: Implementando e avaliando um contínuo de aprendizagem docente*. Projeto de Pesquisa.
Timperley, H. (2001). Mentoring conversations designed to promote student-teacher learning. *Asia-Pacific Journal of Teacher Education, 29*(2), 111–123. https://doi.org/10.1080/13598660120061309
Vaughan, N. D. (2010). A blended community of inquiry approach: Linking student engagement and course redesign. *The Internet and Higher Education, 13*(1–2), 60–65. https://doi.org/10.1016/j.iheduc.2009.10.007
Wang, J. (2019). Teacher mentoring in service of beginning teachers' learning to teach critical review of conceptual and empirical literature. In S. J. Zepeda & J. A. Ponticell (Eds.), *The Wiley handbook of educational supervision* (pp. 281–306). Wiley.
Zeichner, K. (2010). Rethinking the connections between campus courses and field experiences in college-and university-based teacher education. *Journal of Teacher Education, 61*(1–2), pp. 89–99. https://doi.org/10.1177/0022487109347671

CHAPTER 11

NEWLY QUALIFIED TEACHERS AND THEIR SUPPORT IN FINLAND

Vilhelmiina Harju
University of Helsinki

Hannele Niemi
University of Helsinki

ABSTRACT

In Finland, new teacher induction is often project-based, and its organization is the responsibility of education providers and schools. Although early-career support has been emphasized in educational policy discussions, Finland still has no official nationwide policy or guidelines for teacher induction. This chapter introduces the main features of the Finnish education system and new teachers' role as fully qualified professionals in it. It also presents two mentoring cases developed to support new teachers in the induction phase. The chapter concludes by discussing actions that should be considered to offer meaningful nationwide support systems for newly qualified teachers.

This chapter discusses the situation of newly qualified teachers in Finland and the actions taken to help them during the first year of their careers. We begin by describing the key characteristics of the Finnish educational system and the contexts in which new teachers teach after graduation. The focus is especially on teachers in elementary schools and those subject teachers in lower and upper secondary schools. Afterward, we discuss teacher education policy for newly qualified teachers, common induction practices, and plans to support early-career teachers in Finland. In particular, two initiatives on early-career support are introduced: mandatory job orientation and the Teacher Education Forum's initiatives for supporting career-long professional development. Then, we introduce two cases of support activities, peer-group mentoring and mentors' training for the one-on-one mentoring model piloted to facilitate new teachers' professional development. We conclude by highlighting the factors to be considered for successful teacher induction and discussing the need for further research on this topic.

EDUCATION SYSTEM AND TEACHERS IN FINLAND

Teacher education in Finland aims to prepare prospective teachers for a high-standard professional role with much autonomy and many fundamental professional responsibilities, including pedagogical activities and supporting students' learning, collaborating with different partners in the school community, and developing one's work and the school community (Harju, 2020). All primary and secondary school teachers must attend a 5-year teacher education program at the university, which has a relatively long history dating back to 1979 when a master's level degree was required for teacher qualifications (Niemi & Lavonen, 2020).

Finnish teacher education has received much international attention because of Finnish students' high learning achievements in the Programme for International Students Assessment (PISA) measurements. One of the major reasons for high learning outcomes is Finnish teachers' high competencies and strong commitment to the teaching profession (Darling-Hammond, 2010; Sahlberg, 2015; Välijärvi et al., 2002).

Teaching is a much sought-after career in Finland, and teacher education programs attract motivated candidates to become teachers. High-quality applicants seek entrance to university-level teacher education every year, and competition is high. For example, in spring 2020, only 16% of applicants were admitted to primary teacher education programs (Finnish National Agency for Education, 2021). The number of teachers admitted to the programs is based on systematic national forecasting of teacher supply and demand. Even though universities are autonomous in student selection, they agree with the Ministry of Education and Culture about a quota regarding teacher education degrees. Over 95% of basic and upper secondary school teachers are fully qualified, and retention in a teaching career is high (European Commission/EACEA/Eurydice, 2021; Finnish National Agency for Education, 2021). The number of teachers leaving the profession is small compared to many other countries, and most teachers working in Finland enjoy and continue their work (OECD, 2014, 2019; Paronen & Lappi, 2018). One reason for the high retention is teachers' high professional role and freedom of work (Jokinen et al., 2013).

The high professional status, good reputation of teacher education programs, and high student learning outcomes might cause the low interest in developing induction activities and explain why Finland has not launched a national induction program (Bjerkholt & Hedegaard, 2008). According to Heikkinen et al. (2020), the general discussion in teacher education has focused on developing teacher education towards career-long professional development rather than easing the potential challenges faced at the beginning of their career.

However, there have been continuous policy-level discussions about mentoring and systematic induction programs for new teachers (Ministry of Education and Culture, 2016; Niemi et al., 2007). The discussions stem from the political initiatives of the European Commission (1995, 2010), in which mentoring for beginning teachers has been promoted. However, these discussions have focused on the teachers' professional role, administration issues, and financial responsibilities for teacher induction in the Finnish educational system.

Overall, teachers in Finland are highly selective, with few teacher shortage issues. They also receive a 5-year teacher preparation that focuses on developing their professional autonomy in making important decisions and shouldering professional responsibilities regarding what and how to teach. Teachers' autonomy and professional agency are central to Finland students' high performance. In contrast, teacher induction activities have not yet been identified as an issue in improving teachers' work. However, policy discussions of teacher induction emerge around offering mentoring to beginning teachers resulting from the political initiatives of the European Commission.

BEGINNING TEACHERS FACE HIGH PROFESSIONAL DEMANDS

Like many other countries, Finland has experienced social changes, such as increasing multiculturalism and growing school segregation, at least in the largest Finnish cities (Bernelius et al., 2021). It has also legislated inclusion policy to promote equity and inclusion in different levels of the Finnish educational system: Schools need to include students with special needs in mainstream schooling and provide free and high-quality education to all children regardless of their residence, schools, and parents' wealth (Niemi & Isopahkala-Bouret, 2012). In addition, a new understanding of learning has been developed and spread, emphasizing learner-centered education, learning transversal competencies, and enhancing the joy of learning (Finnish National Board of Education, 2016). Schools need to promote the holistic well-being and personal growth of all students (Tirri, 2011), and teachers must develop student-centered and mixed-ability group instruction to facilitate meaningful and different kinds of learning in heterogeneous classrooms (Toom & Husu, 2016).

These social changes, relevant legislation, and new understandings affect the demands of the teaching profession and require diverse competence from a teacher. In Finland, the teaching profession is highly independent and autonomous, and teachers have the freedom to choose the ways they implement teaching and learning activities within the frameworks of national and local curricula (Vahtivuori-Hänninen et al., 2014). It can make the professional requirements overwhelming, especially for newly qualified teachers. Until 1985, beginning teachers in Finland received 2-year probation after their master's level teacher preparation programs before assuming official teaching duty. After graduating from teacher education programs, beginning teachers are fully licensed and expected to independently carry out all the responsibilities on the first day as experienced teachers (Heikkinen et al., 2020). The underlying assumption is that the long teacher preparation, such as the five-year program leading to a master's degree, would develop teachers' great teacher autonomy in teaching and help beginning teachers meet the high requirements and expectations for effective teaching in emerging school contexts.

However, this assumption faces a serious challenge. For example, the researchers (Harju, 2020; Harju & Niemi, 2018) found that despite basic teaching competencies or content knowledge, beginning teachers were found to demand support in several areas, some directly related to the emerging demands. For example, how to help individual students learn, deal with their socio-emotional problems, manage conflict situations, develop local curriculum, collaborate with colleagues and other partners, and become familiar with the administration and contexts of the school community. Researchers (Geeraerts et al., 2015; Harju & Niemi, 2018; Jokinen et al., 2008) also found that beginning teachers need the support to develop the above competencies over a long period using various processes of professional development in addition to their teacher education programs.

In short, societal changes and the relevant registrations demand teachers develop new responsibilities and competencies for promoting the holistic well-being and personal growth of all students, including those from different cultural backgrounds and those with special education needs in their classrooms. However, teacher education, professional autonomy, and agency are insufficient for beginning teachers to carry out their new responsibilities and develop relevant competencies. To develop these competencies, beginning teachers need to be engaged in various professional development processes over a long period.

POLICY INITIATIVES AND CONTRADICTIONS

Despite the recognized needs during the induction phase, most beginning teachers did not receive formal and informal induction training in their school contexts. The latest Teaching and Learning International Survey ([TALIS]; OECD, 2019) shows that only 18% of beginning teachers in Finland's lower secondary schools participated in a formal induction program. In contrast, about 70% of teachers reported not attending induction activities (Taajamo & Puhakka, 2019).

Finland still lacks systematic support and formal nationwide policy initiatives that guide the development and implementation of teacher induction programs for newly qualified teachers. However, several themes emerge from the teacher induction policy discussions. These themes include teacher induction administration and finance, beginning teachers' job orientation, and teachers' in-service training as a career-long process.

Teacher Induction Administration and Finance

The Finnish educational system has become highly decentralized from the late 1980s onward, in which any central control of school administration was gradually diminished (Antikainen & Pitkänen, 2014; Vainikainen et al., 2017). The Ministry of Education and Culture only defines education policy in the current situation, while the Finnish National Agency for Education is responsible for national core curriculum development. Finland has not, for example, had a school inspection as an instrument for educational evaluation since the end of the 1980s (Aho et al., 2006). The national government supports schools only through a minor portion of its budget, mainly for infrastructure, special needs services, and special programs.

In turn, local authorities and education providers, municipalities, and schools are responsible for developing detailed curricula that consider local contexts and deliver the quality of school education (Vahtivuori-Hänninen et al., 2014). A municipality, such as a city, is also responsible for financing and administering educational services, teacher employment, induction, in-service training, working conditions, and well-being. Municipals are independent agencies that traditionally do not favor a national mandatory induction system because of their local differences and the induction costs. Preservice teacher education is funded directly from the Ministry of Education and Culture to universities, but municipalities get local taxes. (European Commission/EACEA/Eurydice, 2022) There exists a continuous debate about who should be responsible for teacher induction expenses at the national level, which has not been resolved by the main actors—the Ministry of Education and Culture, the Ministry of Employment, the employer's unions, and the teacher's trade union (Niemi et al., 2018).

In practice, universities can sell induction services. Many universities and municipalities develop mutual agreements regarding induction programs as part of in-service training in a case-by-case manner (Heikkinen et al., 2020). Over the past years, other actors, such as the Trade Union of Education in Finland, have provided induction programs (Trade Union of Education in Finland, 2021a). Unfortunately, these efforts are typical for project-based reforms, not fully integrated with the schools' activities, and often end after the funding stops.

Beginning Teachers' Job Orientation

In Finland, regardless of the sector, employers must provide a job orientation to all new employees as required by the Occupational Safety and Health Act (Finlex, 2002). A teacher will have a job orientation when entering a new school, sometimes understood as support activities organized for newly qualified teachers. According to the TALIS report (OECD, 2019), in Finland, the most common support for new teachers is job orientation, which includes a general administrative introduction, planned meetings with the principal or experienced teachers, and networking with other beginning teachers.

The Finnish Occupational Safety and Health Act (Finlex, 2002) requires an employer to familiarize a teacher with the school's practices, requirements, and procedures. More specifically, as stated by the Trade Union of Education in Finland (2021b), the main contents of the orientation should include (a) teacher employment and workplace organization, such as salary, working time, organizational and team structure, and occupational health care; (b) legislation and different policies that guide the work; and (c) security and well-being, such as safety instructions and procedures for possible threats and violence.

In addition, job orientation also informs many practical issues to ensure that teachers know their workplace practices and guidelines procedures. These include job responsibilities, work environment, equipment and materials, student groups, collaboration, interprofessional cooperation, and student welfare services (Trade Union of Education in Finland, 2021b). It can also include a teacher development plan, which enhances teachers' professional growth and helps them be aware of the goals and values of their employer and how cooperation in the school community is implemented and supported (Niemi et al., 2018).

In practice, beginning teachers' job orientation can be organized in multiple ways. In some schools, the principal conducts the orientation for new teachers. In others, some teachers are responsible for familiarizing the teachers with their new job (Trade Union of Education in Finland, 2021b). Even though the job orientation can include several elements important for teacher induction activities that support beginning teachers, it is often a short program. In some schools, it only lasts a few hours.

The job orientation itself does not completely meet the definition of teacher induction, which focuses more on professional learning processes (Feiman-Nemser et al., 1999; Olsen et al., 2020). It does not consist of core processes essential in teacher development, such as identity formation, sharing experiences and reflections, and interacting with the school community as identified in the literature (Aspfors, 2012; Eisenschmidt & Oder, 2018; Feiman-Nemser, 2001). However, these dimensions of professional learning have become a part of policy discussions regarding teacher induction. For example, the Finnish Trade Union of Education in Finland (2021b) stressed that new teachers' challenges are often complex and need professional support.

Beginning Teachers in Inservice Training

While widely recognized as important in Finland, teachers' in-service training has been criticized for its variety and fragmentation between municipalities from a career-long perspective (European Commission/EACEA/Eurydice, 2021). Research (FNAE, 2021; Kola-Torvinen & Kumpulainen, 2020) also suggested that early-career teachers were less likely to participate in in-service training in Finland because it may not meet their needs. However, more experienced teachers and principals were more likely to do so.

Consequently, teachers' career-long professional development has recently been sought nationally. For example, in 2016, the Ministry of Education and Culture established the Teacher Education Forum to develop teacher education for the future. The Forum organized national conferences and invited stakeholders, such as researchers, teacher educators, municipalities, teachers' and student teachers' trade unions, to discuss teacher education.

The first task of the Forum was to set future objectives for teacher education (Ministry of Education and Culture, 2021). One of the most important objectives of the future program was to bring together initial teacher education, teacher induction, and teacher in-service training to create a needs-based and goal-oriented entity that supports the development of teachers' competencies. In this objective, teacher induction is not a separate issue but is regarded as part of in-service training.

At the moment, the work of the Teacher Education Forum is ongoing. It has funded 45 research and development projects, including some focusing on teacher induction aligned with its objective as coordinated by higher education institutions in different parts of Finland (Ministry of Education and Culture, 2021). The Finnish Education Evaluation Center was commissioned to conduct an external evaluation of the work of the Teacher Education Forum between 2016 and 2018, focusing on the continuum between pre-and in-service training and the place of induction (Niemi et al., 2018).

The evaluation report highlighted two essential features as important in building the national induction structure: integrating induction and in-service training into preservice teacher education and developing municipalities' educational plans (Niemi et al., 2018). Finnish National Agency for Education, FNAE, has proposed to use development plans to ensure support for teachers, including beginning teachers, to identify their strengths and set targets for developing their competence (Paronen & Lappi, 2018).

In short, teacher induction practices in Finland are decentralized, fragmented, and short. Most of these practices are focused on understanding the procedures, policies, and contexts of teaching, such as job orientation. They are also part of inservice professional development with little attention to the specific needs of beginning teachers. These situations drive national efforts to bring initial teacher education, induction, and in-service training. Beginning teachers' needs are specifically addressed in a needs-based and goal-oriented manner.

TWO CASES OF BEGINNING TEACHER MENTORING

This section reports two cases based on the beginning of teacher mentoring in Finland, focusing on peer-group mentoring and the other on one-on-one mentoring through mentor training.

Case of Peer-Group Mentoring

Peer-group mentoring is a professional development method based on collaborative learning, dialogue, and knowledge sharing (Geeraerts et al., 2015). Since 2010, the Ministry of Education and Culture in Finland has funded peer-group mentoring projects nationwide that have involved teachers and educational staff from different levels of the education system (Tynjälä et al., 2019).

The Finnish Network organizes training of mentors of peer-group mentoring for Peer-Group Mentoring that involves all Finnish teacher education institutions. In practice, peer-group mentoring is offered to teachers by different educational providers, usually municipalities, and the group meetings are organized and facilitated by trained teacher mentors. Each mentoring group involves about four to eight teachers, who meet once a month to discuss their everyday work and the possible challenges in their daily work. The groups work autonomously, and the members decide the topics for group discussions, the rules of the meetings, and the schedule. It is worth noting that the teachers involved in peer-group mentoring are not necessarily beginning teachers. Instead, it is up to education providers to decide who is offered mentoring. Teachers that join peer-group mentoring groups can, for example, come from one or different schools, teach the same or different subjects, or be in the same or different career phase (Tynjälä et al., 2019).

Previous studies (Geeraerts et al., 2015; Tynjälä et al., 2019) have indicated that peer and group mentoring offered professional, personal, and social support to participating teachers and influenced the development of their working community. Peer and group mentoring have also been reported to improve teachers' self-confidence and sense of agency, enhance their professional identity development, and influence their motivation for teaching and well-being as teachers (Tynjälä et al., 2019).

Case of One-on-One Mentoring

Funded by the Finnish National Agency for Education, the mentor–novice mentoring project (Niemi, 2017) was implemented from 2011 to 2013. The project was conducted at the University of Helsinki to build meaningful support activities for early-career teachers through mentoring and, thus, improve their students' learning and well-being. The project modified the mentoring program developed by the New Teacher Centre in California (Lieberman et al., 2012; Moir et al., 2009; Moir & Gless, 2009) and adapted it to the Finnish educational context. The key aim was to explore and create a meaningful model for induction and mentoring training.

In the project, 13 experienced Finnish teachers and the project leader visited the New Teacher Centre to understand how to train high-quality mentors. After that, back in Finland, the 13 teachers attended a mentoring training offered by the university's teacher educators. This training lasted about one and a half years (2011–2013) and was based on the core ideas of New Teacher Centre mentoring. In 2013, the project group members published a handbook (Niemi & Siljander, 2013) describing mentor training, relevant structures, and the administrative practices of induction.

In the mentor–novice mentoring project, a mentor and a beginning teacher were recommended to meet regularly to help the beginning teacher develop the tools and practices that help manage their work all year round and ensure high-quality instruction for all students. Together, they plan how frequently they meet, how often the mentor visits the beginning teacher and observes student learning in the classrooms, and the tools the beginning teacher uses to document their and their students' learning. The project also recommended that the mentors' training program have at least five ECTS (European Credit Transfer System) points, which means about 140 hours of studying on the mentor's part and includes five intensive days over 1–1.5 years. The mentoring training should include themes of mentors' professional growth, identity, and roles; new teachers' needs and support for their professional development; the ethics of mentoring and guidance, especially confidentiality in mentors' work; communication, principles of dialogue, active listening dialogue and the language of mentoring; and tools for e-mentoring and documentation.

Drawing on the interview data from 13 mentor teachers, the authors (Niemi & Siljander, 2013) described the project's effects on the beginning teachers. The analysis revealed that the mentoring developed in the project was described to improve the well-being of beginning teachers and their students. It also indicated that mentors supported their novices in playing roles in the school community and working with parents and other interest groups. It further showed that mentors helped their novices develop their pedagogies by using students' cultural backgrounds as a resource. However, the effects of such mentoring on beginning teachers' instruction, as expected by the emerging demands, is still a question worth further examining.

Although different in their mentoring approaches, both presented mentoring methods (Niemi, 2017, pp. 14–15; Tynjälä et al., 2019) followed national agreements on the role of induction in professional development. They received funding to compensate for participating mentors, support project development and management, and time and space for the project implementations. As a result, both have positively impacted beginning teachers' well-being and agency in teaching and learning to teach. However, their effects on new teachers' instruction and student learning outcomes, as expected, are yet to be established.

CONCLUSIONS AND IMPLICATIONS

In conclusion, teachers in Finland were selective and received long university-level initial teacher preparation, which leaves no issue of teacher shortage.

Their strong autonomy in teaching decisions and agency in taking professional classroom responsibilities also contribute to their high student performance. In addition, the central government traditionally plays a limited role in education administration, curriculum, and finance. These factors shape the characteristics of teacher induction practices in Finland as decentralized, fragmented, short, and less focused on the needs of beginning teachers.

While enabling versatile induction activities based on local contexts and needs, the Finnish decentralized education system lacks coherent guidelines for teacher induction. Beginning teachers often access unequal amounts and quality of induction support. Thus, a national policy for developing and implementing induction programs can be useful to ensure all early-career teachers receive coherent induction support equally. Such a national policy can be especially necessary for supporting beginning teachers to develop new responsibilities and competencies as expected by the social changes and the relevant legislation (Fresko & Nasser-Abu Alhija, 2015; Heikonen et al., 2017).

This policy has become focused policy discussions at the national level (Heikkinen et al., 2020; Niemi et al., 2018; Niemi, 2017), which started to generate initial project-based efforts to transform teacher education, induction, and development (Ministry of Education and Culture, 2016, 2021). While important for creating good induction scenarios and developing new knowledge about teacher induction, the different projects alone cannot meet the need for induction activities on a larger scale. As a result, four important recommendations emerge from this analysis.

First, the framework and guidelines for teacher induction should be negotiated and agreed upon at the national level by different actors, including the Ministry of Education and Culture, the Finnish National Agency of Education, municipal authorities, the Trade Union of Education in Finland, and teacher education departments of different universities. The meaningful induction activities must be developed, implemented, and monitored by national and local administrations following the agreed framework and guidelines.

Second, a coherent yet needs-based continuum of teacher professional development needs to be established structurally between initial teacher education, induction, and in-service training stages. Again, a more constructive collaboration between different actors is needed in coordinating the activities within and across different stages of teacher development. In this way, the overall national objectives for teachers' work and the particular needs of beginning teachers, local curriculum changes, and students' learning can be appropriated in the continuum.

Third, the ultimate goal of teacher induction is to help beginning teachers offer high-quality instruction to all students as expected. Thus, meaningful induction activities must improve teachers' instruction, agency, and well-being to reach this goal. Such improvement, in turn, will increase students' well-being and learning outcomes. Consequently, these induction activities should be developed based on the needs of individual teachers by considering the individual school contexts and needs (Eisenschmidt et al., 2013; Harju, 2020; Livingston, 2017).

Finally, the nationwide or mandatory local induction activities require funding as support, and pilot induction projects often stop when funding ends (Heikkinen et al., 2020; Niemi, 2017). Thus, the national government and local administration need to generate sufficient and stable resources to develop specific guidelines and activities and sustain the efforts in integrating successful projects into a natural part of teachers' professional learning. Such resources are also necessary to support school principals and management create positive learning environments and supportive activities in specific school contexts (Aspfors & Bondas, 2013; Klages et al., 2020).

Future research and policymakers should focus on finding concrete, workable solutions to make induction a permanent and meaningful part of Finland's teacher education and career-long professional development. In developing these solutions, some important questions remain: (a) "What roles should different actors play in organizing teachers' career-long professional development?" (These actors are the Ministry of Education and Culture, the Finnish National Agency of Education, municipal authorities, schools, the Trade Union of Education in Finland, and universities); (b) "What are the goals of induction, and who determines them?" (c) "How is induction funded to become an appropriate way to support the professional development of teachers?"

REFERENCES

Aho, E., Pitkänen, K., & Sahlberg, P. (2006). *Policy development and reform principles of basic and secondary education in Finland since 1968*. The World Bank.

Antikainen, A., & Pitkänen, A. (2014): A history of educational reforms in Finland. In R. R. Verdugo (Ed.), *Educational reform in Europe: History, culture, and ideology* (pp. 1–24). Information Age Publishing.

Aspfors, J. (2012). *Induction practices. Experiences of newly qualified teachers* [Unpublished doctoral dissertation]. Åbo Akademi University. https://www.doria.fi/bitstream/handle/10024/85054/aspfors_jessica.pdf?sequence=2&isAllowed=y

Aspfors, J., & Bondas, T. (2013). Caring about caring: Newly qualified teachers' experiences of their relationships within the school community. *Teachers and Teaching, 19*(3), 243–259.

Bernelius, V., Huilla, H., & Ramos Lobato, I. (2021). 'Notorious schools' in 'notorious places'? Exploring the connectedness of urban and educational segregation. *Social Inclusion, 9*(2), 154–165.

Bjerkholt, E., & Hedegaard, E. (2008). Systems promoting new teachers' professional development. In G. Fransson & C. Gustafsson (Eds.), *Newly qualified*

teachers in Northern Europe—Comparative perspectives on promoting professional development (pp. 45–75). University of Gävle.
Darling-Hammond, L. (2010). *The flat world and education. How can America's commitment to equity will determine our future?* Teachers College Press.
Eisenschmidt, E., & Oder, T. (2018). Does mentoring matter? On the way to collaborative school culture. *Educational Process: International Journal, 7*(1), 7–23.
Eisenschmidt, E., Oder, T., & Reiska, E. (2013). The Induction program: Teachers' experience after five years of practice. *Mentoring & Tutoring: Partnership in Learning, 21*(3), 241–257.
European Commission. (1995). *White paper on education and training: Teaching and learning: Towards the learning society*. Publications Office of the European Union. http://aei.pitt.edu/1132/1/education_train_wp_COM_95_590.pdf
European Commission. (2010). *Developing coherent and system-wide induction programmes for beginning teachers: A handbook for policymakers*. Publications Office of the European Union. https://ec.europa.eu/assets/eac/education/experts-groups/2011-2013/teacher/teachercomp_en.pdf
European Commission/EACEA/Eurydice (2021). *Finland. Teachers and education staff*. https://eacea.ec.europa.eu/national-policies/eurydice/content/teachers-and-education-staff-24_en
European Commission/EACEA/Eurydice. (2022). *Administration and governance at local and/or institutional level*. https://eacea.ec.europa.eu/national-policies/eurydice/finland/administration-and-governance-local-andor-institutional-level_en
Feiman-Nemser, S. (2001). From preparation to practice: Designing a continuum to strengthen and sustain teaching. *Teachers College Record, 103*(6), 1013–1055.
Feiman-Nemser, S., Carver, C., Schwille, S., &Yusko, B. (1999). *A conceptual review of literature on new teachers' induction*. National Partnership for Excellence and Accountability in Teaching. https://files.eric.ed.gov/fulltext/ED449147.pdf
Finlex. (2002). *Occupational safety and health act*, 738/2002. Finland's Ministry of Justice. https://www.finlex.fi/en/laki/kaannokset/2002/en20020738_20060053.pdf
Finnish National Agency for Education. (2021). *Teachers and principals in Finland 2019*. https://www.oph.fi/sites/default/files/documents/Teachers%20and%20principals%20in%20Finland%202019.pdf
Finnish National Board of Education. (2016). *New national core curriculum for basic education: focus on school culture and integrative approach*. https://www.oph.fi/en/statistics-and-publications/publications/new-national-core-curriculum-basic-education-focus-school
Fresko, B., & Nasser-Abu Alhija, F. (2015). Induction seminars as professional learning communities for beginning teachers. *Asia-Pacific Journal of Teacher Education, 43*(1), 36–48. https://doi.org/10.1080/1359866X.2014.928267
Geeraerts, K., Tynjälä, P., Heikkinen, H. L. T., Markkanen, I., Pennanen, M., & Gijbels, D. (2015). Peer-group mentoring as a tool for teacher development. *European Journal of Teacher Education, 38*(3), 358–377. https://doi.org/10.1080/02619768.2014.983068
Harju, V. (2020). *Beginning teachers' support needs for professional development* [Unpublished doctoral dissertation]. University of Helsinki. http://urn.fi/URN:ISBN:978-951-51-6813-9

Harju, V., & Niemi, H. (2018). Teachers' changing work and support needs from the perspectives of school leaders and newly qualified teachers in the Finnish context. *European Journal of Teacher Education 41*(5), 670–687.

Heikkinen, H. L. T., Pennanen, M., Markkanen, I., & Tynjälä, P. (2020). A brief history of the peer-group mentoring model in Finland: Struggling for space in a contested niche. In K.-R. Olsen, E. M. Bjerkholt, & H. L. T. Heikkinen (Eds.), *New teachers in Nordic countries—Ecologies of mentoring and induction* (pp. 107–128). Cappelen Damm Akademisk/NOASP.

Heikonen, L., Pietarinen, J., Pyhältö, K., Toom, A., & Soini, T. (2017). Early career teachers' sense of professional agency in the classroom: Associations with turnover intentions and perceived inadequacy in teacher-student interaction. *Asia-Pacific Journal of Teacher Education, 45*(3), 250–266.

Jokinen, H., Morberg, Å., Poom-Valickis, K., & Rohtma, V. (2008). Mentoring newly qualified teachers in Estonia, Finland, and Sweden. In G. Fransson & C. Gustafsson (Eds.), *Newly qualified teachers in Northern Europe. Comparative perspectives on promoting professional development* (pp. 77–106). University of Gävle.

Jokinen, H., Taajamo, M., Miettinen, M., Weissmann, K., Honkimäki, S., Valkonen, S., & Välijärvi, J. (2013). *Pedagoginen asiantuntijuus liikkeessä—hankkeen tulokset.* (Results from the project Pedagoginen asiantunti—juus liikkeessä) University of Jyväskylä: Finnish Institute for Educational Research. Retrieved from https://jyx.jyu.fi/bitstream/handle/123456789/42778/978-951-39-5557-1.pdf?sequence=1&isAl-lowed=y

Klages, W., Lundstedt, M., & Sundar, P. R. (2020). Mentoring of newly qualified teachers in early childhood education and care centres. Individual or organizational orientation? *International Journal of Mentoring and Coaching in Education, 9*(1), 103–118.

Kola-Torvinen, P., & Kumpulainen, T. (2020). *Opettajat ja rehtorit Suomessa 2019. Opettajien osallistuminen jatko- ja täydennyskoulutukseen, asiantuntijavaihtoon sekä työelämäjaksoille* (Reports 2019: Teachers and principals in Finland 2019). Finnish National Board of Education. Retrieved from https://www.oph.fi/sites/default/files/documents/opettajat_ja_rehtorit_suomessa_2019_opettajien_osallistuminen_jatko_ja_taydennyskoulutukseen_asiantuntijavaihtoon_seka_tyoelamajaksoille.pdf

Lieberman, A., Hanson, S., & Gless, J. (2012). *Mentoring teachers. Navigating the real-world tensions.* New Teacher Center and Jossey-Bass.

Livingston, K. (2017). The complexity of learning and teaching: Challenges for teacher education. *European Journal of Teacher Education, 40*(2), 141–143.

Ministry of Education and Culture. (2016). *Teacher education development programme.* https://minedu.fi/documents/1410845/4183002/Teacher+Education+Development+Programme+2016

Ministry of Education and Culture. (2021). *Opettajankoulutusfoorumi uudistaa opettajankoulutusta (The Teacher Education Forum is reforming teacher education).* https://minedu.fi/opettajankoulutusfoorumi

Moir, E., Barlin, D., Gless, J., & Miles, J. (2009). *New teacher mentoring. Hopes and promise for improving teacher effectiveness.* Harvard Education Press.

Moir, E., & Gless, J. (2009). Quality induction: An Investment in teachers. *Teacher Education Quarterly, 28*(1), 109–114.

Niemi, H. (2017). Towards induction: Training mentors for new teachers in Finland. In B. Hudson (Ed.), *Overcoming fragmentation in teacher education policy and practice* (pp. 49–72). Cambridge University Press.

Niemi, H., Erma, T., Lipponen, L., Pietilä, M., Rintala, R., Ruokamo, H., Saarivirta, T., Moitus, S., Frisk, T., Stylman, V., & Huhtanen, M. (2018). *Maailman parhaiksi opettajiksi – Vuosina 2016–2018 toimineen Opettajankoulutusfoorumin arviointi. (The world's most competent teachers—Evaluation of the teacher education forum in 2016–2018.)* Finnish Education Evaluation Centre.

Niemi, H., Hansen, S.-E., Jakku-Sihvonen, R., & Välijärvi, J. (2007). *Opettajankoulutus 2020* (Teacher education 2020). Ministry of Education and Culture. http://urn.fi/URN:ISBN:978-952-485-432-0

Niemi, H., & Isopahkala-Bouret, U. (2012). Lifelong learning in Finnish society—An analysis of national policy documents. *International Journal of Continuing Education and Lifelong Learning*, 5(1), 43–63.

Niemi, H., & Lavonen, J. (2020). Teacher education in Finland: Persistent efforts for high-quality teachers. In L. Lefty & J. Fraser (Eds.), *Teaching the world's teachers* (pp. 153–178). Johns Hopkins University Press.

Niemi, H., & Siljander, A. M. (2013). *Uuden opettajan mentorointi. Mentoroinnilla oppilaan ja opettajan hyvinvointiin* [New teacher mentoring. Towards students' and teachers' wellbeing through mentoring]. Palmenia Centre for Continuing Education. University of Helsinki.

OECD. (2014). *TALIS 2013 results: An international perspective on teaching and learning*. OECD Publishing. http://doi.org/10.1787/9789264196261-en

OECD. (2019). *TALIS 2018 results (Volume I): Teachers and school leaders as lifelong learners*. OECD Publishing. https://doi.org/10.1787/1d0bc92a-en

Olsen, K.-R., Bjerkholt, E. M., & Heikkinen, H. L. T. (2020). Introduction: Mentoring and induction in the Nordic countries. In K.-R. Olsen, E. M. Bjerkholt, & H. L. T. Heikkinen (Eds.), *New teachers in Nordic countries—Ecologies of mentoring and induction* (pp. 11–26). Cappelen Damm Akademisk/NOASP.

Paronen, P., & Lappi, O. (2018). *Finnish teachers and principals in figures*. Finnish National Agency for Education. https://www.oph.fi/sites/default/files/documents/finnish_teachers_and_principals_in_figures.pdf

Sahlberg, P. (2015). *Finnish lessons. What can the world learn from educational change in Finland* (2nd ed.). Teachers College Press.

Taajamo, M., & Puhakka, E. (2019). Opetuksen ja oppimisen kansainvälinen tutkimus TALIS 2018. *Perusopetuksen vuosiluokkien 7–9 ensituloksia, osa 1* (Teaching and Learning International Survey TALIS 2018. First results of basic education Grades 7–9, Part 1). Raportit ja selvitykset 2019:8. The Finnish National Agency of Education. Retrieved from https://www.oph.fi/fi/tilastot-ja-julkaisut/julkaisut/opetuksen-ja-op- pimisen-kansainvalinen-tutkimus-talis-2018

Tirri, K. (2011). Holistic school pedagogy and values: Finnish teachers' and students' perspectives. *International Journal of Educational Research*, 50(3), 159–165.

Toom. A., & Husu. J. (2016). Finnish teachers as 'makers of the many': Balancing between broad pedagogical freedom and responsibility. In H. Niemi, A. Toom, & A. Kallioniemi, (Eds.), *Miracle of education: The principles and practices of teaching and learning in Finnish schools* (pp. 41–55). Sense Publishers.

Trade Union of Education in Finland. (2021a). *NOPE training for young teachers*. www.oaj.fi/en/membership/oaj-trains-and-educates/nope-training

Trade Union of Education in Finland. (2021b). *Uuden työntekijän rekrytointi ja perehdytys* [Recruiting and orienting a new employee]. https://www.oaj.fi/arjessa/johtotehtavissa-opetusalalla/uuden-tyontekijan-rekrytointi-ja-perehdytys/

Tynjälä, P., Pennanen, M., Markkanen, I., & Heikkinen, H. L. T. (2019). Finnish model of peer-group mentoring: Review of research. *Annals of the New York Academy of Sciences, 1483*(1), 208–223.

Vahtivuori-Hänninen, S., Halinen, I., Niemi, H., Lavonen, J., & Lipponen, L. (2014). A new Finnish national core curriculum for basic education (2014) and technology as an integrated tool for learning. In H. Niemi, J. Multisilta, L. Lipponen, & M. Vivitsou (Eds.), *Finnish innovations and technologies in schools—A guide towards new ecosystems of learning* (pp. 21–32). Sense Publishers.

Vainikainen, M.-P., Thuneberg, H., Marjanen, J., Hautamäki, J., Kupiainen, S., & Hotulainen, R. (2017). How do Finns know? Educational monitoring without inspection and standard setting. In S. Blömeke & J. E. Gustafsson (Eds.), *Standard setting in education: The Nordic countries in an international perspective* (pp. 243–259). Springer.

Välijärvi, J., Linnakylä, P., Kupari, P., Reinikainen, P., & Arffman, I. (2002). *The Finnish success in PISA—And some reasons behind it*. Institute for Educational Research, University of Jyväskylä. https://jyx.jyu.fi/bitstream/handle/123456789/50467/951-39-1377-5.pdf?sequence=1

ABOUT THE EDITOR

Jian Wang is a full professor and Helen DeVitt Jones chair in teacher education at the College of Education, Texas Tech University. His publications focus on teacher mentoring, teacher education, mathematics teaching and learning, and curriculum influences on teacher learning. He has worked on the TIMSS curriculum project, the teacher–mentoring project at the National Center for Research on Teacher Learning, and the design-based research project at the U.S. Prep National Center. He has also served as a co-editor of the *Journal of Teacher Education* and is currently co-editor of the *Educational Research and Development Journal*. His email: jian.wang@ttu.edu

Printed in the USA
CPSIA information can be obtained
at www.ICGtesting.com
CBHW052348191024
15920CB00003B/5